Cambridge International AS & A Level English Language

STUDENT'S BOOK

Author: Beth Kemp
Series consultants: Lisa Small and Tony Fleming

William Collins' dream of knowledge for all began with the publication of his first book in 1819.

A self-educated mill worker, he not only enriched millions of lives, but also founded a flourishing publishing house. Today, staying true to this spirit, Collins books are packed with inspiration, innovation and practical expertise. They place you at the centre of a world of possibility and give you exactly what you need to explore it.

Collins. Freedom to teach.

Published by Collins
An imprint of HarperCollins*Publishers*
The News Building
1 London Bridge Street
London
SE1 9GF

Browse the complete Collins catalogue at
www.collins.co.uk

ISBN 978-0-00-828760-3

British Library Cataloguing-in-Publication Data

A catalogue record for this publication is available from the British Library.

Author: Beth Kemp
Series consultants: Tony Fleming and Lisa Small
Development editor: Sonya Newland
Commissioning editor: Catherine Martin
In-house project lead: Alexandra Wells
Copyeditor: Catherine Dakin
Permissions and picture researcher: Rachel Thorne
Proofreader: Sue Chapple
Cover designers: Kevin Robbins and Gordon MacGilp
Cover illustrator: Maria Herbert-Liew
Typesetter: Jouve India Private Ltd
Production controller: Sarah Burke

Printed and bound by: Grafica Veneta SpA in Italy

With thanks to the following teachers for reviewing sections of the book as it was developed:

- Elizabeth Dunand, Brilliantmont International School, Switzerland
- Woody River, ULink College of Suzhou, China
- Swe Mon, Macau Anglican College, Macau, China
- Constantinos Constantinou, Better English Institute, Cyprus
- Lucy Toop, The Norwood School, London, UK

All exam-style questions and sample answers in this title were written by the author(s). In examinations, the way marks are awarded may be different.

Contents

Introduction

How to use this book

The Collins *Cambridge International AS & A Level Language* Student's Book offers a skills-building approach to the syllabus. It is structured to build skills and knowledge in a clear sequence, with in-depth, up-to-date coverage of each syllabus topic and a stimulating range of international texts to analyse, respond to and inspire your own writing.

In each chapter, you will work with an exciting range of texts from different cultures, chosen to expand your understanding and enjoyment of studying English Language. We aim to encourage and support you in developing a dynamic, personal relationship with language texts and debates which will promote a lifelong interest in the subject.

- **Section A** supports your transition from upper secondary. The two chapters refresh your understanding of key concepts such as audience, purpose and form, and of key elements of language including sentences and clauses. These chapters will be particularly useful for those students who have not studied Cambridge IGCSE™ English (First Language).

- **Section B** develops your analysis and writing skills. Chapter 3 introduces you to different modes of analysis, including contextual, pragmatic, lexical, semantic, grammatical and phonological approaches. Chapter 4 supports you in writing in different forms and for different audiences and purposes, encouraging you to experiment and to learn from the techniques and methods writers employ. These skills will be vital whether you are studying for an AS or A Level.

- **Section C** explores the four A Level language topics in depth. A detailed chapter on each topic introduces the relevant linguistic theories and will help you to begin to apply these ideas in your own arguments and analysis of texts, transcripts and data.

- **Section D** helps you to apply your knowledge and skills to extended language tasks. The chapters offer step-by-step support for responding to a range of tasks. Sample responses are provided to help you assess and improve your work. The tasks, responses and commentaries have been written by our authors, not by the Cambridge International examination board.

- **Section E**, finally, will build your confidence for your examinations, with four complete exam-style practice papers. (Indicative content for the longer questions is provided in the resource for teachers on the Collins website, www. Collins.co.uk/cambridge-international-downloads.)

A number of features have been included to support your learning:

A **Big question** (or questions) provides a clear focus for your learning in each unit and can be revisited at the end of the learning sequence.

A wealth of **activities** throughout encourage you to actively engage with the ideas you are exploring and to apply these ideas yourselves to texts, data or your own writing.

Analysis and writing skills are developed throughout the book. Each unit ends with a **Final task** where you can apply your learning independently. Successful writing is modelled throughout the units. Each chapter concludes with a substantial formative task to test your understanding.

Taking things further sections ask you to explore a concept in greater depth or to develop a more sophisticated skill, to extend your learning.

Key terms are defined on the page where they occur and collated into a full Glossary of key terms at the end of the book.

Any culturally-specific words, phrases or references in the texts have been glossed in a **Vocabulary** box to support your understanding.

A Teacher resource is provided online at collins.co.uk/cambridge-international-downloads including medium-term plans and suggested answers to the Student's Book activities.

We hope that your use of this book will not only help you with preparing for your examinations, but will give you confidence in considering linguistic issues in a range of contexts, inspiring you to explore language's social and cultural aspects, and helping you to develop a lifelong love of all things linguistic.

Beth Kemp

Elements of language

The Cambridge AS & A Level English Language course offers you the opportunity to explore language in greater depth than you have before. You will need to take a more technical approach to language and, at times, to draw on other disciplines, such as psychology and sociology.

Chapter 1 reviews some language essentials that you have probably come across before to secure your understanding. Understanding the core elements of language, including grammatical terminology, is vital for success at higher levels. You need to be able to identify these features in context, to analyse their contribution to a text's meanings and effects, and to know which parts of a text are most significant.

This chapter also introduces some of the course's key concepts:

- the way that *text and context* work together to create meaning, as well as how language choices create style
- the importance of *audience* as both a key part of context and an influence on a writer's or speaker's choice of language
- applying *creativity* when reading and analysing texts in order to appreciate what writers and speakers intend their audiences to feel and experience from language
- using your own creativity in different forms of writing to produce texts that are appropriate and effective for different contexts.

1.1 Sentences and clauses

How can we describe sentences and clauses?

Types of clause

Clauses are the basic building blocks of sentences. They are usually built around **verb phrases** and can be described as main (independent) or subordinate (dependent).

- A main clause can stand on its own as a complete sentence (e.g. 'She laughed.' and 'The girl with black hair had already thought of all those things.').
- A subordinate clause does not work on its own; it may start with a **subordinating conjunction** (e.g. 'Although she laughed') or be built around a **non-finite verb** ('Having already thought of all those things').

Clauses may be linked using conjunctions.

- **Coordinating conjunctions** are used to join main clauses. The name 'coordinating conjunction' reflects the fact that the clauses they connect are of equal value (each could be a sentence in its own right).
- **Subordinating conjunctions** are used to introduce subordinate clauses. This can be at the start of a sentence or following a main clause.

A clause that begins with a subordinating conjunction always keeps the conjunction with it when it moves in the sentence:

> I was late to college today **because** the bus broke down.
>
> **Because** the bus broke down, I was late to college today.

A coordinating conjunction stays where it is, and clauses move around it:

> I was late to college today **and** it was raining.
>
> It was raining **and** I was late to college today.

In a sentence where the subject is the same for two (or more) main clauses, the subject is not usually repeated:

second main clause with implied subject of 'he'

third main clause with implied subject of 'he'

> He got up, went to the window and looked out.

Although 'went to the window' and 'looked out' cannot stand alone as sentences, they are not subordinate clauses; the reader/audience will simply understand that the subject ('he') is implied.

Key terms

verb phrase: a verb with other words that are attendant to it, which function together as a verb

subordinating conjunction: a word or phrase that opens a subordinate clause (e.g. 'because', 'although')

non-finite verb: a verb that is not conjugated to agree in person and number – either an infinitive ('to eat', 'to laugh', 'to go'), a progressive ('eating', 'laughing', 'singing') or a perfective ('eaten', 'laughed', 'sung')

coordinating conjunction: word or phrase that links main clauses or other sentence elements (e.g. 'and', 'or', 'but')

Types of sentence

The table below describes the four major sentence types in English.

Sentence type	Contains	Example
simple sentence	one main clause	Grease the sides of the cake tin.
compound sentence	two or more main clauses	Grease the sides of the cake tin and line the base with a disc of baking parchment.
complex sentence	one main clause + one or more subordinate clauses	If you're using a standard type of cake tin, grease the sides.
compound-complex sentence	two or more main clauses + one or more subordinate clauses	If you're using a standard type of cake tin, grease the sides and line the base with a disc of baking parchment.

In addition to these, you may come across minor sentences. A minor sentence is effectively an incomplete sentence, often lacking a subject or verb. Sometimes this is implied and refers back to the previous sentence (especially in speech), but minor sentences can also be exclamations or interjections:

> How awful!
>
> What a disaster!
>
> Ouch!
>
> 'Are you coming tomorrow?' 'Yes, I am.'

In the last example, it would sound awkward to say the whole thing: 'Yes, I am coming tomorrow.' The minor sentence is the more natural response.

Writing speech

Sentences with speech must also obey the rules for introducing and punctuating speech correctly:

'Are you coming tomorrow?' he asked. — **punctuation inside speech marks**

'Yes, I am,' she replied. — **new speaker requires new line**

Activity I

Read Text I opposite, a recipe for poppy-seed cake. It features all sentence types except minor and simple.

a) Find an example of each type of sentence: compound, complex and compound-complex.

b) Why do you think this text uses the sentence types that it does? (If you find that difficult to answer, try imagining the text using different kinds of sentences – what changes?)

Text 1

Lemon poppy-seed cake

Poppy seeds are used in cakes and many other dishes across the world, their fragrant nutty taste going especially well with the citrus flavour of lemon or orange. There is a lot of milk in this recipe, which makes the crumb very tender and soft. It's baked in a bundt tin, which gives more of a crusty outer layer, though if you don't have one, a standard round cake tin would do just as well, or you could use the mixture to make muffins (see page 12). If you like, you could decorate with candied orange slices (see page 340), placing these on the iced cake instead of sprinkling over the poppy seeds.

Prep time: **10 minutes**
Baking time: **50–70 minutes**
Ready in: **1 hour 40 minutes**
Serves: **10–14**

325g (11½oz) plain flour, plus extra
    for dusting
1½ tsp baking powder
1½ tsp salt
400g (14oz) caster sugar
25g (1oz) poppy seeds, plus
    1–2 tsp to decorate
225ml (8fl oz) sunflower or vegetable
    oil, plus extra for greasing
4 eggs
1 tsp vanilla extract
325ml (11½fl oz) milk
Finely grated zest of 1 lemon
Candied orange slices (see page 340),
    to decorate (optional)

For the icing
200g (7oz) icing sugar, sifted
3 tbsp lemon juice

2.5 litre (4½ pint) bundt tin (about
    23cm/9in in diameter) or 25cm (10in)
    diameter cake tin (see page 336).

Preheat the oven to 180°C (350°F). Gas mark 4, then grease the bundt tin with sunflower or vegetable of and dust with flour. If you're using a standard type of cake tin, grease the sides and line the base with a disc of baking parchment.

Sift the flour, baking powder and salt into a large bowl, add the sugar and poppy seeds and mix together.

In a separate bowl, whisk together the remaining ingredients until combined. Tip this mixture into the dry ingredients and mix together using a wooden spoon to make a smooth batter. You may need to use a whisk briefly to get rid of any lumps of flour.

Tip into the prepared tin and bake for 50–60 minutes (60–70 minutes if using a standard cake tin). When cooked, the cake should feel springy to the touch and a skewer inserted into the centre should come out clean.

Remove the cake from the oven and allow to sit for just 2 minutes then loosen the edges with a small, sharp knife, place a wire rack upside down on top of the cake and carefully turn it over. Gently remove the tin and allow to cool completely (see page 336).

While the cake is baking, or while it's cooling, you can make the icing. Beat the icing sugar and lemon juice together until smooth. Carefully transfer the cake to a cake to a cake stand or serving plate, then drizzle the icing backwards and forwards from the centre to the outside of the cake in a zigzig pattern. Sprinkle over the poppy seeds straight away and the candied orange slices (see page 340), if you're using them, before the icing has a chance to dry.

Rachel Allen, from *Cake: 200 Fabulous Foolproof Baking Recipes*

Activity 2

Write a page of the opening to a short story entitled 'The Secret'. Aim to vary your sentence length and type to control pace and create atmosphere. You could try:

- using a minor sentence to create a break in the narrative
- using a non-finite clause to open a sentence (e.g. starting with 'Having plotted…,')
- moving subordinate clauses around so that some come at the beginning of sentences and some come later
- inserting **adverbials** of time (e.g. 'a few weeks ago'), of manner (e.g. 'very carefully') and of place (e.g. 'in the garden') at the start of sentences or clauses.

Sentence functions

Sentences can be defined by their function as well as their construction. There are four main sentence functions: declarative, interrogative, imperative and exclamatory.

Key term

adverbial: word or group of words that modifies a verb by saying when, how or where the action was performed

Function	Type	Examples	Explanation
declarative	statement	He is very happy with his new job. I like swimming.	Word order is the standard subject-verb. Declaratives are the most common type of sentence.
interrogative	question	Is he happy with his new job? Do you like swimming?	Word order inverts the verb and subject or may add a question word such as 'why' or 'how' before the verb.
imperative	command	Be happy! Swim!	Word order omits the subject and opens with the verb; politeness tokens (e.g. 'please') or hedges (e.g. 'just') can come first.
exclamatory/ exclamative	exclamation	What a great job!	These tend to be minor sentences. Note that not everything with an exclamation mark is exclamatory – imperatives often have exclamation marks too.

A sentence can only fit into one function category. These are grammatical labels for a sentence defined by its word order, not its purpose or its punctuation. This means that if a question is implied through **intonation** only (e.g. 'you like swimming?!' said in an incredulous tone), it is still a declarative. Equally, if a sentence has an exclamation mark but fits a category other than exclamatory, it isn't an exclamatory. For example, imperatives are often written with exclamation marks ('Put that down!') because they might be said emphatically.

Key term

intonation: the rise and fall of the voice while speaking

Activity 3

Look again at the recipe in Text 1. What is the function of the majority of the sentences? Why do you think this is?

Activity 4

Identify the following sentences by type and/or function, then rewrite them to change at least one of these aspects. You can break up the sentence, rearrange it and add elements in order to do this.

a) What are you doing?
b) How dare you!
c) All things considered, it didn't turn out too badly for any of us.
d) I don't know where to go or what to do.
e) The day was wet, cold and threatening to get far worse.

Final task

Return to the story opening you wrote called 'The Secret'. Did you write any sentences that are not declarative? Continue your story, incorporating some dialogue. Aim to include at least three sentence functions.

1.2 Words and phrases

Assessment objectives:
AO3

What are the main word classes? What is a phrase?

What are word classes?

To fully understand the difference between word classes, you need to know what each word class *does*. Word classes can be distinguished by their function and by the way they behave with other words. They can be broadly divided into two types:

- *Lexical* word classes carry information in the sentence – the 'main' words (e.g. nouns, verbs, adjectives, adverbs).
- *Functional* word classes are used to join elements together and transmit grammatical meaning (e.g. pronouns, **auxiliary verbs**, prepositions, conjunctions, **determiners**, articles).

Lexical word classes contain many words, and new words are added to them all the time (e.g. 'screenshot', 'instaworthy'). Functional word classes are smaller and much more fixed – for example, despite suggestions, people have been unwilling to consider a new, gender-neutral pronoun in English. Lexical word classes carry more meaning in a text and are therefore more useful to comment on when you are writing an analysis.

Key terms

auxiliary verb: supports the main verb in constructing the tense or voice (in English, this can only be either 'to be', 'to do', 'to have' or a modal)

determiners: modifying words that limit the field of reference of nouns – article (e.g. 'a', 'an', 'the'), possessive (e.g. 'my', 'his'), numeral (e.g. 'three'), quantifier (e.g. 'many', 'few') or distributive adjective (e.g. 'each', 'any')

stative verbs: verbs that express a state, such as a feeling or emotions, rather than actions

modal verb: a type of auxiliary verb that does not vary according to person and expresses probability, certainty or necessity (must, may, will, would, can could, shall, should)

Lexical type	Used for	Behaviour and conjugation	Examples	Types
noun	labelling things, people, places	works with determiners/quantifiers; may have plural form	teacher American New Delhi	proper/common concrete/abstract (non-)countable
adjective	adding information and detail	works with nouns and **stative verbs**; can have comparative and superlative forms	tall happy informative brave	evaluative emotive descriptive
adverb	adding information and detail	works with verbs and whole clauses/sentences	happily bravely very	sentence time, manner, place degree, frequency
verb	showing actions, processes and states	works with pronouns and nouns; takes endings to show **tense/aspect** and to agree with the subject	go be seem jump	dynamic/stative **modal** auxiliary main/auxiliary
pronoun	replacing nouns and noun phrases	has different forms for different people and cases (subject/object)	I/me you yourself	subject/object possessive reflexive

Key terms

tense: the way a verb phrase indicates time

aspect: the form of a verb that indicates duration or completion

Nouns, noun phrases and pronouns

Nouns provide labels for things. Common nouns are labels for *types* of things, people, animals, locations and so on ('horse', 'teacher', 'ceramics', 'city'). Proper nouns are labels for specific, *unique* individual people, animals, artworks, locations, and so on ('Shergar', 'Mrs Philips', *The Scream*, 'Boston').

Common nouns can be classified as 'countable' (i.e. they are perceived in singular and plural forms) or 'uncountable', also known as 'mass' nouns. Do not confuse mass nouns, such as 'traffic', which we do not think of in singular/plural form, with those having an invariable plural spelling like 'sheep', which still make perfect sense paired with a numerical determiner (e.g. 'three sheep').

Common nouns can be further divided into concrete nouns, which label physical objects or things that can be perceived by the senses ('box', 'chair'), and abstract nouns, which label non-tangible things, such as ideas, beliefs and emotions ('empathy', 'justice'). Note that some nouns can be used in both senses:

> *My father needed heart surgery last week.*
>
> Concrete: The sentence is concerned with the physical organ.
>
> *That guy has a really big heart – he just gave his last dollar to someone he barely knows.*
>
> Abstract: The sentence uses the word figuratively; we know nothing about the man's physical heart.

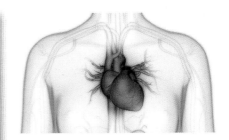

Activity 1

What type of noun is each of the following? Organise them into lists under the headings 'Proper', 'Common', 'Concrete' and 'Abstract'. Some will fit under more than one heading and the lists may not be equal in length.

Adolescent	Doorway	Fluffy	Money	Orange	Steak
Berlin	Romeo	Honda	Oak	Peace	Susan
Communism	Fear	Humiliation	Spoon	Red panda	Traffic

A noun phrase is a noun plus any words that are attendant to it, such as determiners, **demonstratives** and adjectives. To work out exactly which words are included within the noun phrase, replace the whole phrase with a pronoun and see if the sentence still makes sense. It is important to include the whole phrase when quoting noun phrases in an analysis.

Key term

demonstratives: pronouns or adjectives that indicate which one of various possibilities is being discussed (e.g. 'his', 'these', 'that', 'those')

I really wish I hadn't said those terrible words to my poor mother.

- noun phrase headed by 'words'
- noun phrase headed by 'mother'
- pronouns replace the noun phrases

I really wish I hadn't said that to her.

Pronouns replace nouns and noun phrases to avoid repetition. When commenting on a text, you may want to note whether a pronoun is the first, second or third person.

		First person	Second person	Third person
Singular	Subject	I	you	he, she
	Object	me	you	him, her
	Possessive determiner	my	your	his, her
	Possessive pronoun	mine	yours	his, hers

		First person	Second person	Third person
Plural	Subject	we	you	they
	Object	us	you	them
	Possessive determiner	our	your	their
	Possessive pronoun	ours	yours	theirs

Activity 2

Identify the noun phrases and pronouns in the extract below, then identify the type of each noun and pronoun.

> If you are looking for the perfect place to take your family this summer, try your local sports club. It is cost-effective, health-promoting and supports the local economy. Your children will have a great time and will thank you for your trouble and you will all benefit from the healthy activity.

Verbs

Verbs are different from other word classes because they *conjugate*. This means that their endings change in order to:

- make them agree with a subject (pronoun, noun or noun phrase)
- show tense (that is, indicate when the action/state/process they describe happened)
- show aspect (that is, indicate for how long and to what degree of completeness the action/state/process they describe happened).

Verbs may be regular – that is, they follow standard patterns in their conjugations – or irregular. Simple tenses are formed using a single verb, while complex tenses require an auxiliary verb ('to be', 'to have'). Note that there is no future tense as such in English; there are no verb endings to mark the future. Instead a range of different present tense phrases are used with modal or auxiliary verbs, sometimes assisted by adverbs of time, to denote future plans. This is not the same as French or Spanish, for example, where endings are added to the verb stem to show the concept of the future.

'eats' is conjugated with an 's' because it is in the third person and present tense, which suggests Sadiq is eating the orange at the time of speaking *or* Sadiq often eats an orange and the sentence describes a regular event

auxiliary verb 'to be' is conjugated in the first-person present tense, showing that something is happening now to the person who is speaking

progressive verb indicates that the act of walking is in progress (at the time of speaking)

> Sadiq eats an orange.
>
> I am walking to the station.

The table below shows some examples of different tenses with regular and irregular verbs.

	Examples with regular verbs	Examples with irregular verbs
Simple present	I jump He looks They walk	I go He eats They are

	Examples with regular verbs	**Examples with irregular verbs**
Simple past	I jumped He looked They walked	I went He ate They were
Present perfect	I have jumped He has looked They have walked	I have gone He has eaten They have been
Past perfect	I had jumped He had looked They had walked	I had gone He had eaten They had been
Present progressive	I am jumping He is looking They are walking	I am going He is eating They are being
Past progressive	I was jumping He was looking They were walking	I was going He was eating They were being
Forms with modal auxiliaries	I will jump He would look They could have walked	I will go He would eat They could have been

The modal auxiliary verbs express permission, possibility, probability and expectation:

will	would	shall	should	can	could	must	may	might

These verbs do not follow standard patterns of conjugation: they do not take an 's' in the third person present tense. For example, you would not conjugate 'must' as 'I must, you must, he musts'. Also, because modals are *only* auxiliaries, they cannot be used on their own. For example, you cannot say 'I must' on its own in the same way you can other auxiliary verbs such as 'I am' or 'I have'. It needs another verb to make sense:

> I am running; I am a mother; I am happy
>
> I have climbed; I have a job
>
> I could *run*; I could *have* climbed
>
> I could a mother; I could happy; I could a job

In the third line above, the modal verb 'could' is followed by another verb. In the fourth line, however, you can see that the modals cannot be followed directly by a noun or adjective – they need another verb.

Activity 3

Create sentences by placing the following verbs into at least five different tense or tense/aspect combinations. You can add detail using other words and should aim to vary the subject.

- think
- drive
- leave
- cut

For each example, explain the circumstances of your sentence. (When is it happening? How often does it happen? Has it finished? How long ago?) For example, the box on the right shows five variations on the verb 'run', with explanations.

I am running	(happening right now, I am in the middle of it)
He runs	(a regular occurrence, not happening at the moment)
They ran	(is complete, not long ago)
We could have run	(didn't actually happen)
You will run tomorrow	(specific time, not happened yet)

Adjectives and adverbs

	Comparative	**Superlative**
Short adjectives and short adverbs not ending in '-ly'	+er: taller, faster	+est: tallest, fastest
Longer adjectives and adverbs ending in '-ly'	more ___: more intelligent, more beautifully	most ____: most intelligent, most beautifully

Adjectives and adverbs can modify other words to add information and detail to a sentence. Adjectives can modify nouns by appearing within the noun phrase – for example, 'a little boy', 'the tired-looking old man'. This is called *attributive* usage. Adjectives can also be used *predicatively* (after a verb), where they modify the subject of a sentence – for example, 'he seemed tired and old', 'the boy was little'.

Adverbs are most commonly used at the start of sentences or just before verbs, but they can appear in many different positions within a sentence, often with quite different effects.

Both adjectives and adverbs can have comparative and superlative forms, allowing writers and speakers to make comparisons and show relationships. The table on the left shows how these are formed.

Activity 4

Use a range of different adjectives and adverbs to create different descriptive phrases for the following (you may also change the nouns/verbs to be more specific):

- a tree
- a man walking
- a thought
- a child
- a cat hunting

Commenting on word classes in texts

Like nouns, adjectives can form phrases, usually in conjunction with an adverb. It is often worth commenting on whole phrases when analysing texts.

Read Text 2, a review of a novel called *The Scarecrow Queen* by Melinda Salisbury.

Text 2

Be warned: this reviews the conclusion to a trilogy, so there may be spoilers for the first two books. If you haven't read the first two, my advice is simple – do that. It's a cracking fantasy series and I am even more convinced of that now I've read the whole thing. The series showcases lyrical writing and is therefore great as an accessible and enjoyable model of good writing to offer to students alongside the curriculum.

I would especially recommend it if you tend to notice poor female representation creeping into books and media that claim to have 'strong female characters' or to be 'for girls'. These books will *not* let you down. Mel's ethics shine through in her realistically portrayed and therefore flawed characters (note: strong female character does not equal robotically tough) and her commitment to offering her female characters genuine choices, great relationships (and by that, I mean friendships as well as romance possibilities) and real growth.

Text 2 is taken from a blog aimed at teachers, which reviews children's and teenagers' books. Patterns in the text relate to the following factors:

- its *form* – the fact that it is a review
- its *audience* – the fact that it is written for teachers
- its *subject* – the fact that it is about books.

Key phrases worth commenting on are:

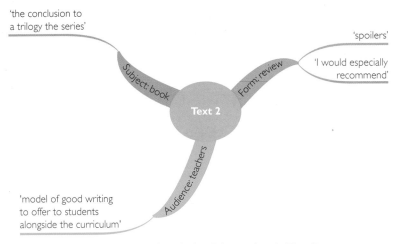

'the conclusion to a trilogy the series'

Subject: book

Form: review

Text 2

Audience: teachers

'spoilers'

'I would especially recommend'

'model of good writing to offer to students alongside the curriculum'

Now read the following good analysis of the review in Text 2.

> The writer uses language suitable for reviewing, such as the evaluative adjective 'lyrical', which explicitly makes a judgment about the quality of the writing. The extended noun phrases 'an accessible and enjoyable model of good writing' and 'poor female representation' also serve this purpose, as well as being particularly suitable for the teacher audience, who are likely to be concerned about what students could learn from ideologies in their reading.

Activity 5

Extend the analysis above, adding one or two sentences commenting on an aspect of the review's content – what it chooses to focus on. How does this relate to either its teacher audience or its form as a review and/or blog? Use at least one quotation from the review to support your point.

Text 3

Mrs. Cratchit made the gravy (ready beforehand in a little saucepan) hissing hot; Master Peter mashed the potatoes with incredible vigour; Miss Belinda sweetened up the apple-sauce; Martha dusted the hot plates; Bob took Tiny Tim beside him in a tiny corner at the table; the two young Cratchits set chairs for everybody, not forgetting themselves, and mounting guard upon their posts, crammed spoons into their mouths, lest they should shriek for goose before their turn came to be helped. At last the dishes were set on, and grace was said. It was succeeded by a breathless pause, as Mrs. Cratchit, looking slowly all along the carving-knife, prepared to plunge it in the breast; but when she did, and when the long expected gush of stuffing issued forth, one murmur of delight arose all round the board, and even Tiny Tim, excited by the two young Cratchits, beat on the table with the handle of his knife, and feebly cried Hurrah!

Charles Dickens, from *A Christmas Carol*

Final task

Reread the recipe in Text 1 and then read Text 3 below. Choose five or six phrases from each extract that would be useful if you were writing an analysis of the presentation of food and its preparation in each text. Think about how they show the food and the stages of its preparation. How could you make links between the language used and the form of each text? Use the analysis above as a guide.

1.3 Images

What is imagery?

Similes and metaphors

Imagery is figurative language – language used in a non-literal way. The most common figurative techniques are similes and metaphors.

- A simile compares two objects using 'like' or 'as' (e.g. 'The tree branches swayed like gymnasts' ribbons').
- A metaphor compares two objects by saying one *is* the other (e.g. 'The tree branches were gymnasts' ribbons in the wind').

There are two key differences between similes and metaphors:

- There is a difference in **tone**: metaphors are more direct in their imagery, while similes are more obviously a comparison.
- Similes allow you to use stronger and more interesting verbs, which state what the similarity is (e.g. 'sway'), while metaphors often leave the reader to **infer** the link(s).

To create an effective simile or metaphor, it is important to select an unusual but appropriate point of comparison. In the example above, the trees appear to be swaying gently and elegantly. If the writer had intended to suggest that the wind was fierce or dangerous, the comparison to gymnasts' ribbons was the wrong imagery to choose!

Key terms

tone: the attitude of a writer towards a subject (similar to the tone of voice that a speaker uses)

infer: to work out what a writer means by using evidence from a text

Activity 1

a) Imagine you are writing about a small animal moving along the ground. What impression of the animal's movement would each of the following comparisons create?

- water rushing over rocks
- a ball bouncing downhill
- ants in a line

b) Which impression do you feel is most effective? Why?

c) Write up the most effective comparison into a simile and a metaphor.

Key term

cliché: an overused idea, phrase or image

When using similes and metaphors, it is important to avoid **cliché**. However, it is also important not to try so hard to come up with something original that the imagery sounds wrong. A good image is surprising, but that surprise should come from the way in which the image illuminates something about the object being described. The use of figurative language should point out a feature that the reader might not have noticed otherwise, in relatively few words.

Activity 2

Look at the two examples of imagery below. What is the problem with each one? Think about their **connotations** as well as the originality of the images.

- His stomach gave a rumble like a lion's roar.
- The children flew out of school like bees from a hive.

Key term

connotations: the emotional or sensory associations that a word has

Activity 3

Write similes and metaphors for the following using the steps below.

| a smile | a child running/playing | a sunset |

- Identify at least three possible objects of comparison.
- Think through all possible associations for each object of comparison in order to decide which is best.
- Write out your favourite ideas as both simile and metaphor before deciding which works best in each case.

Personification and pathetic fallacy

Personification is another type of imagery in which an inanimate object, or sometimes an animal, is given human-like qualities:

> The run-down house was in dire need of love.

Houses are not able to experience emotions, so the house cannot literally be 'in dire need of love' – the writer is *personifying* the house. The effect of this is to engage the reader's sympathy and appeal to their emotions.

Pathetic fallacy is a more specific type of personification, in which an aspect of nature is given emotions that reflect the mood of the text or a character. For example, in *Wuthering Heights*, Emily Brontë describes a storm on the night that Heathcliff disappears:

> About midnight, while we still sat up, the storm came rattling over the Heights in full fury. There was a violent wind, as well as thunder, and either one or other split a tree off at the corner of the building; a huge bough fell across the roof.

The anger and violence attributed to the weather in the highlighted words reflect the characters' violent emotions on this turbulent night.

Activity 4

Write the opening paragraph to a descriptive piece, describing either a mountain or a forest scene. Use personification and/or pathetic fallacy to create a sorrowful atmosphere.

Extension: Write a contrasting opening paragraph of the same scene, creating a pleasant atmosphere.

Sound imagery

As well as visual imagery, writers use language to create a rich soundscape in their work. They use several different language features to achieve this.

Language feature	Explanation	Example
alliteration	repeated consonant sounds in a sequence of words	Peter Piper picked a peck of pickled pepper.
sibilance	repeated 'ss' and 'sh' sounds in a sequence of words (a sub-type of alliteration)	She sells seashells on the seashore.
assonance	repeated vowel sounds in a sequence of words	How now brown cow?
onomatopoeia	words that create a sound which they are trying to describe	Bang Whoosh
rhyme	matching sounds at the ends of words	Twinkle, twinkle little star How I wonder what you are

These features, especially alliteration and sibilance, are popular in headlines and advertising texts as they help to create memorable phrases. Beyond that, though, the nature of the sounds used can also create impressions that contribute to the imagery, mood or tone. Harsh consonantal sounds like 't's and 'k's will establish a different tone to the use of sibilance, for example – which could be used to evoke the sound of whispering or to create a calm, soothing atmosphere.

When commenting on sound imagery, it is important to distinguish between **graphemes** (letters) and **phonemes** (sounds). Alliteration between 'f' and 'ph' is perfectly possible, for example, as is sibilance using both 's' and soft 'c'. However, 'thundering torrent' is not an example of alliteration, as 'th' and 't' are two different sounds.

Key terms

grapheme: the smallest written representation of meaning (that is, a single letter or symbol)

phoneme: the smallest spoken representation of meaning (that is, a single sound)

Activity 5

Draw up a list of as many advertising slogans, company names and jingles (e.g. from the radio) you can think of that use sound-based techniques. Identify the techniques used in each one.

End-of-chapter task

Choose two songs that you know reasonably well by different artists, preferably of different styles, and find and print out copies of the lyrics. Annotate these lyrics, labelling examples of sound imagery and figurative language. Is there a difference in their use of imagery? Do these choices make sense to you with reference to their musical style?

Chapter 2 Elements of texts

Chapter 2 refreshes your understanding of the key elements that you will need to consider when creating and analysing texts: form, purpose and audience. To do this well, you need to be familiar with the conventions of different forms. Chapters 3 and 4 will develop your analytical and writing skills more specifically, but this is the place to review basic terminology and essential information to revise, consolidate and fill any gaps in your existing knowledge.

Key concepts covered in this chapter include:

* the way that *text and context* work together to create meaning.
* the importance of *audience* as both a key part of context and an influence on a writer's or speaker's choice of language
* applying *creativity* when reading and analysing texts in order to appreciate what writers and speakers intend their audiences to feel and experience from language
* using your own creativity in different forms of writing to produce texts that are appropriate and effective for different contexts.

2.1 Form

What is form?

Form is the *type* of text – for example, a leaflet, an article or a letter. In your study of English Language at AS and A Level, both written and spoken pieces are considered 'texts'. You will therefore be working with forms such as speeches, transcripts and podcasts, as well as more familiar written forms.

Different types of text can be identified by their conventions. These are not rules as such but are established ways of writing that most texts of that type will follow. Conventions can include content, structure and language. When analysing a text, it is worth noting where it deviates from the standard conventions of its form, as the author will usually have done this for deliberate effect.

Commercial forms

Commercial forms include: advertisements, brochures, flyers and leaflets.

These texts share some key features, including:

- headings
- branding such as logos, slogans or official colour schemes
- simple and clear text, often in short paragraphs, single sentences or bullet points.

Of these, advertisements are perhaps the most varied. Print advertisements often include few words – sometimes none at all, choosing to rely on images instead. Advertisements that do use language are likely to do so creatively,

heading: bold title with pun on 'taste'

large image of product dominates

branding: company colour-scheme and font

simple text

often including imagery. Spoken advertisements for the radio (or to be inserted into podcasts), and multimodal ones for TV are often dialogue-heavy and may play out a scenario with different characters. Or they may present a brand to the audience, making use of emotive language and comparative or superlative adjectives to highlight the product's or service's superior qualities.

Activity 1

Write the text to a full-page magazine advertisement for a snack-food product aimed at teenagers. Name your product and invent its qualities. You may need to think about the page layout, but you do not need to draw it or otherwise indicate it in your text.

Journalistic forms

Journalistic forms include:

- editorials
- news stories
- articles and columns
- reviews
- investigative journalism.

You will come across different types of journalism, as listed above, but most of them share features such as a headline/title and internal features such as subheadings and pull-quotes. The differences between them lie in their general content, their overall style and the key language features they use. The table below outlines some of the conventions in journalistic forms.

	Key content angle	General style	Typical language features
Editorial	presents the official opinion of the publication	detached and formal	written in the third person (but this can vary by publication)
News story	describes the news events	varies by publication, but often neutral	many complex sentences to fit in a lot of information
Article (feature and opinion) and column	explains the writer's opinions or discusses a topical issue	personal and often chatty; varies according to personality of writer	written in the first person
Investigative journalism	gives in-depth information about a topical issue that the journalist has discovered	usually detached and formal; avoids sensationalist and emotional comment	includes statistics, dates and times, images of documents and so on, as evidence
Review	offers an evaluation of a product or collection of products	personal but well-informed	often uses jargon relating to the type of product (e.g. film-related language)

Activity 2

Look at a newspaper or news magazine or use an online news source. Find examples of at least three of the forms outlined in the table. For each one:

- find a good quotation to demonstrate the style described
- find an example of the language feature listed as 'typical'
- suggest at least one further language feature to add to the 'typical' column.

Online forms

Online forms include:

- blogs
- podcasts.

Online texts may vary depending on their subject and purpose, and of course, blogs and podcasts take different forms – one written, the other spoken.

A blog is a website (or part of a website) that displays articles (posts) on a central topic or set of related topics. Some blogs are essentially diaries relating a person's experiences, while others provide information and/or opinions. A podcast is an audio recording, usually one of a series, again themed around a central topic, with one or more hosts to organise the content. Some podcasts tell a story – effectively audio plays – but most, like blogs, provide information and/or opinions on a range of sub-topics around the core topic. Blogs and podcasts each follow some key conventions.

Blog posts usually start with a heading and the date. The posts are usually written in the first person and tend to feature hyperlinks to other posts and external sites. There may also be images, which could be captioned and hyperlinked. Posts often end with a list of tags – brief descriptions of the sub-topics mentioned in the post. A blog website usually has different categories, and posts are 'filed' in an appropriate category. Both categories and tags help the reader find their way around the blog.

Podcasts will not usually be fully scripted, but they are likely to have been planned ahead of time and/or edited after recording. They often feature interviews with guests and may include jingles and sound effects. Many podcasts have more than one host, as speaking uninterrupted alone is very difficult, as well as being harder to listen to. Therefore, turn-taking features are often more explicit, to help listeners who cannot see who is talking. For example, comments such as 'I believe Mary has some views on this' are much more likely to be heard in a podcast than in real conversation.

Blogs and podcasts are both likely to have a regular audience, and they may address this audience directly (e.g. 'Those of you who heard last week's show will remember…'). Both also have strong links to social media. The examples below show some of these key conventions.

Blog

direct address to regular audience

clear statement in first person for first-time readers

informal phrasing keeps tone casual

As those of you who are regular readers of The Bookish Blog will know, I am a big fan of fantasy novels in particular, so was very excited to see this hit my Kindle.

Podcast

conversational way of opening sentence

direct reference to regular audience

clear, direct reference to podcast

talks about books in familiar way as audience likely to also be readers

Of course, as regular listeners will know, we here at The Bookish Pod are all big fantasy readers, so we were very happy when this title arrived for review.

Activity 3

Choosing either a blog or podcast form, write or script two paragraphs reviewing a book, film or piece of music that you have enjoyed recently. In your writing you should:

- welcome readers/listeners
- introduce the object you are reviewing
- give an overview verdict and describe the object, perhaps comparing it to other similar items (that is, other books/films/albums in the same genre)
- use appropriate conventions.

Personal forms

Personal forms include:

- letters
- diaries
- travel writing
- autobiographies
- memoirs.

Letters and diaries are often produced only for a very limited audience – usually just the writer themselves or, in the case of a letter, one other specific person. The key conventions of letter form are:

- the placement of the addresses
- the salutation ('Dear…' or equivalent)
- the closing ('Yours sincerely', and so on).

Everything else in a letter is a matter of style and will depend on its audience and purpose.

Travel writing is a kind of journaling in which someone records a trip in descriptive writing. This may be intended purely as a personal record for the traveller, or it may be written with a wider readership in mind. Published travel writing will usually be more specific and precise in its descriptions than private travel writing.

Autobiography and memoir are personal forms of writing in which someone shares their life story, or specific experiences from it, with an audience. Both forms are usually written as narratives in order to make the events clear and engaging.

Travel writing, autobiographies, memoirs and diaries are all likely to be written in the first person and the past tense. They will use plenty of descriptive detail, and events are often recorded in chronological order. Diaries tend to have dates to organise their information; they may also use abbreviated language, or even codes, to simplify the recording of information.

Activity 4

Write about an event from your life for your autobiography. Choose the most interesting and important details to include, making sure you clearly set the scene for your readers. Follow the key conventions:

- write in the first person
- use descriptive and imaginative language
- include your thoughts and feelings about the experience you are describing
- give your reader an insight into your life and personality.

Formal texts

Many of the text forms already discussed in this unit can be written in a formal way, especially editorials and news stories. However, some types of text are inherently formal, including essays and scripted speeches.

Essays:

- have a formal structure – an introduction and a conclusion, surrounding a detailed discussion of a topic
- usually require clear evidence and a strong sense of logic, which can be clearly indicated through the use of **discourse markers**.

Scripted speeches:

- follow formalities such as acknowledging the institution and/or context in which the speech is being given by making appropriate thanks or greetings
- contain repetition and formal **rhetorical devices**, as the audience is listening to the words rather than reading them.

Look at this extract from a speech, and the annotations which highlight some common conventions of formal speeches.

Key terms

discourse markers: words or phrases that signal a change of topic and may provide a link between parts of a conversation or text

rhetorical devices: language techniques used for effect, such as questions that make a point rather than seeking an answer

repetition with expansion

inclusive address

metaphor is also common in speeches

complex and less-common vocabulary used to show seriousness of the topic as well as formality of the context

> I urge you to consider the possibility, the very serious possibility, that our country is drowning under a tidal wave of callousness.

Activity 5

Read this opening to a formal essay. Identify as many of the conventions of the form as you can.

> There is a strong case to be made for revising the laws regarding animal ownership in this country. At the present time, it is legal for anyone who does not have a specific ban to own an animal. Such bans are allocated, for example, in the case of conviction for animal cruelty. Surely, rather than allowing animals to suffer at the hands of the heartless, it would be better to require a demonstration of responsibility first?

Literary forms

Literary forms are:

- narrative writing (which may be presented as prose, drama or poetry)
- descriptive writing (which is most likely to be found in prose form).

The key conventions of a prose narrative:

- It has a clear sense of action or direction – something must be happening, either externally in the world or internally within the characters.
- It has a deliberate perspective – it may be told from the point of view of one of the characters, by an external narrator or in the third person.

- It requires a decision about chronology: narrative must have a beginning, a middle and an end, but they do not have to appear in that order (some narratives start **in medias res** (mid-action) or **in ultimas res** (with the ending) with flashbacks or occasional backwards references to fill in the gaps in the story).

Narrative told in drama has additional conventions, including:

- a script layout, such as character names to indicate who is speaking when
- stage directions
- a story told through dialogue and (occasionally) unspoken action/ interaction (there is no place for description or explanation).

Descriptive writing has few conventions. However, it is important to include detail to help your reader picture the scene and to create a strong atmosphere in your descriptive writing. The aim of description is to draw your audience into the time and place you are describing, and that requires clear physical, sensory detail, ideally using more than one of the senses. Imagery such as metaphor, simile and onomatopoeia are also common in descriptive writing.

The skills required for literary writing are also useful in other forms. For example, narrative writing skills can be applied to biography and autobiography, and descriptive writing techniques are useful in travel writing for evoking a sense of place.

Key terms

in medias res: 'in the middle of things' – a structural term used for a narrative opening in the middle of the story

in ultimas res: 'at the end of things' – a structural term for a narrative which opens with the ending or the outcome of the story and then goes back to explain how it all happened

Activity 6

How can you tell that this is a story? Identify the conventions of narrative.

> So, I was walking along the road when I noticed this man behind me. I got scared so started walking more quickly and that was when he started jogging. That really freaked me out, so I ran. I charged around a corner, terrified, and ran straight into a woman, who asked me what the matter was. I was just telling her that a man was chasing me, when he caught up with me. 'You dropped your purse back there,' he said.

Note that the terms 'narrative' and 'descriptive' can apply to the *purpose* of a piece of writing, as well as its *form*. For more information on the purposes of writing to narrate and writing to describe, see Unit 2.2.

Final task

Choose one of the topics below (you may make it more specific) or a topic that you are passionate about.

- wildlife
- fashion
- sport

Produce two texts about that topic, using different forms. Try to make them as different as possible. For example, if you were passionate about reading, you might write:

- a leaflet for parents on how to encourage your child to read more
- a passage from your autobiography detailing how you felt when you first read a book on your own.

2.2 Purpose

What is purpose? What kinds of purpose can texts have?

What do we mean by 'purpose'?

A text's purpose is the reason it has been produced or the function that it serves. Key purposes you should be familiar with are writing to:

- persuade
- argue
- analyse
- critique
- narrate
- describe
- inform
- instruct.

Some forms of writing are linked to particular purposes, but most forms can be produced for a range of different purposes. For example, narrative prose is written to narrate. A letter, on the other hand, might be written to persuade, to argue, to describe, to inform…

Writing to persuade, argue, analyse or critique

These purposes are related in that all are clearly non-fiction purposes, concerned with putting across ideas to an audience that may potentially disagree. When writing for each of these purposes, a different aspect may be prioritised.

In persuasive writing, you are trying to convince your audience to adopt your own point of view. There is a clear assumption that at least some of the audience will not agree with you at the start, and you are trying to bring them round to your way of thinking. This kind of writing often uses techniques that exploit the audience's feelings, such as rhetorical questions to make them question ideas and emotive language to provoke strong feelings.

Argumentative writing is less emotional and more logical. It prioritises the argument and is less concerned with getting the audience to agree. Clarity and reasoning are significant in this kind of writing, so there is an emphasis on clear structure and sequencing, and on providing evidence to back up an argument or evaluate different views.

Analytical and critical writing offer judgments, but analysis is much more in-depth than critical writing. On this course, you will be analysing the language used in texts, but there are other types of analytical writing, such as texts that analyse politics or the law. Critical writing – such as film, book or restaurant reviews – offers opinions and personal responses for consumers from a position of professional expertise. Analysis, on the other hand, is intended to be read by other experts and will therefore use more precise, expert language.

Look at this example of the difference between an analytical approach and a critical approach:

> **Analysis of a novel**
> The first-person voice is used by the writer to focus the reader's attention on the narrator's experiences.
>
> **Review of a novel**
> I loved how the first-person narration kept me sharply focused on Emma's feelings and experiences.

Activity 1

Write a short letter to persuade your school or college management to improve its catering options for students (e.g. to increase the vegetarian options or provide for students with special dietary requirements). Use techniques to appeal to your reader's emotions and make them take your case seriously.

Writing to narrate or describe

Narration is organising events into a story. This may be to write a novel, to relate what happened last week or to tell a joke. All these are narrative texts, which depend on the same features to work.

In narrative writing, it is important to plunge your audience into a different version of reality. Readers need to engage strongly with characters in fiction and to understand their motivations. In order to do this, everything must make sense and be believable. A story is not just things happening; it is a *plot* – everything must happen for a reason. It must be plausible and fit together.

The purpose of both descriptive and narrative writing is, essentially, to entertain. The key difference lies in their organisation. Narrative requires structure, order and causation, while descriptive writing is lyrical, slow-paced and enjoyable. It is the kind of writing to savour. This is the place to use extensive vocabulary and enjoy more obscure imagery. Unlike narrative writing, descriptive writing should not have a plot; nor does it need a lot of action. Narrative writing aims to guide a reader through a story; good descriptive writing aims to take a reader to a place and immerse them in it. It is all about capturing a scene, a mood, an atmosphere, although it still needs a structure to shape the experience.

Activity 2

Choose a story that you know well (it can be a film or other storytelling medium if you prefer).

a) Write an additional scene for the story in prose format. This could be a prologue, a scene inserted in the middle of the action, or it could take place after the existing story. Make sure that you describe the action clearly for readers who may not know the characters as well as you do.

b) Write an extended descriptive passage (half to one typed page in length) to accompany the scene you have just written. The relationship between the two is up to you – it may be the main setting or come before or after your scene. Try to evoke appropriate atmosphere and emotion through the description you write. Remember to use more than just visual description – evoke other senses, too.

Writing to inform or instruct

Both informative and instructional writing convey information, but their purposes are slightly different. Informative writing passes on facts that educate the reader; instructional writing enables the reader to do something.

Examples of informative texts include:

- a documentary on bird life in the Gulf region
- an encyclopedia entry on Albert Einstein
- a flyer on the importance of recycling.

Examples of instructional texts include:

- a YouTube video on braiding hair
- a recipe for cinnamon rolls from a cookbook
- a health leaflet on increasing physical activity.

Both informative and instructional texts need to be very clear, so they often use organisational features such as headings and/or discourse markers (such as 'firstly'), bullet points or numbering that make the order of information clear. Depending on the subject and audience, both these types of text may include jargon (technical vocabulary).

Activity 3

Write an instructional text for a task you perform regularly. This could be a common activity such as making breakfast, or something more unique to you (e.g. a job you do or an unusual hobby). Try to include every step and make it easy for anyone to follow the instructions.

Putting purposes together

In practice, texts often have more than one purpose. For example, a letter written to persuade people to give money to a charity will also inform them about the charity's work. Texts intended to entertain often have a secondary purpose beyond simple narration. *A Christmas Carol*, for example, tells the story of Ebenezer Scrooge. This seasonal tale was written by Charles Dickens in the Victorian period to challenge the way people thought about the poor and to encourage them to be more charitable. In Text 3 in Unit 1.2, Scrooge is shown a scene in the house of his employee in order to shame him into realising how little he pays Bob Cratchit and yet how good a man Bob is.

Activity 4

What other books and entertainment narratives (films, TV shows, and so on) are you aware of which have a secondary purpose? Try to be specific about what that purpose is – for example, *A Christmas Carol* could be described as persuasive or critiquing. Whatever you choose, make sure you have a clear argument for your claims.

Final task

Like letters, leaflets can be produced for a range of purposes. How many purposes can you plan a leaflet for? Make a list of ideas. The start of an equivalent list for letters might be:

- a letter to a politician telling them to support your local hospital (persuasive)
- a letter to the local newspaper explaining why the local council is wrong to change school traffic rules (argumentative)
- a letter to your elderly grandfather explaining how to view your family's shared photos folder on the cloud on his phone (instructional).

2.3 Audience

What do we mean when we talk about 'audience'? How do writers aim texts at different audiences?

Intent and audience

The audience of a text is the person or people it was produced for. Never describe an audience as 'anyone' – writers always have a type of person in mind when writing. For example, in theory, anyone *could* read this book, but they would not be likely to. The audience is people studying for the Cambridge International AS or A Level in English Language, and their teachers and tutors.

When analysing a journalistic text, you can often find clues within it to the intended audience:

- If the source has a place name in the title, it may be a local newspaper/magazine and therefore intended for people from that area.
- If the text uses a wide vocabulary range (that is, including complex words), it is likely to be intended for a well-educated readership that prefers a precisely worded text.
- If the text features the writer heavily (e.g. with a picture or large font for their name), they may be a featured columnist, in which case the writer is likely to have a fan base which makes up their primary audience.
- If the piece uses cultural or political references (whether you can follow them or not), they can help you assess the audience. Are they highbrow or specialist (e.g. arts-related)? Do they focus on popular culture (such as reality TV or popular sports)? These will tell you whether the piece/paper is aiming at a more educated audience or a mass one (note the label of a 'mass' audience not a 'lower-class' or 'less educated' one).

You are more likely to be asked to read articles from higher-end newspapers (sometimes known as broadsheets) than mass-audience (tabloid) newspapers or magazine articles, so it is useful to familiarise yourself with their style and features.

For all texts, whether journalistic or other varieties, the aspects to guide you when considering audience are:

- the subject of the text – a leaflet about the dangers of smoking is obviously intended primarily for smokers, but it may also be designed to put off anyone who is about to start
- how people access the text – a flyer put through people's doors in a particular place is obviously intended to target a specific geographical area; online texts are usually found by searching or following links in other texts
- the way the text is written – as above with journalism, look for clues to the ideal audience's social class/level of education, interests and expertise level in the subject.

Multiple and secondary audiences

While texts are likely to have a single intended primary audience, a secondary audience may well read or discover a text. This is especially true for anything online, as people can easily find online material that aligns with their interests. For example, a newspaper column may appeal to additional readers in any one week due to the subject chosen.

Activity 1

Who would you identify as the *intended* audience of the following texts? Can you see any likely additional audience(s)? Copy and complete the table.

Text	Intended audience
a leaflet sent home with schoolchildren about healthy family cooking to avoid child obesity	parents or carers of school-aged children
an opinion article by Gene Weingarten, well-known humour columnist in the *Washington Post*, about playing Scrabble on his phone	
a letter seeking donations to an animal welfare charity, received inside a wildlife magazine and addressed to 'Dear Supporter'	
a post on a beauty blog reviewing a selection of organic skincare products	
an episode of a regular nostalgia podcast about 1990s children's TV, featuring an interview with a writer from *Doug*	

Directing text to an audience – tone and effect

To write for a specific audience, then, you need to use relevant language and references. It is also important to think about tone and the effect this will have.

Look at the following two annotated examples.

The crisis of plastic waste in our oceans has reached epic proportions. Helpless sea creatures are starving after swallowing fragments of our discarded coffee cups and microbeads from beauty products.

- **first-person plural possessive pronoun implies responsibility**
- **mildly emotive language, as it suggests a quest, a problem to be solved**
- **strongly emotive language**

neutral phrasing removes responsibility and concern from the reader

modal verb makes it sound less likely, with formal scientific verb creating detached tone

neutral description presents situation as a given, not as anyone's fault/responsibility

> Ocean plastics are a new crisis facing the planet. Fragments of plastic may be ingested by sea life, leading to their death, or they may become entangled in the mass of plastic bags littering the seas.

The first example has an emotive, personal tone, while the second is more neutral. This may mean that the first has a more powerful effect on the audience, but it would also make it inappropriate for some contexts, such as scientific journals.

Tone is an important way of creating an effect on your audience; it is also something that you can comment on when analysing texts. Tone is largely about word choice. For example:

- In the first extract, using the personal pronoun 'our' to create an inclusive address contributes to the personal tone and establishes a clear sense of responsibility. This is then built on with the emotive language.
- In contrast, a neutral tone is constructed in the second example through scientific language such as the verbs 'ingested' and 'entangled'. The modal verb 'may' is a powerful way to introduce a sense of detachment by implying that these are mere possibilities, while the first example presents the scenario 'sea creatures are starving' as a clear fact, using the present progressive to show that it is happening right now.

End-of-chapter task

Write a brief diary entry describing an interesting event that occurred in the last week. Then turn it into a text for a different audience (that is, not just yourself). Choose one of the following:

- a blog entry
- a newspaper column
- a short story.

If you are not sure of how to write any of these, find an example first to check the form.

Chapter 3

Key analytical skills: Approaching texts linguistically

What do you already know about analysing texts? How systematic is your approach? For example, are you aware of whether and when you are using semantic methods or grammatical ones?

This chapter will provide you with a range of essential terminology for analysing texts in greater depth. The units take a broadly 'outward-in' approach, looking at contextual aspects of texts themselves first, such as the audience they are intended for, before zooming in on the texts in an increasing level of detail – from words to nuances of meaning to sounds.

This chapter covers a number of the course's key concepts:

- investigating *context*, including purpose, *audience* and form, examining how these aspects influence a writer's choices and contribute to a text's *meaning*
- describing aspects of *style* by exploring a range of ways to comment on the choices writers make
- applying *creativity* in your thinking, interpretation and expression as you engage analytically with texts and produce texts of your own.

3.1 Approaching texts in their context

How does context affect writers' and speakers' choice of language? What concepts are used to discuss context and language?

Context as spatial

The most obvious definition of context is spatial – it is about physical location. In this sense, context affects the language we use in everyday life, not just in formal or professional writing. For example, most people make slightly different language choices when they are speaking at work than they do when speaking at home or in a social context.

Activity 1

What differences are there between how you speak in class and how you speak with your friends? Try to identify ways in which your speech is broadly different (e.g. in structure), as well as individual words and phrases that might be specific to each context.

Key terms

dialect: a regionally-specific non-standard variety of language, including accent, grammar and word variations from the standard variety (e.g. 'I done it')

sociolect: a non-standard variety of language spoken by a particular social group

accent: non-standard and regionally-specific pronunciation features of language

ellipsis: the omission of words or phrases

elision: the omission of sounds or syllables

Other features of spatial context affect how people use language, too, such as whether or how well they know the person they are speaking to. People are more comfortable making certain language choices with those that they know well – for example:

- informal word choices such as slang, **dialect** or **sociolect**
- **ellipsis** (missing words out) e.g. 'You ok?' instead of 'Are you ok?'.
- features of informal pronunciation such as **accent** or **elision** (e.g. 'an' that').

Note that 'dialect' is a term used by linguists to mean a variety of language, but we can also talk about 'accent' and 'dialect' as separate features of language. Accent refers to the way sounds are pronounced differently from the standard form, while dialect refers to differences in the words and grammar used.

Context in terms of audience, purpose and form

Context is a combination of factors that exist outside the text, but which inform a text and might therefore inform your assessment of it. As such, it is important to consider context in the early stage of any text analysis.

Context = location + audience + purpose + form + mode

For more information on audience, purpose and form, see Chapter 2.

Activity 2

Copy and complete the following table to identify the audience and purpose of each of these texts.

Text	Audience	Purpose
a broadsheet newspaper article about a new trend in gardening	readers of that newspaper interested in gardening	to inform and entertain
a highly illustrated book about the life of an actor or rock star		
a leaflet found in a doctor's surgery about reducing the risk of heart disease	people at risk of heart disease	
a conversation between friends to plan a holiday trip		transactional (to get something done)
a young-adult fantasy novel		
a piece describing a trip to Egypt, published on a travel blog		
a scripted speech introducing a documentary about the wildlife of the Serengeti		
a review of a hotel left on a travel website		

As well as audience and purpose, the form of a text is also an important factor in its context. This is not just the case in written texts; spoken exchanges such as a chat with friends or an interaction with a bus driver also have specific forms. At a broad level, spoken texts can be described as **transactional** or **interactional**.

- Transactional conversations are about getting things done – whether that is buying a bus ticket, arranging where to meet someone or planning what to have for dinner.
- Interactional conversations can cover a far broader range of topics (personal, political, ideological, and so on) but ultimately the point of an interactional conversation is social – to get to know someone better or to express a relationship. Some linguists have compared interactional conversation to animals' grooming behaviours.

In reality, most conversations are a mix of transactional and interactional, so you will probably identify elements of both types in a transcript.

Look at Text 1 below, a transcription of a conversation about homework between a mother (who is a teacher) and her 14-year-old daughter. Note the conventions of a transcription – it does not use standard punctuation or capital letters and instead shows pauses timed in seconds. In effect, micropauses (less than half a second) and pauses are like punctuation. A transcription aims to record spoken language as precisely as possible, without interference from the written form. For this reason, it is not edited (as written language usually would be) to 'tidy up' repeated words or take out **fillers** like 'um' and 'er', or to add capitals and punctuation, which are ways in which we organise written language.

Key terms

transactional: describing a conversation which has a clearly defined purpose or function

interactional: describing a conversation whose purpose is entirely social

filler: a word used to avoid pausing too long or frequently

Text I

Mother:	have you got homework ↗
Daughter:	erm (.) ive got english sort of ongoing reading homework ↘
	//
Mother:	oh yeah the read a classic thing yeah ↘
Daughter:	erm (.) and i think (1) in two weeks we have do an a4 (.) sheet (1) basically just (.) its just based around what weve already learnt from [the book (.) so theres a lot of <u>different</u>
	//
Mother:	oh right (.)
	what youve found out so far ↘
	//
Daughter:	options or you can make your own up
	so you can do like character profiles(.) you can do summaries (.) er you can do like spider diagrams sort of just sort of <u>things</u> you <u>know</u> (2) its just to sort of prove that youve read it really ↘
Mother:	have you got a deadline to have read the book BY ↗
Daughter:	erm (4) its by the end of the topic ↘ which i dont know when the topic ENDS
Mother:	they didnt tell you that ↗ (2) how you sposed to
	//
Daughter:	well (1) i think she mentioned it ↘ but i dont
	remember (3)
Mother:	ok ↘ (4)
Daughter:	i dont know (2) erm (7) i dont know cause i wouldve wanted to like divide it up ↘ an
	//
Mother:	yeah
Daughter:	be like (.) make sure ive read THIS much by (.) then
Mother:	yeah
Daughter:	i think its the end of the year ↘
Mother:	you think its by (.) july ↗
Daughter:	yeah (1) erm
Mother:	i dont think a shorter deadline would be fair ↘ (.) given that
	//
Daughter:	dont you ↗
Mother:	some are reading like pride and prejudice
	//
Daughter:	ok erm because she s that YEAH this is our <u>final</u> topic ↘ she said that yeah yeah yeah i remember now sorry (.) its just come back to me yeah

Transcription key

(.) micropause
(1) pause timed in seconds
<u>underline</u> stressed word or syllable
EMPHASIS (words said with more emphasis)
// simultaneous speech (said at the same
time as the line below/above
↘ downward intonation
↗ upward intonation
{laughs} non-speech sounds

Activity 3

Is the conversation in Text 1 mostly transactional or mostly interactional? When making your decision, consider:

- whether and to what extent it exchanges information
- how necessary or useful that information seems to be
- how social or interactional this conversation is
- whether and to what extent the participants appear to be doing or planning something together
- what each participant might individually want out of the conversation (that is, do they have separate purposes?).

When commenting on the form of conversations, you can be more specific than simply describing them as transactional or interactional. For example, you might describe a sales pitch as a 'persuasive transactional speech' or an exchange between a customer and a shop assistant as a 'transactional service encounter'.

In analysis of any text type, be as specific as possible and link points about the form of a text to the language chosen. For example, in an analysis of the transcription above, you might note that it is clearly the start of a planning conversation, or a negotiation in which plans are being made. The mother asks a lot of questions or gives prompts that enable the daughter to identify what she needs to do.

Activity 4

Copy and complete the table below, explaining how each language choice is appropriate for the form it has been used in. The first row has been completed for you.

Text type	Language choice	How does the language fit the form?
an advice leaflet on choosing a career, aimed at teenagers	subheadings	it organises the information and enhances clarity for the reader
an opinion column on litter from a broadsheet	first-person address	
a crime novel	metaphor	
the script for a television advert for toothpaste	alliteration	

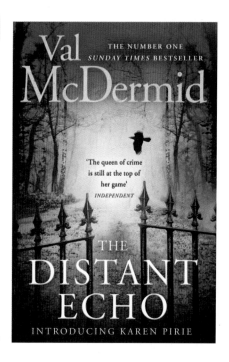

Val McDermid

THE NUMBER ONE
SUNDAY TIMES BESTSELLER

'The queen of crime is still at the top of her game'
INDEPENDENT

THE

DISTANT ECHO

INTRODUCING KAREN PIRIE

Using context in analytical writing

Read the text below, which is an article about the importance of getting enough sleep.

Text 2

Taking Sleep Seriously

By Mark Parkinson

The weight of evidence is so strong that we really have to kill off all the macho, heroic myths around sleep deprivation. I remember that, years ago, there was much talk about how Margaret Thatcher only needed four hours of sleep each night when she was Prime Minister of Great Britain. I've also seen similar claims related to Tony Blair.

In my student days, it was almost seen as a badge of honour when you put yourself in the situation to 'pull an all-nighter' to get an assignment completed and handed in with minutes to spare the next morning.

Now I'm older, and hopefully a bit wiser, I can see that it was a basic equation between prioritising time for what was necessary/important or what was fun, immediate and wanted. I don't think I can really remember a single occasion when a night spent working and getting no sleep wasn't the result of bad judgement and lack of self-control/regulation rather than genuine volume of responsibilities and necessity.

I've been writing for some time about how sleep deprivation is exacting a toll on students and limiting their learning potential. Here's a very well written and presented article from McKinsey & Co that looks at another perspective – the organisational costs of insufficient sleep, especially when leaders are making decisions without getting enough shut-eye.

McKinsey – The Organisational Cost of Insufficient Sleep

The article sets out a very strong case that the implications are so great that this must really matter to organisations. Rather than perpetuating cultures where people are recognised and rewarded for appearing to make personal sacrifices by going without sleep, organisations need to see that they potentially pay a heavy price when people are operating in less than effective states.

In other words, they have to educate their workforce and help them to develop positive and healthy habits. Two days ago, I wrote about the Netflix culture. Interestingly, that was very clear that there should be rewards or recognition for people according to how long they spend on the job or how much time they put in to work. Recognition should link purely to outcomes and the link to time should be de-emphasised.

I think it's often quite hard to change such habits in adulthood. As a result, the right habits need to be established from an early age. This means:

a) Developing good routines and patterns around sleep and bed time for very young children,

b) Not treating staying up late as a special treat (too many do it with junk food as well).

c) We should teach our children about the basics of the science related to sleep, so that they understand why it's important (not just tell them to do what we say),

d) We need to set good examples to our children about getting a healthy amount of sleep, including things like switching off devices an hour before bed.

When we are at a less than optimal level of effectiveness due to lack of sleep, we should acknowledge this to our children.

In the past, we really didn't know just how harmful these sleep issues could be. Ignorance is no longer an excuse, so we must change our ways.

From www.newdelhitimes.com/taking-sleep-seriously

Text 2 appeared in the *New Delhi Times* and can also be found on the newspaper's website. This tells us that it will have multiple audiences, including:

- regular readers of the newspaper
- readers of this writer's columns
- people who find the article online by looking for material about sleep in particular.

Activity 5

The writer is clearly a regular contributor to the *New Delhi Times* ('Two days ago, I wrote about the Netflix culture.'). What does this tell you about his purpose for writing this column? Organise the following statements from most to least likely (you can do this as a triangle with several 'most likely').

- to build an audience
- to create a relationship with an audience
- to tell people about sleep
- to share his opinions about sleep
- to persuade people to get better sleep
- to improve his reputation as an expert on sleep
- to show he can write about a range of topics.

Now look at the following sample analysis. As you read, consider how effective it is in showing how context influences the language of this text.

In the article, the writer makes his case strongly straight away with clear and direct language, to achieve his primary purpose of making an argument. The article uses the metaphor 'killing off … myths' together with words from a **semantic field** of manliness like 'heroic' and 'macho' to support his argument that in the past, not getting enough sleep has been presented as something that tough people do. By opening with this concept of destroying myths, he makes his position immediately clear and also shows the reader what to expect throughout the piece. This lives up to the title of 'taking sleep seriously', demonstrating that this is a serious article. At the same time, by referencing other articles he has written and by maintaining a personable and friendly tone ('Now I'm older, and hopefully a bit wiser'), he is also writing to build rapport with his audience in the hope that they will read more of his articles in the future.

Key terms

semantic field: a group of words that belong to the same category of meaning (e.g. 'bicycle', 'car' and 'truck' all belong to the semantic field of vehicles)
lexical field: the topic of the text

Case study: **Schema theory**

A schema is a system for understanding something. Schema theory, as popularised by the psychologist Piaget (1896–1980), is the idea that people have schemata, or frames, to help them make sense of things – that is, they organise knowledge into chunks, or units. It is a well-established concept that originated outside of linguistics, so it is not associated with any one individual; however, Goffman's (1922–1982) frame theory (as described below in relation to context) can be cited as an example of a specific type of schema within linguistics.

The frame theory states that when children are at school, for example, they have a pre-established set of ideas (a frame) about how they should behave linguistically in that context. They expect to answer and ask questions, to request permission before speaking and to receive explicit feedback on their contributions. All these things would be out of place in other contexts, but because they are the norm in school, they slot into place for children (after the first year or so) as soon as they step into class. It is therefore the context that cues this schema or frame.

Activity 6

Think of two different 'frames', like the school example in the case study above. Describe the linguistic behaviours you would expect in each of these frames. Consider:

- who any interactions would take place between
- whether there are routines and protocols (like schoolchildren needing permission to speak in some circumstances)
- what kinds of speech will take place (like children asking and answering questions in school, and receiving feedback on their answers).

Possible frames include: doctor/dentist, sports club, place of worship or working as, for example, wait staff.

So, different contexts cause different linguistic choices. This might be about selecting appropriate words and phrases to have the desired effect on an audience. Or it may be about meeting the conventions of a specific form, which includes operating within a schema or frame. Sometimes, however, a different context can impose a different meaning on the same set of words.

Activity 7

In each of the following scenarios, imagine that your friend replies to your question with 'I like your blue top'. How does the meaning change? Note down how you would react to each response and why.

Scenario 1: 'What should I wear tonight?'
Scenario 2: 'Do you like my new green top?'

Context and mode

Mode is another factor worth discussing when considering context. Broadly speaking, mode is the way in which a text, whether written, spoken or a hybrid such as an electronic text, is transmitted from the producer to the receiver. However, mode is really more complex and interesting than that. Discussing it as either one thing or another – written or spoken, for example – is likely to hinder any in-depth analysis, so it is better to think of it as a question of degree: not 'is this text written or spoken?' but 'how written (or spoken) is this text?'

The table below outlines the key features associated with mode. You will see that they go in pairs. When analysing a text use these features to ask yourself '*How* … is this text?' rather than '*Is* this text …?'

visual	This relates to the concept of 'channel' – how the message of the text is received, via either the eyes or ears. Different kinds of features are effective depending on whether the text is seen or heard, such as the use of bold font and embedded images or volume for emphasis.	auditory
permanent	How long is the text expected to last? An ephemeral one is not intended to have any life after production at all: in conversation, we speak and it is gone, or we throw away the shopping list, whereas a printed book or recorded speech is forever the same. Interestingly, although we talk about the internet being 'forever', if you 'bookmark' a webpage and return to it, it may have changed – the same cannot be said of a physical book page.	ephemeral
planned	Classic conversation is truly spontaneous, whereas the printed word will have been planned, drafted and edited before being seen by its audience. Of course, some types of speech may be planned before production, and even some informal online writing may be edited before sending.	spontaneous
monologic	A monologic text is one with a single voice, while interactivity is about a multiplicity of voices – for example, a conversation between two or more participants, or an online chat with multiple voices. It can also be used to describe an online text where the reader/viewer participates (e.g. through selecting a particular pathway).	interactive
transactional	This is about whether the text fulfils a concrete or social need, and is rarely fully at any one end of the scale.	interactional
asynchronous	This comes from the Greek *a* (not) *sun* (together) and *chronos* (time) and is a measure of whether participants are present at the same time in the interaction. For example, when you speak, your audience hears your words immediately (synchronous) but when you send messages electronically, there is a slight delay and you have the opportunity to correct what you are saying without your audience knowing you made a mistake.	synchronous
formal	This relates both to the structure of the text or interaction and the language used. Are there clear rules governing the speech or text? Is informality appropriate?	informal

It is helpful to consider these not as binary opposites, but as continuum lines. Plotting different text types onto a set of these lines can help you to see how the different features work together and how you might use them in an analysis. It is rarely – if ever – the case, that a text would produce a straight vertical line down the grid.

To take the example of a broadsheet column such as Text 2, tracking the continuum lines would produce quite a mixed profile. The article scores highly for planning, but relatively low for permanence (newspapers are not intended for a long life). The text is received visually but does not make as much use of this as some texts (for example, a poster), and is monologic. In terms of transactionality, it has a purpose but also aims to keep readers coming back to the newspaper, so there is a kind of interactionality to it. It is definitely asynchronous and the formality is mixed (probably because of the transactional/interactional mix mentioned above).

visual	auditory
permanent	ephemeral
planned	spontaneous
monologic	interactive
transactional	interactional
asynchronous	synchronous
formal	informal

Activity 8

Create mode diagrams like the one above for the following texts. For each diagram, write a paragraph explaining your choices.

Text A (a video of a virtual tour of a zoo)
Watch Robert Irwin's virtual Australia Zoo tour on YouTube.

Text B (a diary entry)

Today I enjoyed the zoo and getting to see all the animals. I was a little disappointed we didn't manage to find the capybaras but we did get to see the otters playing with stones right by the glass. I even managed to get some cute pictures of them all! We were very lucky as it had stopped raining by the time we were wandering around the outdoor areas.

Text C (an extract from a tourist brochure)

ARCTIC
What happens here, doesn't stay here

CANADA GOOSE ARCTIC GALLERY

The new Canada Goose Arctic Gallery is a window on the intimate connection between people and nature in Canada's North. Discover this region through authentic specimens and artefacts. Walk through real ice as part of a National Film Board of Canada multimedia experience. #ArcticAtTheMuseum

When writing about features of mode, be selective. It is best to choose features that are unusual for the text type, or which stand out as interesting, rather than to list all the typical ones. When writing about mode as part of an analysis of Text 2 on page 40, for example, you might focus your comments on the interactional and informal elements, as these are the most unexpected for its form (a newspaper article) and therefore the most interesting.

It should be possible to pair these with linguistic features (that is, choices of words and phrases) for more detailed and incisive comment. For example, the writer of Text 2 shows an interactional intention through the use of first person address. He uses 'I' to give his opinion, but also refers to 'our children', switching to an inclusive plural form of first person to create a link with his readers. This may also help fulfil his persuasive purpose – people are likely to listen to advice given by someone positioning themselves *alongside* rather than *above* them.

Activity 9

Analyse the following language choices from Text 2 by making connections to either its audience, form, purpose or an aspect of its mode:

- the lettered list of habits that children need to establish
- 'Now I'm older, and hopefully a bit wiser'
- 'Ignorance is no longer an excuse, so we must change our ways.'

Final task

Analyse and compare the three texts from Activity 8, all of which are about tourist attractions. Focus your comparison on the *contexts* of the extracts, so identify the key contextual factors:

- Who is the intended audience?
- What purpose(s) was the text produced for?
- What is the text's form?

For each text, choose at least *two* factors that you think are the most important, and find a language choice that exists because of each factor. Write these up into sentences, so that you have a clear paragraph about each text.

3.2 Approaching texts on a pragmatic level

What is pragmatics? What concepts are used to discuss pragmatics in texts?

What does pragmatics mean?

> ### Activity 1
>
> Find the meanings of the following words in a dictionary. They derive from the Greek root *pragma*, meaning 'deed'.
>
> * pragmatic (adjective)
> * pragmatist (noun)

In everyday speech, we use the adjective 'pragmatic' to describe someone or something that is practical. In linguistics, pragmatics is the study of the practicalities of language – what speakers and writers are intending to do with their words. A pragmatic approach to a text usually means looking at several different things:

* the intentions that the person producing the text had and how they have fulfilled them
* any differences between what the language of the text appears to say and what it means to its intended audience (e.g. using sarcasm or **idiom**)
* how producers and audiences of the text (need to) cooperate to make the text work (e.g. using **inference**)
* how texts make reference to their contexts, such as language, to negotiate power differences between participants or routine structures for politeness (e.g. greetings).

Why pragmatics?

Pragmatics is a useful branch of linguistics for focusing on what language is for: communication. Linguists who primarily concern themselves with pragmatics study how language is used cooperatively – how people work together to arrive at meanings – for example, using **implicature** and inference.

Key terms

idiom: a typical phrase common to a language (e.g. 'dead funny' meaning 'really funny'; 'a right laugh' meaning 'a lot of fun')

implicature: the meanings intended in what someone says or writes which are not stated explicitly

inference: the meanings drawn out of a text by a listener or reader

Case study: **Grice's cooperative principle**

The philosopher H. P. Grice believed that all human communication is founded upon the cooperative principle: basically, that we work together to make sense of what each other says/writes. If something does not make sense, we assume there must be something in the context that we need to identify in order to rectify that.

Look at this dialogue:

Person A: Where is the TV remote?
Person B: The children were watching cartoons earlier.

This may initially appear to make no sense, but when you consider it more carefully, the pragmatics of Person B's response are that Person A should be addressing the question to the children. Although Person B's contribution may at first appear irrelevant (uncooperative), in fact it is pragmatically perfectly useful.

Grice outlined four maxims which he maintained that speakers follow unless there is a good reason not to (in which case they 'flout' the maxim):

- maxim of relation: speakers make contributions that are relevant to the conversation
- maxim of quantity: speakers say neither too much nor too little
- maxim of quality: speakers say what they know to be true or what they have evidence for
- maxim of manner – speakers organise their speech to make it clear

Working from a common background

Speakers often understand one another because they share the same background and therefore the same frame of reference. This is known as **shared resources** and is a way of referring to the common knowledge or cultural understanding that an audience is likely to have. This may include general knowledge facts, but also broad cultural information. Pop culture references also fall into this category, as do bigger cultural ideas such as references to Greek or Roman mythology in the West.

Shared resources

It is often possible to identify the audience of a text by its references to shared resources. Sometimes these resources will be ones in your own 'set'; at other times, you may recognise that a reference is being made but not fully understand it. While this may be difficult when you are trying to analyse a text, it does at least tell you that you are probably not its intended audience! In these cases, it is acceptable to identify that 'X' appears to be a reference to shared resources that the specific audience is expected to have access to, thus showing a relationship between the writer and the reader.

For example, a newspaper article may make a historical reference by comparing someone in the news to a historical figure. These range from broad references such as 'Napoleonic' or 'like Attila the Hun' to suggest that someone is empire-building, to much more niche references (for example, to specific battles). It is usually possible to tell what comparison is being made from the way the reference is used, even if it is not familiar to you.

> **Key term**
>
> **shared resources:** the sum of knowledge and references that it is reasonable to expect members of a culture to have access to

Activity 2

Look at the references below, taken from journalistic texts produced for an educated audience. Explain the intended meaning of each reference in terms of what it is supposed to convey to the audience. How might each reference make the audience feel?

- *The great thing about him is that he never asked what anyone could do for him, but what he could do for them. And, quite naturally, for that we loved him.* (about the leader of a youth sports team)
- *A startling figure in business, she was gathering companies with all the compassion of a Viking taking villages.*

Intertextuality

Intertextuality (or intertextual reference) is a type of reference to shared resources – to another specific text, or a specific type of text. Again, these are usually culturally specific, and often resort to mythology and folklore (e.g. Grimm-type fairy tales for the West). Intertextual reference is also common in song lyrics, and you will find phrases from well-known speeches in all sorts of other texts.

Intertextuality is particularly common in media texts, as it allows quick associations to be made. For example, an advert may show a girl in a red cape, intending to convey meanings of innocence and vulnerability. Equally, such references can be used to construct imagery in an abbreviated way, such as describing a glare as 'like a Gorgon' to evoke the idea that the expression has the power to turn to stone. If you are not familiar with the stories of Little Red Riding Hood or Medusa, the meaning will be lost on you. In most cases, however, references help a writer/speaker to not only connect with a set of meanings quickly, but also to make a connection with the audience, as the person understanding that reference feels they are part of something by having made the link. This is particularly effective in texts like advertisements – if the audience feels good, they may buy the product!

Key term

Intertextuality: the ways in which texts are interrelated and the meanings that arise out of this

Activity 3

Find examples of uses of shared resources or intertextuality. Try looking in:

- song lyrics
- sitcom scripts
- advertisements on television and in print
- stand-up comedy routines
- newspaper articles.

Remember to look for either things that *do not need explaining* – the audience is just expected to know – or *references to other texts*, whether high or popular culture.

The use of shared resources can contribute to a text's tone by tapping into a wider set of ideas economically and allowing the reader to apply atmosphere from those ideas to the text more broadly. For example, for the 'Viking business woman' reference in Activity 2, the text as a whole would be quite likely to be humorous as this reference is slightly **hyperbolic** in the way that it is used, with the clash between 'compassion' and 'Viking'.

Activity 4

Look at the dataset below – a collection of headlines on the topic of modern cinema.

Headline	Topic of article
A Minion to One Chance	how a film franchise became so successful that children no longer know the word minion existed before the films
Sisters Are Doing It For Themselves	focus on women filmmakers
Offers They Couldn't Refuse	discussion of the recent trend in remaking films from the 1970s, 80s and 90s
The A-Lister Team	red carpet season roundup
Movies by the Book	round-up of film adaptations from novels

Analyse the use of intertextuality, shared resources and other features in this dataset. The information provided about the topic of each article should help you, but searching for phrases that sound similar to the title will also help.

How has the use of shared resources helped each writer connect with the audience and make a point? What does each suggest about the tone of the article to come?

Representation

The concept of representation refers to how language is used to build up an image. It is therefore another key area to consider in terms of what people *do* with language, or how language works pragmatically. Ultimately, language is a symbolic system: words stand for things; they carry meanings. In some cases, the meanings words accumulate over time form a web of complex social ideas that may have little to do with the thing originally labelled by that word.

For example, take the word pair 'bachelor' and 'spinster'. According to dictionary definitions, these words are equivalents, both meaning 'unmarried'. However, for most speakers of English, the words *represent* very different types:

- bachelor = young, fun, trendy (note the phrases 'eligible bachelor', 'bachelor pad', 'bachelor party')
- spinster = old, unwanted, needy (note the use of 'bachelorette party' rather than 'spinster party').

Activity 5

How many meanings for the word 'represent' can you find? How does the word break down? Which possible meanings seem to contribute to the concept of 'representation' being discussed here?

Analysing representation in texts

In the context of text analysis, representation is usually more about the overall effect than the weight of meaning of individual words. In using a particular set of images, or even in choosing a particular tone, a writer or speaker can set up a clear representation. To comment on this in an analysis, you need to make inferences and state what the writer/speaker is implying through their choices.

A useful concept here is that of **positioning**, which explores where the speaker/writer places three key components of the text: the audience, themselves and the subject. For example, a newspaper columnist might place themselves and their reader together against the problem being written about: 'We can tackle this together.' Or a writer may position themselves as an 'expert' – above the audience – and show this by writing in a way that seeks to inform and educate. Often, it is enough to talk about audience positioning, as this informs writer and subject positioning as well. For example, in a heavily persuasive text, the writer probably believes that the audience does not already hold the position that he or she wants them to.

Within a text, the main subject may have several representations. For example, in Text 2 in Unit 3.1, sleep is represented in the following ways:

- as something that people use to show toughness by 'only' needing a small amount
- as valuable – this does not need explaining
- as something many adults are getting wrong
- as being worth educating children about
- as having habits set in childhood.

Key term

positioning: a description of where, symbolically, the writer, audience and subject of the text are located in relation to one another

Taking things further

The theories of the linguist Norman Fairclough are largely about power relations in texts. One example of this is the concept of **synthetic personalisation**, or texts creating fake relationships. Synthetic personalisation is used regularly in advertising and in commercial texts, where the business wants to appeal to the audience, making people feel like they have understood their needs and can provide the perfect product to meet those needs. A range of linguistic techniques are used to achieve this, from the very simple (e.g. addressing the audience directly using 'you'), to the subtler and more sophisticated (e.g. choosing particular accents that people relate to more readily).

Key term

synthetic personalisation: the use of inclusive language when addressing mass audience to make them feel like they are being addressed individually

Final task

Return to the texts in Activity 8 in Unit 3.1:

- a video 'virtual tour' of a zoo
- a diary entry about a zoo trip
- an extract from a brochure about a museum.

Having looked at their contexts in some detail, you are now going to apply what you have learned about pragmatics.

- What reference to shared resources or uses of intertextuality can you see in the texts? Explain their effects, referring back to the audience.
- What representations does each text create? Describe up to three of the most significant representations for each text and select a quotation for each one as evidence.
- How are the writer and audience positioned in relation to one another in each text? Demonstrate with a quotation in each case.

3.3 Approaching texts on a lexical level

What is lexis? What does the type of lexis used add to a text?

What is lexis?

In your study of English Language, you will need to investigate issues such as the complexity of the words used in a text, their tone and the kind of language style associated with them. All this is about approaching texts in terms of their lexis – that is, their vocabulary. ·

Key term

synonym: a word with the same or similar meaning as another

Activity 1

Bearing in mind that 'lexis' is a **synonym** for 'vocabulary', which of the following extracts are acceptable usages and which are not?

- The writer has used the lexis 'blackest' to evoke the depth of the darkness…
- The lexis in this text, for example, 'unmistakably wrongfooted', contributes to the positioning of the writer as sophisticated…
- The text has a melancholy tone, created by the writer's use of lexis, for example, 'somnolent trees'…
- This is quite a simple text, seen in the monosyllabic lexis 'saw'…
- Lexis such as the adjective 'remarkable' and the noun 'astonishment' helps to create a sense of wonder in the text…

When analysing the words used in a text, it can be useful to comment on their character as a whole, or to slice that whole up into parts and discuss sections of the vocabulary that have been used to create different effects. Considering lexis is essentially an assessment of the words en masse; it is not an analysis of individual words or phrase choices in terms of their meaning. Examining the lexis as a whole will allow you to comment on the tone of a text and/or its audience (or the writer's attitude toward the audience).

Activity 2

Tone can be associated with lexical formality. For each trio of synonyms below, rank each word by its formality, where 1 is the most formal and 3 is the least.

ask	interrogate	question
problem	impediment	snag
debilitated	fatigued	tired
employment	vocation	work

The reason that English has such a large word stock is its complex linguistic history. This is a result of a series of invasions and cultural shifts that took place in Britain over several centuries. Viking, Roman and Norman invaders brought Norse, Latin and French influences on the language respectively.

Both Anglo-Saxon and the version of Anglo-Saxon with Norse influences are known as Old English. Old English is not intelligible to most speakers of contemporary English, but many words in modern English are derived directly from Old English. By the time Norman French had become the official language of England, the native tongue of the country had become Middle English. Early Modern English starts in the 16th century and it is in this period that many Latin and Greek words came into the language.

XXXII. How the Worm came to the Howe, and how he was robbed of a cup; and how he fell on the folk.

NOT at all with self-wielding the craft of the worm-hoards
He sought of his own will, who sore himself harmed;
But for threat of oppression a thrall, of I wot not
Which bairn of mankind, from blows wrathful fled,
House-needy forsooth, and hied him therein,
A man by guilt troubled. Then soon it betided
That therein to the guest there stood grisly terror;
However the wretched, of every hope waning

The ill-shapen wight, whenas the fear gat him,
The treasure-vat saw; of such there was a many
Up in that earth-house of treasures of old,
As them in the yore-days, though what man I know not,
The huge leavings and loom of a kindred of high ones,
Well thinking of thoughts there had hidden away,
Dear treasures. But all them had death borne away
In the times of erewhile; and the one at the last
Of the doughty of that folk that there longest lived,
There waxed he friend-sad, yet ween'd he to tarry,
That he for a little those treasures the longsome
Might brook for himself. But a burg now all ready
Wonn'd on the plain nigh the waves of the water,
New by a ness, by narrow-crafts fasten'd;
Within there then bare of the treasures of earls
That herd of the rings a deal hard to carry,
Of gold fair beplated, and few words he quoth:

Page from 'The Tale of Beowulf' in Old English

For more on this topic, see Unit 5.2.

Activity 3

Using a dictionary or the internet, look up the **etymology** (origin) of each of the words in Activity 2. What patterns do you notice – for example, are there any links between formality and etymology?

Register and frequency

It is important to be as precise as possible when talking about the **register** of a text, as this can help when discussing tone or contextual factors such as audience. If a field is clearly defined, it is possible to give it its own register – for example, it is better to talk about a 'medical register' than a 'high register' or a 'specialist register'.

Frequency is a concept that is often discussed alongside register, because frequency can be used to support claims about the formality or complexity of the register. High-frequency lexis is lexis that is used often, while low-frequency lexis is not frequently heard. Note that low-frequency lexis does not necessarily equate to a particular end of the register scale – it might be low frequency because it is extremely formal, or because it is taboo or obscene.

When looking at etymology, **morphology** can be useful. For example, words using the suffixes '-ology' or '-metry' are more likely to be of Greek origin, and to belong to a technical register.

Read the following transcription of a conversation between a 19-year-old (the teenager) and her mother. F is the older girl's 14-year-old sister.

Key terms

register: a description of the level of formality or specialism of the lexis of a text

frequency: a measure of how often a word/phrase is used in everyday language/by the average speaker

morphology: the study of how words are built from morphemes, for example, 'runs' = 'run' + 's' (verb + present tense marker)

Text 3

Teen:	hi
Mother:	what dyou want
Teen:	charming
Mother:	sorry (.) im just really busy (.) so what DO you want
Teen:	i just (1) I wanted to (.) dont worry about it (.) sorry
Mother:	no its fine (.) im sorry (1) come back
Teen:	i was wondering if we could (.) me and F (.) if we could go to the cinema later

Transcription key

(.)	micropause
(1)	timed pause in seconds
CAPITALS	raised volume

Activity 4

Answer the following questions about the transcription.

a) Why is the lexis all low register and high frequency?
b) Why does Teen say 'charming' in her second turn?
c) How is 'charming' different from the rest of the exchange in lexical terms?

Chapter 3 Key analytical skills: Approaching texts linguistically

Identify what is good about this analysis following Activity 4.

> The form of the transcription is a mostly transactional conversation – Teen has a specific request and the talk is mostly quite business-like, apart from the pragmatics, as Mother is 'really busy'. Because she is busy and replied initially bluntly, she seems to have offended Teen, which Teen signals with her slightly sarcastic comment 'charming'. This one example of slightly lower-frequency lexis stands out – it was clearly chosen to have the effect of shaming her mother slightly for the careless initial reply. It is effective in this, setting off a chain of apologies, and restoring balance.

The register of spoken language is often lower than that of written language. For example, you are more likely to hear **colloquialisms** such as 'hi' or 'yeah' than to see them written down. Dialect forms (such as 'me duck' as a term of address) or **slang** (such as 'quid' or 'buck' as money terms) are also more commonly spoken than written.

Colloquial language is used mainly (though not exclusively) in speech, while dialect words are regionally specific. You are most likely to see them written down in forms that record or mimic speech, such as dialogue in novels. Slang is a particular kind of colloquialism, having a time-limited or social group-specific element to it. Slang goes out of date, and different types of people use it differently – your parents' slang is unlikely to be the same as yours.

Key terms

colloquialisms: language used commonly in conversation and informal contexts
slang: highly informal language used in speech by a particular social group or used for a short time

Activity 5

Note down some familiar examples of colloquialisms, slang and local dialect. Which words do you say that you would not write in your school/college work, for example? Classify each example as slang, colloquialism or dialect.

In looking at lexis, you may also have to consider an occupational or other specialist context, which could lead to the use of **jargon**. It is important to think about whether jargon is being used negatively (excluding others/creating a hierarchy/hiding meaning) or positively (including others/creating a team ethos/helping to understand). Note that the *intention* may not have been this positive or negative use. In describing the usage as negative or positive, you are commenting on the jargon's *effect*.

Key term

jargon: technical terminology used within a specific field of study or work

Activity 6

What do you think the effect of each example of jargon below would be on the audience? For example, would it be likely to improve their understanding of the situation, increase their trust in the healthcare context, or create a negative emotional effect such as fear or confusion?

- (in a leaflet on heart disease) *Coronary Angiogram – A doctor will put some coloured water into your arteries to see if they are blocked.*
- (spoken to a teen patient on arrival into hospital after an accident) *Have you taken any analgesia?*

Lexis and characterisation

Key term

characterisation: the creation of a fictional character in a narrative text, establishing their distinctive features

In narrative writing, lexis can make a useful contribution to **characterisation**. For example, register can clearly indicate many details about the narrator of a story. Text 4 below is an extract from a novel published in 1885. It is easy to identify that the narrator, Huckleberry Finn, is young and relatively uneducated because the writer includes dialect forms and colloquialisms or slang. The overall tone — which also comes from the way the sentences are put together — reads clearly like a boy speaking.

Text 4

You don't know about me without you have read a book by the name of The Adventures of Tom Sawyer; but that ain't no matter. That book was made by Mr. Mark Twain, and he told the truth, mainly. There was things which he **stretched**, but mainly he told the truth. That is nothing. I never seen anybody but lied one time or another, without it was Aunt Polly, or the widow, or maybe Mary. Aunt Polly — Tom's Aunt Polly, she is — and Mary, and the Widow Douglas is all told about in that book, which is mostly a true book, with some stretchers, as I said before.

Now the way that the book winds up is this: Tom and me found the money that the robbers hid in the cave, and it made us rich. We got six thousand dollars apiece — all gold. It was an awful sight of money when it was piled up. Well, Judge Thatcher he took it and put it out at interest, and it fetched us a dollar a day apiece all the year round — more than a body could tell what to do with. The Widow Douglas she took me for her son, and allowed she would sivilize me; but it was rough living in the house all the time, considering how dismal regular and decent the widow was in all her ways; and so when I couldn't stand it no longer I lit out. I got into my old rags and my **sugar-hogshead** again, and was free and satisfied. But Tom Sawyer he hunted me up and said he was going to start a band of robbers, and I might join if I would go back to the widow and be respectable. So I went back.

Mark Twain, from *Huckleberry Finn*

Glossary:
stretched: lied about
sugar-hogshead: a barrel, which Huck had used as a bed in their hideout

Activity 7

Select three quotations from Text 4 to analyse and demonstrate how Mark Twain creates Huckleberry Finn's voice and character in this opening to the novel.

Now read Text 5, which is an extract from a short story.

Text 5

The boy raised his head when the door scraped open. His heart leapt with a relief that surprised him, then he closed his eyes and sank back on the floor.

'Gertrude?' His father's voice was gruff.

The boy didn't answer. He peeped under his arm at the man's dark shape leaning against the door. He held a bundle in his right hand; in his left he balanced his machete. The boy watched his father's shape double as he dropped the bundle and the cutlass in the corner near the door.

'Gerty!'

The boy pressed his face into the bedding until the floor was hard against his cheek. He felt the weight of his father's boots sinking in the floorboards as he stepped over the little girl, then the younger boy and finally himself.

The room darkened further as the man's shadow fell on him. His father reached for the tiny kerosene lamp on the table and turned it up.

The boy knew that the man was staring at the bed against the wall. He waited, fearing the wrath that would follow when he saw that the bed was rumpled and empty.

His father's silence was unbearable, his breathing low and deep.

The boy's body bunched when the man's hand dropped on his back and he went through the motions of someone just awakened.

'Stanford! Fordy, wake up, boy. Stan boy! Where you' modder? Tell me, where your modder is?'

When the boy sat up and raised his eyes, he stared directly into his father's. He shifted his gaze to the paper-pasted board walls across the room. From outside came the drone of jeeps, and louder, sharper sounds. He knew that beyond the flimsy house the darkness threatened.

'I talking to you, boy!' This time his father shook him.

'Sh ... Sh ... She gone!' the boy said, and the pain of the day and the night began to show on his face. His father's eyes followed the trickle down his cheeks. The man raised his hand and the boy shrank back. His father brushed away the tears with a knuckle.

Jacob Ross, 'Dark Is The Hour' from *Tell No-one About This: The Collected Stories 1975–2017*

Further reading

David Crystal, *The Story of English in 100 Words* (Profile Books, 2012)
Steven Pinker, *The Seven Words You Can't Say on Television* (Penguin, 2008)
Tony Thorne, *Shoot the Puppy: A Survival Guide to the Curious Jargon of Modern Life* (Penguin, 2007)

Final task

Analyse Text 5, paying particular attention to its lexis. To do this, consider:

- the register chosen and its overall effect
- the likely origin/etymology of any particularly interesting words or groups of words
- the voice created through lexical choices in dialogue and narration.

3.4 Approaching texts on a semantic level

What is semantics? What features can you discuss when looking at a text semantically?

What is semantics?

You may already be familiar with the term 'semantics'. In everyday speech, it is used in contexts such as when people are arguing over what something means ('but that's just semantics'), or making a joke based on words that are similar to one another.

In linguistics, the study of semantics is the study of meaning, so a semantic approach to a text will explore:

- what words mean (individually or in combination)
- why words might have been chosen for the precise nuances, or shades of meaning, they have
- the relationships words share based on their meanings.

Since semantics is concerned with meaning, it has links with pragmatics (what a writer or speaker intends to convey). However, the two are not quite the same. A semantic approach focuses on words and their particular meanings; pragmatics explores the social and practical results of language in the world – what language is used to do. Of course, this intended outcome can depend on the words selected, so you may be able to comment on aspects of a text in terms of both semantics and pragmatics. Semantics is a rich source for linguistic analysis, as meaning is such an important aspect to consider.

Denotation and connotations

Key terms

denotation: the dictionary definition of a word

connotations: the cultural, social or personal associations surrounding a word

When talking about the meaning of a word, it is useful to discuss both its **denotation** and its **connotations**. The denotation of a word is the standard definition that you would find in a dictionary, which does not change rapidly over time or vary much between individuals. A word's connotations are its associations. Mostly these will be cultural – for example, the colour red has connotations of danger in several countries and is therefore used in road-safety signs in these countries. Connotations may also be personal, such as snow having positive connotations for a ski fan and frightening connotations for someone who associates it with falling and breaking a leg.

Connotations can greatly influence word choice, and add tone and mood to a text.

Look at the following examples:

- He returned to his residence.
- He returned to his dwelling.
- He returned to his home.

The nouns have different connotations, suggesting different kinds of living situations. In turn, this may add to the characterisation, giving further information about the man's social status or taste, because readers may have assumptions about what kind of person would live in a 'dwelling' or a 'residence'.

Activity 1

Explore the differences in connotation between each word in the following word groups. Think about in what context the words could be used and put them into sentences. Do they fit with the same context? Does the meaning change?

dwelling	residence	home
childlike	youthful	juvenile
willowy	skinny	emaciated

Write a brief explanation of the differences between the three words in each group. You can include references to the sentences you used or other words that you used in your sentences.

Figurative language

One key aspect of meaning is whether words are meant to be taken literally or figuratively. When words are meant literally, the audience is intended to understand exactly what the words say – no additional meaning is meant to be drawn from them. When a figurative meaning is intended, however, the audience is supposed to understand something other than the denotative meaning of the words being used. For example:

Pull your socks up!
Literal meaning: your socks are falling down and need to be adjusted.
Figurative meaning: your behaviour is falling short of the standard expected and needs to be adjusted.

Figurative language can also be used **euphemistically**, to avoid being direct, such as describing someone's pet as having 'gone to the farm' instead of being literal and saying it has died. As an umbrella term, 'figurative language' describes a range of features. **Metaphor**, **simile**, **personification** and **hyperbole** are the most common.

Key terms

literal meaning: the exact, dictionary meanings of words/phrases
figurative meaning: the metaphorical meanings of words/phrases
euphemism (euphemistically): a phrase used to avoid saying something thought to be unpleasant
metaphor: a figure of speech comparing two unlike things to highlight the qualities of one
simile: a figure of speech that compares two things using the word 'like' or 'as'
personification: attributing human qualities to an inanimate object or an animal
hyperbole: exaggeration for effect

Activity 2

Copy the table and put each of the phrases in the correct column. Add examples of your own to each list. (If you cannot come up with any, try thinking of song lyrics, advertisements and poems that you know.)

Metaphor	Simile	Personification	Hyperbole

conniving cat

peace fell over the house

I've told you a thousand times

fingers as deft as a spider

fists like hammers

the trees whispered

faster than the speed of light

my Dad is as old as the hills

the house tucked them in

her empty heart

he sighed like the tide going out

haunted by his guilt

You might think of figurative language as something very literary and deliberately crafted, but metaphor is used in spoken language all the time, too. In fact, many metaphors have become so overused in speech that they are considered 'dead metaphors' because they are no longer effective. Consider how often you hear people say the following (or similar) without meaning them literally:

* I'm starving.
* My head's killing me.
* I'm going to kill him.

Related to this is overused hyperbole in phrases like 'I've told you a thousand times…'.

Semantic fields

A semantic field is a collection of words that are linked by meaning. In other words, they all belong to the same category – or at least the things they refer to (their referents) do.

In a semantic field, the category title is known as the 'hypernym', and the words in the field are 'hyponyms'. Some hyponyms can also be hypernyms of a new field. You can see this in 'cat' in the example below – it belongs to the semantic field of 'mammals', so is a hyponym there, but it is also a hypernym because it heads a new semantic field containing words such as 'leopard', 'lion' and 'tiger'. If a text had the words 'leopard', 'lion' and 'tiger' in it, it would be more precise to say that it contained a semantic field of 'big cats' than one of 'mammals' or 'animals'. In an analysis, it can be useful to list 'hyponyms from a semantic field of…' to show a pattern in the writing – they do not need to appear close to one another in the text.

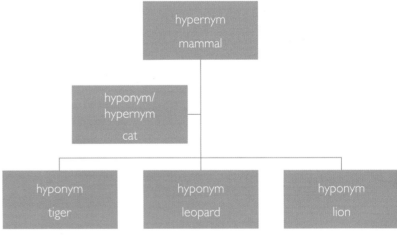

Activity 3

Create a semantic field for each of the hypernyms below and identify where the hypernyms and hyponyms are as in the example above. Try to include more than one layer of hypernym.

* furniture
* emotion
* music

It is useful to identify and analyse the semantic fields in texts, particularly when those fields do not precisely fit the topic under discussion. Obviously, in a report on a sports match you would expect to find a lexical field relating to the game. However, you may also identify a secondary semantic field being used metaphorically – perhaps a semantic field of war through the use of lexis such as 'triumph', 'challenger' and 'hero', and phrases such as 'tore through the defences' being used to create an impression of the match as a battle. Read Text 6 below, which is taken from a newspaper report on a swimming challenge.

Text 6

Great Gold v Great White: Olympic legend Michael Phelps on what it's like to take on ocean's most fearsome predator

Backed by a 15-strong army of divers underneath him for protection, he'll emulate the shark's shape and swimming conditions while racing over 100 m. With 23 Olympic gold medals to his name, no one could blame swimmer Michael Phelps for wanting a bit of a challenge.

But the human super-fish threatened to bite off more than he could chew when he threw down the gauntlet to the greatest challenger he could think of.

This time it's one with fins rather than legs, and a pretty fearsome reputation to boot – the Great White Shark.

In an astonishing experiment, the king of the pool has taken on the king of the ocean for a new documentary.

From *Daily Mirror*, 18 July 2017

Look at this sample analysis of Text 6. Think about how it links detailed linguistic labels to strong comment on meaning.

> Text 6 builds a semantic field of fighting to create an extended metaphor of Phelps and the shark competing against one another. Twice the text uses parallel noun phrases: 'Great Gold vs Great White' and 'king of the pool … king of the ocean' to create a sense of the shark and the swimmer as opponents, while verb phrases such as 'taken on' and 'threw down the gauntlet' from a semantic field of challenging imply that Phelps has approached the shark to request the competition.

Taking things further

Always take the opportunity to combine approaches for a sophisticated analysis – we have only separated them out in this book to help you understand what each involves. The trick to detailed analysis is to pull ideas together, using all the methods available to you. For example, the analysis on the left uses grammatical labels in what is mostly a semantic analysis, commenting on semantic fields and figurative language. How could you build on this analysis to show an awareness of the text's mass-market newspaper context?

Read Text 7, an extract from a travel article about a visit to a war memorial.

Text 7

A WALK WITH THE VALIANT

On the eve of Remembrance Day, Bruce Holmes takes an emotional journey through now-peaceful battlefields of World War I.

It's 8 o'clock and the large crowd waits silently, as they do every evening, while the buglers take their positions. And the notes of the Last Post ring out, reminding us why we are here. In the Belgian city of Ypres in West Flanders stands the Menin Gate, unveiled in 1927 as a memorial to the soldiers of the British Empire who fell in the First World War and especially to the missing "who have no known grave". On the stone walls of the Menin Gate are inscribed the names of 6191 men of the Australian Imperial Force, many of whom were killed in the Third Battle of Ypres in September 1917.

Keeping the connection alive, the entry to the Australian War Memorial in Canberra is guarded by two restored lions, which before WWI stood either side of the gateway to the Menin Road.

No visitor to Ypres should miss the In Flanders Fields Museum in the Cloth Hall. This building, dating from the 13th century, lay ruined after German shelling in WWI but was rebuilt after the war.

The museum displays objects of war as well as newsreel footage. But what is most moving are the words, in poems and letters from soldiers or, most poignantly, in letters from home that were probably never received. In one:

"Dear Jack, We haven't heard from you for six weeks and even from a great distance that does seem slow. Aunt Effie asked after you since she'd heard you'd been unwell..."

There is audio, too. A voice reads Wilfred Owen's poem 'Dulce et Decorum Est', which recalls the physical horror of the gassing victim: "The blood come gargling from the froth-corrupted lungs."

This is not a museum that is easily forgotten.

A short drive from Ypres is Hill 60. This strategically important hill was where those who'd been miners at home turned their skills to tunnelling to create mineshafts under the German positions, fill them with explosives and blow it all up on June 7, 1917, as part of a new offensive, which all went to plan thanks to the First Australian Tunnelling Company. Today it's a quiet spot with a memorial to the Australians, a ruined pillbox and, well, a lot of holes in the ground.

Close by, we see blood-red poppies by the roadside, evoking the words of that famous poem: "In Flanders fields, the poppies blow/ Between the crosses, row on row/ That mark our place…"

In northern France, just west of Lille, is the Australian Memorial Park at Fromelles, also known as VC Corner. Here, in 1916, the Australians suffered massive losses trying to prevent the Germans sending reinforcements south to the Somme. There's a bronze sculpture titled Cobbers, which depicts one soldier carrying another to safety.

Heading south, visitors arrive in the area of the Somme, where some of the bloodiest battles of 1916 and 1917 were fought. The village of Peronne is a good place to begin; its Historial de la Grande Guerre museum is well worth a look, with its field kits and machine guns but also various items indicative of daily life for those at home.

Bruce Holmes, from
'A walk with the valiant'

Activity 4

a) Which words in Text 7 would you select to exemplify the lexical field of World War 1? Which words would help you to show that the writer uses a semantic field of memory?

b) Write a brief paragraph of analysis using your findings, following the example on page 61.

The meaning of phrases

There are three main types of phrase that it is useful to identify and comment on in analysis: idiom, proverb and cliché. These are explained in the table below and can all affect the character of a text by capturing a particular register or contributing to the representations within a text.

Type of phrase	Explanation	Example
idiom	a phrase or saying that usually doesn't make much sense if you haven't heard it before and which cannot be figured out by looking up the individual words; idioms are culturally specific and very difficult – sometimes impossible – to translate between languages	raining cats and dogs
proverb	a saying with a metaphorical meaning, which applies a wider lesson to a specific example; meaning can be inferred from the phrase	Don't cry over spilled milk.
cliché	an overused phrase or saying – idioms and proverbs can become clichéd through overuse; some phrases become clichés for a time then die out as people lose interest in them	At the end of the day…

Many clichés and idioms began as sports metaphors and found their way into everyday usage by way of the business world, which adopted phrases such as 'ballpark figure', 'down to the wire' and 'in pole position'. Now they can be heard in casual conversations and also in media representations of office workers and managerial types.

Activity 5

Write down as many idioms, clichés and proverbs as you can think of in five minutes. Then try to classify them. Do you know where any of them came from? Choose two or three interesting ones to research in more detail.

It's a play on words

The meaning of words, and the fact that sometimes similar-sounding words mean different things, can be a source of humour. Linked with other linguistic concepts, therefore, semantics is a key component in creating comedy through language.

The idea of a 'play on words', or a pun, usually works by playing with both sound and meaning, as well as using pragmatics (the intended outcome is to create laughter). There are three key types of pun:

- a **homographic** pun uses words that look the same (they may sound the same or different): 'The duck said to the store owner, put it on my bill.'

Key term

homograph: a word that is written in the same way as another, but which has a different meaning

Key terms

homophone: a word that sounds the same as another word, although it may be spelled differently
collocation: words commonly found near or next to one another

- a **homophonic** pun uses words that sound the same (though are usually spelled differently): 'The wedding was so emotional that even the cake was in tiers.'
- a **collocational** clash uses a word similar to a word that 'belongs' in the phrase or pair, so the audience almost gets what they are expecting, but not quite: Tan Tropez (tanning salon).

These examples demonstrate an important way in which humour works. People usually laugh when they hear or see something unexpected, so one style of comedy operates on the principle of a gap between expectation and result. Certain jokes and some sitcoms work in this way, setting the audience up to expect one thing before the punchline overturns that expectation. This can also be achieved with more narrative forms of comedy – for example, by following a structure, with all its conventions, then doing something unexpected at the end.

Activity 6

Identify the type of pun (or any other feature you can see) at work in each of the following. Write a short explanatory analysis for each one.

Shop names	Tabloid headlines	Children's jokes
Karl's Plaice	Zoo Escape Causes Otter Chaos to Local Fish Population	How do turtles talk to each other? They use shell phones.
Hair Today, Gone Tomorrow	The Silence of the Hams	Why did the spider go online? To check his website.
The Codfather		What do you get when you cross a snake and a pie? A pie-thon.
Austin Flowers		How do you fix a broken tomato? With tomato paste.

Putting together a semantic analysis

Look back at Text 2 in Unit 3.1. There are several elements that it would be worth noting in a semantic analysis. Read the sample analysis and the annotations below.

clear identification of secondary field – examples of hyponyms would support this

examples offered here with an explanation of exactly what they do

clear explanation of how the different references within the fields help the writer

This text is very tightly focused on its core topic of sleep, with a related secondary field of science to support this. Lexis such as 'evidence' and 'strong case' show the writer's desire to prove his arguments. This is also emphasised by the references to the different realms of education and business, which he uses to back up his claims by showing that they have broad relevance.

Further, the writer makes use of two metaphors in the course of this text to support his arguments. The first comes at the very beginning of the text, when he writes of 'macho, heroic myths' to evoke the idea that people present themselves as masculine warriors when they deprive themselves of sleep. This metaphor works instantly to connote the figure of a business executive or hardworking professional bragging about how little sleep they get to promote themselves as working harder and being tougher than everyone else. Use of the word 'myth' in this metaphor further foregrounds that the writer's argument is going to be that this is false.

useful topic sentence

clear highlighting of how the metaphor works

good to end the paragraph with a statement about meaning

The second metaphor follows quite soon after and is used to characterise students as making decisions on how to spend their time. The writer presents this as an 'equation', which he goes on to criticise as poor prioritisation. The mathematical metaphor here actually portrays the decision as more planned than such decisions probably really are, adding weight to his argument that we do have choices about how to spend our time. The idea of an 'equation' also has connotations of balance and of there being different sides which could be brought into line – in this case, sleep, work and fun activities.

clear description of representation

concise point about what the metaphor represents

useful reminder of the text's purpose

again, good to close the paragraph with interpretation of meaning

Final task

Using the sample analysis above as a model, write a semantic analysis of Text 7 on page 62. You should consider:

- use of semantic fields in the text, including any secondary fields
- use of set phrases such as idiom, cliché or proverb
- the balance of literal and figurative language, and detail and features of figurative language.

You could also consider:

- use of lexical register
- how any of the features you note link to the text's context
- any pragmatic elements you notice.

3.5 Approaching texts on a phonological level

What is phonology? Which aspects of language are analysed in phonological analysis?

What is phonology?

Activity 1

microphone	phonograph	saxophone	telephone
megaphone	cacophony	phonics	headphones
phonetic	xylophone	homophone	gramophone

How many of the words above do you know the meaning of? What do they all have in common? Can you work out the meaning of 'phonology' from this ('-ology' means 'study of')?

Phonology broadly means the study of sounds. Some forms of writing demand it more than others, and some writers make considerable use of phonological features, while others do not. Some linguists distinguish between *phonology* – the deliberate use of features that create sound patterns – and *phonetics*, which describes sounds more specifically, whether or not they are deliberately manipulated by the writer/speaker.

Phonology allows you to make comments on both the bigger picture and the fine detail in an analysis. Some sound features are about structural features, such as links between words (rhyme schemes, for example). At the same time, a more phonetic approach may look at tiny details, such as the specific sounds within words.

Phonological effects in texts

Poems and spoken texts require the closest attention to phonology in analysis, as these are often designed to be heard. Features such as rhyme, assonance and alliteration (including sibilance), as well as onomatopoeia are more likely to be found in such texts. This is not to say that there are no phonological features in other written texts (many persuasive texts make strong use of alliteration, for example), but phonology is more relevant when exploring texts written to be heard. Casual speech is also less likely to include such features but contains other sound-related aspects.

For basic information and definitions of phonological features such as rhyme, assonance and alliteration, see Unit 1.3, page 20.

Read Text 8, which is an extract from a lullaby.

Text 8

> Hush little baby, don't say a word,
>
> Papa's gonna buy you a mockingbird.
>
> And if that mockingbird won't sing,
>
> Papa's gonna buy you a diamond ring.

Activity 2

How does the manipulation of sound (e.g. features such as those mentioned on the previous page) help to create meaning in Text 8? If you know this lullaby, can you remember any other verses? What phonological features help you to do this?

Phonology and casual speech

When analysing conversations, there is a different range of sound-related aspects to consider. Look at this example conversation.

Speaker 1:	but youre not really gonna go (.) right ↘
	//
Speaker 2:	well (.) i re ↗ally want to ysee an (.) ive (.) its just ive waited ages for this to come up (i) yes i know ↘ its not what i should do
	//
Speaker 1:	TOO right its not what you should do ↘ (2) sorry (.) sorry (.) i know that was a bit harsh but its always you ↗ that has to give in

The features you can identify in casual speech include the following:

- **prosodic features**: Prosodic features are those, such as pitch, intonation and rhythm, which span more than one word.
- **pitch** and **intonation**: With pitch, you are assessing how high or low a voice is being used, whereas intonation is about the variation of that pitch – for example, whether a speaker increases pitch at the end of an utterance (perhaps to denote a question). Pitch and intonation are not always evident in transcriptions.
- **stress** and **emphasis**: Emphasis is when a speaker leans a little more on a word or part of a word to bring it to the hearer's attention. Multisyllabic words can generally be said to have a stress pattern, where one syllable is emphasised slightly more than the other(s), but where emphasis is more individualised, for example if one word is picked out in the context of the whole sentence, it is usually shown in transcripts by underlining.
- pauses: Pauses act like punctuation for speech; **micropauses** of less than half a second are like commas, and longer pauses are more like sentence-end punctuation. It is not true that pauses always show hesitation or uncertainty, although it is possible for this to be the case.
- non-verbal sounds: All speakers use non-verbal sounds such as **voiced pauses/non-verbal fillers** or laughter – they are not a sign of a non-fluent speaker.

Key terms

prosodic features: category of terms which includes phonological features applying to speech and affecting more than a word, e.g. rhythm, intonation, pitch

pitch: the measure of whether a voice is high or low.

intonation: the pattern of pitch within speech, which varies according to meaning

stress: the pattern of emphasis within a spoken word, usually common within a language or dialect

emphasis: giving a little more volume or time to a word to show its importance in an utterance

micropause: a pause of less than half a second

voiced pause/non-verbal filler: a non-verbal sound like 'um' used to avoid pausing too long or too frequently

filler: a word used to avoid pausing too long or frequently

Activity 3

Record yourself talking with one or more friends for five minutes or longer (ideally, enough time to forget about the recording and begin to speak normally). Listen to the last minute of the recording and transcribe it using the following rules:

- Include everything everyone says, including fillers and repetitions.
- Time any pauses in seconds.
- Use capitals for any emphasis/extra loud words or parts of words.
- Write any non-verbal sounds in brackets like '(laughs)'.
- Include any overlaps (where people talk over each other) and show this by lining them up on the transcript and putting // on the line in between (see the example above).

Phonetic descriptors

To talk about sounds precisely in an analysis, you need to use a set of specific labels. To begin with, it is important to understand the difference between the spoken and written word, so you need to be able to separate letters (graphemes) from sounds (phonemes).

In fact, graphemes are an imperfect system when it comes to describing linguistic phenomena. This is because there are 44 phonemes in standard British pronunciation of English (other English dialects or international variants of English have a different number), but only 26 graphemes with which to record them – and often several different ways of writing down the same sound.

Key term

Standard English: the most widely used form of English that is not specific to a particular location or region

Activity 4

How many ways can you spell these vowel phonemes? Can you think of a different word to exemplify each different possible spelling in **Standard English**?

a) 'oo' as in 'moon'
b) 'ee' as in 'cheese'
c) 'ie' as in 'pie'
d) 'oa' as in 'coat'
e) 'ay' as in 'day'
f) 'ir' as in 'bird'
g) 'or' as in 'for'
h) 'eer' as in 'deer'

The International Phonemic Alphabet (IPA) is a way of recording phonemes that is consistent across languages. It has a single symbol for each possible phoneme to avoid the complications you explored in Activity 2.

Activity 5

Using the table of IPA symbols opposite, write the following in IPA:

- English Language
- (your full name)

Consonants	
p	pen, copy, happen
b	back, baby, job
t	tea, tight, button
d	day, ladder, odd
k	key, clock, school
g	get, giggle, ghost
tʃ	church, match, nature
dʒ	judge, age, soldier
f	fat, coffee, rough, photo
v	view, heavy, move
θ	thing, author, path
ð	this, other, smooth
s	soon, cease, sister
z	zero, music, roses, buzz
ʃ	ship, sure, national
ʒ	pleasure, vision
h	hot, whole, ahead
m	more, hammer, sum
n	nice, know, funny, sun
ŋ	ring, anger, thanks, sung
l	light, valley, feel
r	right, wrong, sorry, arrange
j	yet, use, beauty, few
w	wet, one, when, queen
ʔ	(glottal stop) depar'ment, foo'ball

Vowels	
ɪ	kit, bid, hymn, minute
e	dress, bed, head, many
æ	trap, bad
ɒ	lot, odd, wash
ʌ	strut, mud, love, blood
ʊ	foot, good, put
iː	fleece, sea, machine
eɪ	face, day, break
aɪ	price, high, try
ɔɪ	choice, boy
uː	goose, two, blue, group
əʊ	goat, show, no
aʊ	mouth, now
ɪə	near, here, weary
eə	square, fair, various
ɑː	start, father
ɔː	thought, law, north, war
ʊə	poor, jury, cure
ɜː	nurse, stir, learn, refer
ə	about, common, standard
i	happy, radiate, glorious
u	thank you, influence, situation
n̩	suddenly, cotton
l̩	middle, metal
ˈ	(stress mark)

Although you do not explicitly need to learn the symbols of the IPA for studying English Language at AS Level, it is still useful for identifying specific sounds in texts, such as those representing dialect in speech. If you continue to A Level study, you will need it when studying young children's speech or describing different accents.

Manner of articulation

Being able to talk about some key types of sound is useful in analysing texts. It is worth commenting on an abundance of similar or related sounds in texts, as they contribute to mood and tone. These sounds can be identified according to both how and where they are articulated – that is, how the sound is produced and where in the mouth it originates. This is known as 'manner of articulation' and it focuses exclusively on the consonant sounds.

Within this, there are two groups: **plosives** and **fricatives**. The plosive sounds are sudden consonant sounds that require air to be released out of the mouth all at once. You cannot extend a plosive sound (except by putting a vowel after it). The fricative sounds are made using friction over the tongue or lip; you can keep a fricative sound going as long as you have breath.

Taking things further

For a challenge, revisit the transcription you made of yourself and your friend(s) in Activity 3 and select one or more words or phrases to code into IPA. Try to either find:

- words/phrases with non-standard pronunciation (that is, where you are aware that your/your friend's accent is apparent)
- words/phrases which are not spelled phonetically.

Key terms

plosive: a set of consonant sounds produced by expelling all the air at once
fricative: a set of consonant sounds produced using friction

Activity 6

Each of these tongue twisters is based on a different consonant sound group. Which one uses plosives and which fricatives?

- She sells sea shells on the sea shore.
- Peter Piper picked a peck of pickled peppers.

Place of articulation

Consonant sounds are also differentiated by *where* they are made in the mouth. Most consonant sounds require the tongue to move, so the place of articulation tends to be labelled for where the tongue strikes or is pressed against.

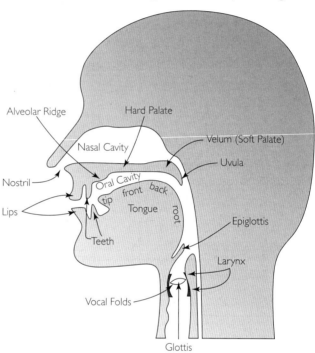

Activity 7

The table opposite shows the English phonetic alphabet as it relates to English consonants. Work out definitions of the terms in the top row of the table.

- Make each of the sounds in the table (refer to the list on page 69 to remind yourself what the sounds are).
- Figure out where they are happening in your mouth/on the diagram (that is, where your tongue strikes).
- Note down what each term in the IPA chart means.
- Write a definition for each of them in your own words.

THE INTERNATIONAL PHONETIC ALPHABET (revised to 2005)

CONSONANTS (PULMONIC)   © 2005 IPA

	Bilabial	Labiodental	Dental	Alveolar	Postalveolar	Retroflex	Palatal	Velar	Uvular	Pharyngeal	Glottal
Plosive	p b			t d				k g			ʔ
Nasal	m			n				ŋ			
Trill											
Tap or Flap											
Fricative		f v	θ ð	s z	ʃ ʒ						h
Lateral fricative											
Approximant				r			j				
Lateral approximant				l							

Where symbols appear in pairs, the one to the right represents a voiced consonant. Shaded areas denote articulations judged impossible.

Voicing

The final definition of a consonant sound is that it can be voiced or unvoiced, which relates to the involvement of the vocal cords. Many sounds (for example, b/p) appear in pairs in the chart above as they are produced in the same manner and the same place. The difference between them lies in the 'voicing'. When you say the word 'bit', your vocal cords vibrate for the 'b'; if you say 'pit', the vocal cords do not vibrate for the 'p', so a different sound is produced.

You do not need to discuss vowels in terms of place or manner of articulation, but it is worth noting that it is often differences in vowel sounds that we notice in accents. And of course it is the combination of vowels and consonants that creates words and therefore meaningful communication.

Final task

Choose your favourite song and analyse its effectiveness phonologically, considering the following:

- Which sound groups (e.g. plosive, fricative) does it play with?
- Does it use rhyme? If so, which words does the rhyme serve to foreground?
- Does it use any other phonological features?
- How do the lyricist's phonological choices support the song's lexical and semantic effects?

3.6 Approaching texts on a grammatical level

What do we mean by grammar in this context? How is grammar useful in analysis?

What use is grammar in analysing a text?

In the context of your English Language studies, the word 'grammar' is used slightly differently to how it may be used in everyday language.

Activity 1

Which *four* of the following can be used to accurately complete the phrase 'Grammar is…'?

- a science (e.g. 'hard and fast' or absolute)
- a way of describing patterns in the system of how language is used
- about how words can be adapted (e.g. take endings)
- about how words can be put together into phrases, clauses, sentences
- about how words sound or are pronounced
- applicable to speech as well as writing – but differently
- punctuation or spelling.

Grammatical knowledge is obviously important in studying language. However, the grammar of a text by itself does not usually tell you very much. You need to consider the meaning(s) of a text first, then to show your grammatical knowledge alongside that. What this means is that you:

- assess the text's context
- consider any pragmatics issues or points to make
- look at lexis (e.g. for tone and approach to audience)
- look at semantics and note relevant fields, figurative usage, and so on
- consider phonology
- look at the quotations you have already highlighted/selected and see what grammatical labels you can add to those
- consider whether any other grammatical aspects of the text fit with other points you want to make.

Sentences

Sentences can be discussed in two different ways, by their type or function:

- Type looks at sentence structure in terms of clauses.
- Function looks at sentence form in terms of its elements.

For more information on sentence types and functions, see Unit 1.1.

For example, Text 7 in Unit 3.4, contains this sentence:

No visitor to Ypres should miss the In Flanders Fields Museum in the Cloth Hall.

subject of the sentence

verb phrase

object

The sentence is declarative, because it follows the standard basic construction: subject–verb–object. If the function labels were purely pragmatic, this sentence could be labelled as imperative, because it is telling the reader what they should do – the sentence's effect is to say, 'do not miss the In Flanders Fields Museum'. However, because of the way it is structured, it must be labelled as declarative. Remember, sentences only fit into one function category. An imperative version of the sentence might read: 'Do not miss the In Flanders Fields Museum.' Forms such as 'no visitor should miss', or 'it must be labelled' avoid a bare (or bald) imperative.

When commenting on sentences, only remark on those that stand out as particularly interesting or worthy of note. It is rarely worth discussing what type of sentence dominates in a text, for example, or trying to identify one of each type simply to show that you can. You need to demonstrate that you can analyse with *meaning*, selecting the most appropriate parts of the text to comment on.

Clauses

In analysis, it is often simpler – and more useful – to talk about clause types than sentence types. There may be more than one way to label a clause. The table below outlines two useful examples of subordinate clauses that can be removed from a sentence without affecting its sense.

Clause type	Purpose	Examples
comment clause	indicates that the speaker/writer is sharing their opinion	I think/suppose, and so on to be fair putting it bluntly what's surprising to me is
relative clause (sometimes called adjectival/adjective clause because it functions like an adjective)	begins with a relative pronoun ('who', 'which' or 'that') and adds more information about a noun/noun phrase – a type of subordinate clause	'who fell in the First World War' (from Text 7)

Remember that often there is more than one possible label for a feature, particularly if you are considering more than one level of language (or approach). For example, some clauses might also be described as verb phrases. If you cannot decide between two or three labels, that does not mean you are wrong – all of them could be correct.

Look at these samples of an analysis of a sentence from Text 7.

main clause

subordinate (non-finite) clause

noun phrase acting as subject

phrasal verb in present tense

progressive verb

first person plural object pronoun

verb phrase – first person plural present tense

noun phrase linking to semantic field of World War 1 and remembrance

verb phrase with connotations of bells or clarion call

enigmatic reference to reason through complement implies reason does not need to be stated

> Clause labels:
>
> And the notes of the Last Post ring out, reminding us why we are here.
>
> Word class and phrase labels:
>
> And the notes of the Last Post ring out, reminding us why we are here.
>
> Combined analysis (most useful points):
>
> And the notes of the Last Post ring out, reminding us why we are here.

Read Text 9, the beginning of an autobiography in which the writer reminisces about his international cricket career, which ended in 2013.

Text 9

'Son, life is like a book. It has numerous chapters. It also has many a lesson in it. It is made up of a wide variety of experiences and resembles a pendulum where success and failure, joy and sorrow are merely extremes of the central reality. The lessons to be learnt from success and failure are equally important. More often than not, failure and sorrow are bigger teachers than success and happiness. You are a cricketer and sportsman. You are fortunate to be representing your country, and that is a great honour. But never forget that this too is just another chapter in the book. Typically, let's say a person lives for seventy or eighty years or so. How many years will you play sport? Twenty years; if you are very good, maybe even twenty-five years. Even by that yardstick, you will live the majority of your years outside the sphere of professional sport. This clearly means that there is more to life than cricket. I am asking you, son, to keep a pleasant disposition and maintain a balanced nature. Do not allow success to breed arrogance in you. If you remain humble, people will give you love and respect even after you have finished with the game. As a parent, I would be happier hearing people say, "Sachin is a good human being" than "Sachin is a great cricketer" any day.'

My father's words, which I often heard while growing up, encapsulate my life's philosophy.

I was born to a very close-knit Maharashtrian family in Mumbai's Bandra East and lived in the Sahitya Sahawas colony, a residential co-operative for writers. I am one of four children, with two brothers and a sister. Nitin, Ajit and Savita are all older than me, and not only am I the youngest in the family but I was also the worst behaved.

Sachin Tendulkar, from *Playing It My Way*

Activity 2

What comments might you make about sentences and clauses in Text 9?
Try to link them to context, representation or intended meanings.

Word classes

A key skill you will need is being able to identify word classes, for example
separating nouns from adjectives and then identifying abstract and concrete
nouns. This is best achieved through practice – just looking at definitions is not
an effective way to learn this type of material. Learning the main word classes
is really about getting to know how they are different, and for this you need
to understand what each word class does and how it is used.

For more information on word classes, see Unit 1.2.

Some useful things you can do to approach learning language terminology,
including grammatical terms, are:

- write a glossary for yourself, in your own words – this could be in a
  notebook or folder, or using index cards
- practise applying terms to language that you encounter around you,
  such as food packaging, media texts and overheard conversations – get
  used to asking yourself 'what kind of word was that?' or 'that was funny –
  why was that?'
- test yourself regularly using your glossary (or ask someone else to test you).

Activity 3

Copy and complete the table below to help your understanding of the word classes.

	Examples	What do we do with it? (function)	What types are there?	How does it behave grammatically? (form)	What other words can it go with? (syntax)
noun		label objects, people, places			
verb				takes endings to show who is carrying out the action (subject), when (tense) and whether it has finished (aspect)	
adjective					nouns (a happy boy) and verbs (he is happy)
adverb			time, manner, place, degree, sentence		
pronoun	I, we, us, himself				

Writing notes in your own words is a good way of remembering word classes. Having clear examples that are familiar to you can also help if you are uncertain of a word when reading a text, as you can test it by swapping it with words that you are more confident with. For example, if you wanted to comment on the phrase 'lay ruined after German shelling' and you were not sure whether to classify 'ruined' as a verb or an adjective, you could test it out by swapping it for words that you were more confident with:

- lay walked after German shelling
- lay dirty after German shelling.

From this, you can work out that 'ruined' is being used adjectivally in this instance.

Activity 4

Often, in English, word families can be created by adding suffixes and prefixes to words to create new ones. Certain endings are associated with particular word classes – for example, '-ness' and '-age' are noun endings, while '-ical' and '-ful' are adjectival.

Copy and complete the table with words related to the ones provided. (Do not limit yourself to one per word class.) Can you think of other words that produce similar word families?

Noun	Verb	Adverb	Adjective
			active
		busily	
beauty			
conversion			
trial			

Further reading

David Crystal, *Rediscover Grammar (3rd Edition)* (Longman, 2004)
David Crystal, *Making Sense of Grammar* (Longman, 2004)
Caroline Coffin, *Exploring English Grammar: From Formal to Functional* (Routledge, 2009)

Activity 5

Read Text 7 again. What further points can you make about the use of word classes in this text?

Verbs in more detail

Verbs can be separated according to meaning: into dynamic and stative verbs. Dynamic verbs are verbs of action, while stative verbs are those describing states such as 'be' and 'seem', processes, emotions and perceptions, such as 'think', 'like' and 'see'.

Read Text 10 opposite, which is an extract from a tourist leaflet advertising an exhibition at the Canadian Museum of History.

Text 10

HOCKEY

March 10 to October 9, 2017

For millions of Canadians, winter means hockey and hockey means everything. Be there when the puck drops on Hockey. Watch historic highlight reels. Get close to the greats with one-of-a-kind artefacts. Share your passion with interactive components. Find out why hockey holds pride of place in the hearts of Canadians.

Look at the sample analysis of this text. Note how it clearly links grammatical features to meanings created.

> This text uses mostly stative verbs to express what the audience of tourists is expected to do: 'be', 'get', 'share', with 'watch' and 'find' the only dynamic verbs they would be expected to be involved in. All of these verbs are also used in the imperative form, to direct the audience's actions. As an advertising leaflet, the text also engages in the sharing of ideology, by contributing to the representation of hockey as quintessentially Canadian, through the stative verb 'means' in the present tense, which has the effect of presenting the concept of 'hockey means everything' as an eternal truth.

Activity 6

Find three dynamic and three stative verbs in Text 9 on page 74.

Verbs can also be described in terms of their tense and aspect. Tense is about the time period in which the event took (or is taking or will take) place, while aspect is about duration and completeness. So, how do you break it down and describe the verbs in a sentence? The verb component of a clause is usually one verb phrase, even if there are several verbs with other words between them, as long as they are all operating together.
Look at these examples:

- I am going out later.
- I am probably going out later.
- I am almost certainly not going out later.
- I went out yesterday.

In all these examples, there is one verb phrase in each clause, with adverbs such as 'probably' and adverbial phrases separating the auxiliary verb 'am' from the main verb 'going'. Single-word tenses are defined as 'simple' tenses. Those using auxiliaries are 'complex', and the tense label is taken from the auxiliary. So, in the previous examples, there is a complex present tense and a simple past one. To identify the complex form more precisely, you need to look at the main verb, which here is in the **progressive** form, so it is a present progressive. **For more information on verbs, see Unit 1.2.**

In an assessment, you are not likely to be given a list of words or phrases out of context and asked to identify them grammatically. Rather, you need to be able to identify words in context – those that you consider interesting for semantic or pragmatic reasons.

Activity 7

What kinds of verb phrases are used in Text 9 on page 74 and how do they relate to the text's context? What is the effect of this?

The active and passive voices

One final way that verbs can be discussed in greater depth is by noticing active and passive voice. In practice, it is most useful to notice the passive voice, as this is used less often and may have an interesting effect.

Voice	Example	Explanation
active	The government changed the law.	subject ('the government') – verb ('changed') – object ('the law')
passive	The law was changed by the government.	object ('the law') – verb ('was changed') – subject ('by the government') The verb changes from simple past to past perfect and uses 'to be' as the auxiliary, and the preposition 'by' is added.
agentless passive	The law was changed.	object ('the law') – verb ('was changed') The original subject has disappeared.

It is particularly worth noting agentless passives, as they hide responsibility. Because they are concise, they are a common feature of headlines, but they can be discussed in terms of representation and subject positioning. In the agentless version, it can almost appear like a natural occurrence that the law changed, as though no one brought it about and no one is responsible. This can be a deliberate choice.

Note that passives are grammatically formed by using the auxiliary 'to be' in the same tense as the active voice sentence would be, together with the **perfective** aspect. Be careful not to interpret 'passive' in the everyday sense of not very active, as this sometimes leads to stative verbs being identified as passive constructions.

Activity 8

Identify the voice (active or passive) of the following constructions.

a) The policeman was shot by a bank robber.
b) Animals were screaming as protestors tore through the zoo.
c) Sufiya was struck by a flying branch.
d) Bystanders were shocked at the child's behaviour.
e) The cooker exploded on impact.

Final task

Plan for a full analysis of Text 9, by gathering the key features to comment on in a list, mind map or table. Consider:

- the text's context as a personal memoir of an internationally known sportsman
- how the writer uses lexis and semantics to engage the audience
- the extent to which phonology might be relevant in your analysis
- which grammatical knowledge you can demonstrate in your analysis.

End-of-chapter task

Use a table like the one here to plan a full analysis of Text 11 overleaf, considering how it uses language to suit its context.

	Quotation(s)	Comments (e.g. effect on audience, link to purpose, link to form, likely intention)
pragmatic features		
lexical features		
semantic features		
grammatical features		

Text 11

Will coffee in California come with a cancer warning?

How do you like your cup of cancer in the morning? I take mine with fake sugar and skim milk. Lame, I know. But there's no accounting for taste in carcinogens. Or, in this case, coffee.

You've probably seen the bemused headlines: "Coffee in California may soon come with a spoonful of cancer warnings." There's wacky California, doing its liberalism-through-regulation schtick again.

At issue is a lawsuit brought by the Council for Education and Research on Toxics against coffee purveyors such as Starbucks for not warning consumers about a potential carcinogen in their product. Although the suit was first filed in 2010, a ruling from the Los Angeles County Superior Court is expected soon.

The alleged culprit is acrylamide, a compound formed when coffee beans are roasted. Under Proposition 65, passed in 1986, any company of more than 10 employees has to warn its customers about the presence of one of nearly 900 toxins on a state list. Acrylamide is on that list. Yet the state's leading purveyors of caffeine failed to disclose that fact. That omission could cost them millions in penalties and fees.

But is coffee-based acrylamide really a threat to public health — possibly a major one, given that we're a nation of caffeine junkies?

"Coffee is connected to cancer development by the fact that coffee is sometimes drunk by living people and only living people develop cancer," said Robert A. Weinberg, an oncologist at the Massachusetts Institute of Technology. I took that as a "no".

Kathryn M. Wilson agreed. A cancer epidemiologist at Harvard University, she has studied the effects of acrylamide on the human body. "I think the evidence that acrylamide makes a difference for human cancer risk is pretty weak," she said. Wilson explained that studies connecting acrylamide to ovarian or endometrial cancer for women were based on questionnaires about how often the subjects consumed coffee. The link to ovarian cancer was discounted through subsequent research based on blood analysis.

From *Los Angeles Times*, 2018

Chapter 4

Key writing skills

How varied is your writing experience? For example, how much opportunity have you had to write different kinds of texts? To what extent do you think about your audience when writing?

This chapter will help you shape your writing more carefully for a range of forms and purposes, and get you thinking about how best to meet your audience's needs. Each unit considers a different writing purpose and explores a variety of forms, including writing for a listening audience as well as for readers. You will think about the language features you encountered in Chapter 3 and experiment with these in your own writing. In the final unit, you will draw together the principles of both chapters in this section. You will use both your analytical and writing skills to reflect on how you have crafted your work, commenting clearly on how it is constructed for effect.

This section covers a number of the key concepts:
- investigating *context*, including purpose, *audience* and form, examining how these aspects influence a writer's choices and contribute to a text's *meaning*
- describing aspects of *style* by exploring a range of ways to comment on the choices writers make
- applying *creativity* in your thinking, interpretation and expression as you engage analytically with texts and produce texts of your own.

4.1 Writing analytically

How can analytical writing be structured? What are effective ways of approaching analytical writing?

Planning for analytical writing

Planning any kind of writing is important, for several reasons.

- It allows you to sort through ideas and select the best ones before starting.
- It helps you work out a clear direction.
- It divides the work into two stages, making the writing itself more efficient:
  Step 1: *What* do I write?
  Step 2: *How* do I write it?

Many students do not do as well as they could in their writing assessments because, without proper planning, they tend to only think about *what* they should write not *how* they should write it. Planning also helps you move beyond the most obvious ideas and onto deeper levels of thought at an early stage, thus avoiding writing a superficial response.

Activity 1

The three examples below are all plans for a full analysis of Text 11 at the end of Chapter 3. The task they are planning for is:

How does this text use language appropriate to its context?

Which of these plans do you think would produce the best answer? Give reasons for your choice.

Plan A

- Context of text
- Use of lexis
- Use of semantics
- Use of pragmatics
- Use of grammar
- Use of phonology
- Conclusion

Plan B

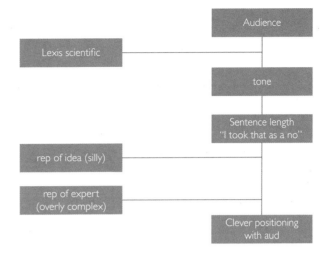

Plan C

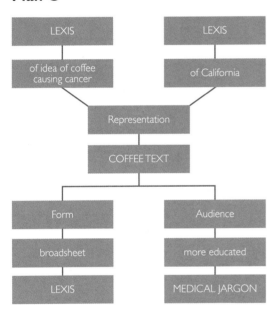

The best way to approach an analytical task is to annotate the text first, to help you identify the key ideas. The goal of the planning stage is to organise and refine those ideas into a sensible shape. When it comes to the writing, you do not need to incorporate every annotation you made in the planning – you will almost certainly identify features on a first reading that you later decide not to use. It is important to be selective. Laying out your initial ideas clearly will give you space in the writing stage to think about *how* to express those ideas, rather than having to think about *what* to say. This is what makes Plan B above effective: it selects appropriate material and makes clear connections to the meanings created by the text and its context.

Structuring your writing

There are different ways of structuring analytical writing, and they all have different strengths and weaknesses. Broadly speaking, the weakest approach is one that follows the order of the text. This is because such an approach:

- can lead to repetitive comments, since many features are similar across a text (as seen in the plans above, which cluster similar ideas together)
- does not allow you to demonstrate sophisticated selection of points, as you are just going through the text in order
- may cause you to overlook important features if they all appear at the end of the text and you become short of time
- gives a less thoughtful impression as you are being less selective.

The differences between the other approaches lie in how their features are organised. The following activity explores these approaches.

Activity 2

Look at the three approaches in the table below. (The examples are from Text 11 in Chapter 3.)

Language-led exploration	Context-led exploration	Text-led exploration
Organising your ideas according to the language levels. For example: - Para 1: lexical points (e.g. scientific jargon) - Para 2: pragmatic points (e.g. references to Californian 'type')	Organising your ideas according to the contextual factors. For example: - Para 1: form is an article, so uses direct address - Para 2: mode is quite interactive, so uses jokey references early on	Organising your ideas according to the ideas within the text. For example: - Para 1: key point is coffee having cancer warnings, so uses scientific jargon - Para 2: writer's opinion is also important, shown by humour and rhetorical questions

For each approach, note down its possible strengths and weaknesses. Think about:

- how easy/difficult it would be to use each approach in an assessment situation
- how effective each approach would be in analysing any text
- how helpful each approach would be in making sure you respond effectively to the task.

What other effective structures for analytical writing can you think of?

Activity 3

Produce a clear plan for the following task:

Analyse Text 11 on page 80, focusing on audience, form and language.

Guiding your reader

As well as helping you to eliminate obvious ideas and reach deeper levels of thought, planning ensures that you know the overall shape of your answer before you begin writing. This will give your work a solid structure and allow you to deliver a logical, well-presented analysis throughout, including:

- a strong introduction
- clear and logical links between paragraphs
- a sound conclusion.

Writing a good introduction

A strong introduction can set up your overall argument effectively and assure the reader that you know where you are going and have firm control over your material.

Read Text 1 below, which is the beginning of a podcast.

Text I

Mary:	This episode of 'Writing Excuses' has been brought to you by our listeners, patrons and friends. If you would like to learn how to support this podcast, visit www dot patreon dot com forward slash writing excuses. Season thirteen, episode two. {sound of typewriter keys plays in background over next turn}
Brandon:	This is Writing Excuses! Writing Active Characters
Mary:	Fifteen minutes long, because you're in a hurry…
Maurice:	…and we're not that smart.
Brandon:	I'm Brandon.
Mary:	I'm Mary.
Amal:	I'm Amal El-Mohtar.
Maurice:	I'm Maurice Broaddus.
Brandon:	Great, and we are recording with what we call our Chicago team this week. You'll be hearing from them every second week of the month and I would like them to introduce themselves.
Amal:	Hi, my name's Amal. I'm an author, critic, poet. I write short fiction and poetry, mostly, I write reviews for NPR and very recently for the *New York Times* and {hesitatingly} I recently won a bunch of awards: the Nebula, Locus and Hugo Award for a short story of mine, called 'Seasons of Glass and Iron'.
Maurice:	Nice. I'm Maurice Broaddus and I'm a science-fiction, horror and fantasy author. I wrote the urban fantasy trilogy *The Knights of Breton Court*. I've a short story collection out right now. I've written, I've had published close to a hundred short stories and most recently out is my novella *Buffalo Soldier*.
Mary:	And he's also an editor as well.
Maurice:	Oh yes {laughs}.
Brandon:	And we're gonna talk about active characters today. I bring this up early in the season because it is something that I notice a lot of my students do and I notice that I did it a lot early in my career, is that I would set a story with a character observing events or who was very passive at the beginning of the story. This isn't always a bad thing, but we generally in writing, we wanna push our characters toward making decisions, being a part of events and that sort of thing, so I'm gonna ask the podcasters how do you go about making your characters more active?

Transcribed from writingexcuses.com 'Writing active characters'

A task based on this podcast might be to analyse the podcast, focusing on form, structure and language. Look at the following two sample introductions for a response to such a task.

Introduction A

> In this essay, I will analyse the podcast 'Writing Excuses', focusing on form, structure and language. It is important to consider form because this text is a podcast so will be structured in a certain way to engage its audience. It is also important to look at the way the participants in the text use language because this is how they create communication and meanings together.

never start essays by saying you will answer the question

do not explain why a feature is important in a general sense

implies the form of other text types is not important

this is true of all texts

Introduction B

clear identification of form and an audience feature

strong statement that implies a direction for the analysis

demonstrates clear understanding of podcast form

introduces another key aspect of podcast form, setting up a more detailed exploration

> Text 1 is a podcast, produced for a listening audience. This form is the most important aspect of the text's context and affects all the language and structural choices made by the participants. The speakers may be speaking together but, unlike a regular conversation, they are not addressing each other but a third-party audience. This aspect governs many of the choices available to the speakers. Also crucial to our understanding of this text is the serial nature of the podcast, which is reflected in many of the lexical choices as well as influencing the text's structure.

Introduction B is clearly far stronger than A. It considers specific features of the text, but only in the context of setting up an overall consideration of what is most important about this particular text. It is clear that the analysis will go on to explore this angle in greater depth by discussing these and related features. Introduction A is too general – all the points it raises could apply to any language in any text, which means they are not worth making.

Activity 4

Refer back to the plan you made in Activity 3. Write a good introduction for this analysis.

Writing a good conclusion

Conclusions are also important in guiding your reader, marking arrival at your endpoint. While your introduction should indicate where your analysis is headed, your conclusion should tie up the main thrust of your argument. It should not introduce any new arguments or details of analysis but should highlight your key ideas and show what you have learned through the process of the analysis. In conclusions, you can:

- re-state key points in a new way
- draw several analytical points together into one overall point (e.g. to highlight patterns of meaning, or to link different aspects together)
- make some evaluation (e.g. that one aspect of the text is more important than another in achieving the writer's purposes, or matching the text's context)
- make sure you are answering the question by focusing on the elements asked about in the task.

Look at the following two sample conclusions for an analysis of Text 1.

Conclusion A

In conclusion, this opening section of the 'Writing Excuses' podcast episode serves to introduce new participants to a regular show. The explicit use of names and credentials, along with the clear explanation as a topic marker for the episode, are all ways of making the content clear and easy to follow for the listening audience. The participants' experience and awareness of the context is clear in the text's structure, as there are no overlaps and they all collaborate to signal things for the audience.

— **clear and concise statement of the extract's overall purpose**

— **brief listing of features discussed in the essay**

— **clear focus on aims of the text and what its effects are**

— **useful summary of structural elements, linking them to meaning/intent**

Conclusion B

To conclude, this is a successful podcast extract which introduces the topic and cast of the episode. As I have discussed, the text shows a range of language features which enable the speakers to achieve their purposes, such as the question at the end 'how do you go about making your characters more active?' This interrogative sentence is used to prompt the others to talk and will make the podcast more successful in starting off their discussions.

— **attempt to evaluate the text's success**

— **vague statement**

— **this level of detail does not belong in a conclusion – it seems to be new information and should therefore be in the main analysis**

Logical connections

As well as considered the overall shape of your analysis, it is also worth looking at how the writing works on a more detailed level. A key aspect of the structure of your argument is how your ideas connect to one another. Think carefully about how you join ideas – your choice of linking words (discourse markers and **connectives**) is important.

For more information about discourse markers, see Unit 2.1, page 26.

Key term

connective: a word or phrase that joins ideas together

Activity 5

Sort the connective words and phrases in the box into the three categories below. Add some more connective words of your own to each category.

- adding a contrasting idea
- building on the last idea
- moving onto a new idea

Additionally	Furthermore	However	In terms of…
It is also interesting to note		On the other hand	

Connectives and discourse markers are also useful in discursive writing.

Making logical claims

It is crucial to make only *logical* claims in your analytical points. If you make a point about the effect of a particular feature, it should clearly link to the word/phrase cited or to the feature itself.

For example, returning to Text 11 in Chapter 3, writing this sentence would be a vague and not particularly interesting claim:

'The alliteration in the first sentence "How do you like your cup of cancer" makes the reader read on.'

- The alliteration is not especially strong (being just two words and with a word between them).
- The alliteration is not the most surprising or interesting feature of that sentence.
- It is the first sentence of the article, so the reader is unlikely to stop there anyway!
- It does not tell us anything about this example of alliteration – it has not engaged with *these words*.
- 'Makes the reader read on' is an over-used claim that rarely impresses.

Activity 6

Improve the comment on the first sentence of Text 11. Consider the points above and try to write something more specific that is not just focused on the alliteration.

Now read Text 2 below, which is an extract from US President Franklin D. Roosevelt's inaugural speech, given in 1933.

Text 2

I am certain that my fellow Americans expect that on my induction into the Presidency I will address them with a candor and a decision which the present situation of our Nation impels. This is preeminently the time to speak the truth, the whole truth, frankly and boldly. Nor need we shrink from honestly facing conditions in our country today. This great Nation will endure as it has endured, will revive and will prosper. So, first of all, let me assert my firm belief that the only thing we have to fear is fear itself – nameless, unreasoning, unjustified terror which paralyzes needed efforts to convert retreat into advance. In every dark hour of our national life a leadership of frankness and vigor has met with that understanding and support of the people themselves which is essential to victory. I am convinced that you will again give that support to leadership in these critical days.

In such a spirit on my part and on yours we face our common difficulties. They concern, thank God, only material things. Values have shrunken to fantastic levels; taxes have risen; our ability to pay has fallen; government of all kinds is faced by serious curtailment of income; the means of exchange are frozen in the currents of trade; the withered leaves of industrial enterprise lie on every side; farmers find no markets for their produce; the savings of many years in thousands of families are gone.

More important, a host of unemployed citizens face the grim problem of existence, and an equally great number toil with little return. Only a foolish optimist can deny the dark realities of the moment.

From Franklin D. Roosevelt's first inaugural speech, 1933

Activity 7

Select one part from each column to construct logical claims about how Text 2 is effective in presenting ideas to its audience.

Quotation	Language technique	Effect
'time to speak the truth, the whole truth, frankly and boldly'	personification via expanded abstract noun phrase	expands theme into abstract
'fear itself—nameless, unreasoning, unjustified terror which paralyzes needed efforts to convert retreat into advance'	semantic field of money used literally and then also metaphorically	implies speaker is on oath and therefore trustworthy

Read Text 3, which is an extract from US President Barack Obama's inaugural speech, given in 2013.

Text 3

Each time we gather to inaugurate a President we bear witness to the enduring strength of our Constitution. We affirm the promise of our democracy. We recall that what binds this nation together is not the colors of our skin or the tenets of our faith or the origins of our names. What makes us exceptional – what makes us American – is our allegiance to an idea articulated in a declaration made more than two centuries ago:

"We hold these truths to be self-evident, that all men are created equal; that they are endowed by their Creator with certain unalienable rights; that among these are life, liberty, and the pursuit of happiness."

Today we continue a never-ending journey to bridge the meaning of those words with the realities of our time. For history tells us that while these truths may be self-evident, they've never been self-executing; that while freedom is a gift from God, it must be secured by His people here on Earth. The patriots of 1776 did not fight to replace the tyranny of a king with the privileges of a few or the rule of a mob. They gave to us a republic, a government of, and by, and for the people, entrusting each generation to keep safe our founding creed.

And for more than two hundred years, we have.

Through blood drawn by lash and blood drawn by sword, we learned that no union founded on the principles of liberty and equality could survive half-slave and half-free. We made ourselves anew, and vowed to move forward together.

Together, we determined that a modern economy requires railroads and highways to speed travel and commerce, schools and colleges to train our workers.

Together, we discovered that a free market only thrives when there are rules to ensure competition and fair play.

Together, we resolved that a great nation must care for the vulnerable, and protect its people from life's worst hazards and misfortune.

Through it all, we have never relinquished our skepticism of central authority, nor have we succumbed to the fiction that all society's ills can be cured through government alone. Our celebration of initiative and enterprise, our insistence on hard work and personal responsibility, these are constants in our character.

From Barack Obama's second inaugural speech, 2013

Further reading

Kim Ballard, *The Frameworks of English: Introducing Language Structures (3rd Edition)* (Palgrave Macmillan, 2013)
Jonathan Culpeper, Paul Kerswill, Ruth Wodak, Tony McEnery, Francis Katamba, *English Language: Description, Variation and Context* (Palgrave Macmillan, 2018)
Sara Thorne, *Mastering Advanced English Language (2nd Edition)* (Palgrave Macmillan, 2008)
Dan Clayton, *Textual Analysis* (Cambridge University Press, 2018)

Final task

Plan for, and then write, an analysis of Text 3, focusing on how it is appropriate for a listening audience. Your analysis should:

- have a logical structure
- guide the reader
- explain the text's context and relate language choices to these factors.

4.2 Writing narrative

How should narrative writing be approached? What techniques can make narrative writing stand out?

What is narrative writing?

Narrative writing is a type of 'imaginative' writing – a term that also includes descriptive writing. When we talk about imaginative writing, as opposed to discursive or critical writing, for example, we are really talking about what the writing is for, or what its *purpose* is. In this model, imaginative writing is set apart from transactional writing, or writing for an audience, which is writing assumed to have a specific purpose and audience. Imaginative writing is intended primarily to entertain.

For detailed information on descriptive writing, see Unit 4.3.

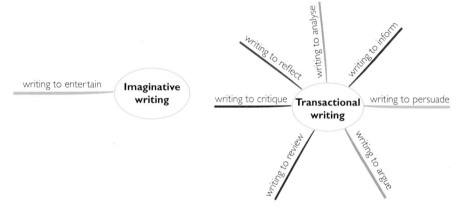

Activity I

List all the ways in which you have experienced narrative writing (storytelling) over the past week. You do not need to have seen the actual writing; experiencing the end product (for example, watching a movie) is fine.

In your AS Level study, your narrative writing will be focused on forms such as short stories. In narrative writing, particularly in short forms, language choices are crucial in creating atmosphere and setting, and in suggesting characters' motivations and moods. A poorly chosen simile can create the wrong mood entirely, while an effective metaphor can save a lot of space in crafting atmosphere.

Activity 2

What are the connotations of each description below? Which would be more effective in a story about old friends realising they had grown apart?

- The snow smothered the ground like the thick cloying blankets of Jesse's childhood.
- The snow fell heavily, softening the edges of the kerbstones as Jesse stepped into the street.

Key elements of a story

Writing creatively requires a range of skills to achieve as much as possible with few words. In narrative writing, you need to think about the following areas:

- character
- atmosphere/tone
- pace
- plot
- setting.

You would not address all these features in every sentence but, in short fiction especially, a sentence must reflect on more than just one feature.

Activity 3

Look at the following three openings.

- Berenice Dougherty had always hated cats. So why was she spending her day off fundraising for a cat shelter in the rain?
- 'The thing is,' he said, 'my job is, well, it isn't going to exist anymore, so we're going to need to make some changes.' I watched him fidget with the BMW keys as he spoke.
- The forest floor is waterlogged and my feet keep slipping, but I must keep running.

Comment on which of the five areas listed above activity 3 each opening introduces or helps to set up the story. Which does each opening do well? What can you tell about the story from these lines (e.g. the type of story)? What does each opening leave you wanting to know?

A good opening often either withholds information or makes ideas very clear right from the start. Whichever approach you choose, it is important to establish what type of story it is going to be as quickly as possible in terms of:

- genre (e.g. realistic, crime, historical, romance, fantasy)
- pace (e.g. is it likely to be thriller-pace throughout or leisurely and gentle?)
- emotional content (e.g. is it going to be upbeat, heart-warming or dramatic?).

Once you have established the type of story, you need to make sure you deliver that consistently throughout. For example, if your story opens as though it is going to be a heart-warming family tale and then everyone is murdered at the end, it will not be successful because you have broken your 'promise' to the reader.

Activity 4

Write one or two sentences to open a story. It should introduce a character and a setting, and create an appropriate atmosphere. Choose from the following topics:

- a story called *Brave New Day*
- a story in which someone loses something important
- a story developing a scene in which two people meet who have not seen each other for years.

In short fiction, where you have a limited number of words, it is usually better to use realistic scenarios and ideas about everyday life rather than trying to build a complicated fantasy world. The most effective short fiction is usually fairly simple, with few characters and not too much action.

Read Text 4 below, which is the opening of a short story. In it, the writer explores a turning-point in a relationship. A couple's electricity is cut off for one hour each night, and the story tells how they deal with it. At first they are surprised by the notice that they have received about the matter, and have not prepared, so they do not have candles ready. The story is effectively a snapshot of their relationship and the writer uses description of small details to reveal and build character and their relationship.

Text 4

The notice informed them that it was a temporary matter: for five days their electricity would be cut off for one hour, beginning at eight p.m. A line had gone down in the last snowstorm, and the repairmen were going to take advantage of the milder evenings to set it right. The work would affect only the houses on the quiet tree-lined street, within walking distance of a row of brick-faced stores and a trolley stop, where Shoba and Shukumar had lived for three years.

'It's good of them to warn us,' Shoba conceded after reading the notice aloud, more for her own benefit than Shukumar's. She let the strap of her leather satchel, plump with files, slip from her shoulders, and left it in the hallway as she walked into the kitchen. She wore a navy blue poplin raincoat over gray sweatpants and white sneakers, looking, at thirty-three, like the type of woman she'd once claimed she would never resemble.

She'd come from the gym. Her cranberry lipstick was visible only on the outer reaches of her mouth, and her eyeliner had left charcoal patches beneath her lower lashes. She used to look this way sometimes, Shukumar thought, on mornings after a party or a night at a bar, when she'd been too lazy to wash her face, too eager to collapse into his arms. She dropped a sheaf of mail on the table without a glance. Her eyes were still fixed on the notice in her other hand. 'But they should do this sort of thing during the day.'

'When I'm here, you mean,' Shukumar said. He put a glass lid on a pot of lamb, adjusting it so only the slightest bit of steam could escape. Since January he'd been working at home, trying to complete the final chapters of his dissertation on agrarian revolts in India. 'When do the repairs start?'

'It says March nineteenth. Is today the nineteenth?' Shoba walked over to the framed corkboard that hung on the wall by the fridge, bare except for a calendar of William Morris wallpaper patterns. She looked at it as if for the first time, studying the wallpaper pattern carefully on the top half before allowing her eyes to fall to the numbered grid on the bottom. A friend had sent the calendar in the mail as a Christmas gift, even though Shoba and Shukumar hadn't celebrated Christmas that year.

'Today then,' Shoba announced. 'You have a dentist appointment next Friday, by the way.'

He ran his tongue over the tops of his teeth; he'd forgotten to brush them that morning. It wasn't the first time. He hadn't left the house at all that day, or the day before. The more Shoba stayed out, the more she began putting in extra hours at work and taking on additional projects, the more he wanted to stay in, not even leaving to get the mail, or to buy fruit or wine at the stores by the trolley stop.

Jhumpa Lahiri, from 'A Temporary Matter' in *Interpreter of Maladies*

Activity 5

Read the first paragraph of Text 4 again. Which features of the story are introduced? What promises is the writer making to the reader?

Show, don't tell

'Show, don't tell' is a commonly repeated rule of storytelling, meaning that you should leave something for the reader to infer. For example, rather than telling the reader 'the man's words made him angry', *show* his anger: 'He clenched his fists as he listened to the man's words'. There is greater emotional power in something that the reader has noticed for themselves.

Activity 6

Reread Text 4. Find a range of phrases the writer uses to show that Shoba and Shukumar's relationship has become more distant in the time leading up to the story.

Key decisions in narrative writing

Once you have decided on your core story, you have several choices about how to tell it:

- First- or third-person perspective?
- Past or present tense?
- What structure?

Imagine that you want to tell a story about a girl who lets down a friend, regrets it and tries to put it right. You have two obvious choices for perspective:

- the girl herself, telling the story in the first person
- a neutral, omniscient third-person perspective (as in 'A Temporary Matter').

You could also use a different narrator, such as a teacher or the friend. This might be more interesting structurally (they could be relating the story a long time later to make a moral point to a new class or child, for example). However, you will need to bear in mind that this is likely to also make the story longer, as you are adding a new character, with additional points.

Activity 7

When deciding on perspective and tense, consider the main benefits and drawbacks of each method. Copy and complete the table opposite with the associated benefits and drawbacks. Consider the following:

- features such as intimacy and immediacy
- ease of writing and control
- ability to include features, such as description, characters' motivation.

	Key benefits	Key drawbacks
first person		
third person		
past tense		
present tense		

If you choose to use a first-person point of view, remember that you need a narrator who will be present for the whole story, or you will need some means of them finding out about the scenes they are not part of. First person gives writing more immediacy, but sometimes a third-person perspective offers greater descriptive opportunities.

The key thing to remember about tenses is to remain consistent in whatever you choose. It is fine to change tense for a specific reason – for example, if you start in present tense but want to use **flashback** – but multiple changes in tense suggest a lack of coherence and control in writing.

In terms of structure, in shorter forms it is best to begin as close as possible to the most important scene. You want to spend as much time as possible on the main scene.

Key term

flashback: a literary device in which the narrative of a story jumps back in time to tell about an earlier event

Case study: **Freytag's pyramid**

The 19th-century German dramatist Gustav Freytag described dramatic structure as following five acts and peaking like a pyramid. Each point in the diagram represents a stage in the story (or an act in the drama):

- Exposition: characters and setting are introduced.
- Rising action: the story builds (following an inciting incident in more modern terminology) and tension rises.
- Climax: point of greatest tension.
- Falling action: a reversal happens (things go wrong for the protagonist), the protagonist either wins or loses in this stage.
- Denouement: the ending, everything is resolved/explained.

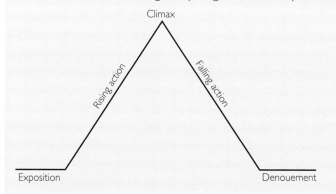

This model was conceived for longer-form stories, but it can also work when applied to short stories and even episodic forms, such as TV series.

As well as Freytag's model, other structures might also be used:

- In short fiction, the denouement might be incomplete, with the denouement left to the reader's imagination (but take care with this one – there is a difference between a clever open ending and just not finishing).

- Starting with the 'big scene' or climax, with the bulk of the story as a flashback explaining how this came to happen.
- Ending with a hint that the resolution is in fact not a resolution and either the story will repeat or a new problem is about to occur.

Crafting a voice

Having decided on perspective and tense, the 'voice' of your story will start to become clear. But voice is also about other choices, such as register and **syntax** – the tone of your writing helps to create the voice. For example, look at these two story openings. They describe similar scenarios and use the same perspective and tense, but they create different voices:

> Walking through the door after work that evening, Jameela slammed it shut behind her as usual, with a cheery 'hi', before stopping herself short at the look on her parents' faces.
> 'What's up?' she asked.

> The door ricocheted into the frame.
> 'Hi –' Jameela stopped herself mid-greeting. This was not to be her usual post-work return. 'What's up?'

Key term

syntax: the arrangement of words into well-formed sentences

Taking things further

For more on the ingredients of successful stories, the TED Talk entitled 'The Clues to a Great Story' by Andrew Stanton, who writes movies for Pixar, is worth watching online.

Further reading

Steven King, *On Writing*, Hodder, 2012
Anne Lamott, *Bird by Bird*, Anchor, 1995
John Yorke, *Into the Woods: How Stories Work and Why We Tell Them*, Penguin, 2014

Activity 8

Take one of the everyday scenarios below and write it in two different ways. The content should be the same, but you should write it in different styles. (Think about different genres of writing – how would a romance writer, as opposed to a science-fiction or a thriller writer, spin it?)

- Someone eats a piece of fruit.
- Someone writes down an address.
- Someone leaves the room.
- Someone brings a chair to the dinner table.

Final task

Write a story entitled 'No Looking Back', which presents someone making a difficult decision. You should aim to show emotion and create tension in your writing. Write between 600 and 900 words.

4.3 Writing descriptively

How is descriptive writing different from narrative writing? How should a descriptive writing piece be approached?

What is descriptive writing?

Descriptive writing requires many of the same creative writing skills as narrative writing, such as showing not telling and setting a scene. You will also call on of the same linguistic features as for narrative writing, such as metaphor and careful lexical choice. The biggest difference between descriptive and narrative writing is the structure and sense of movement that each requires. Narrative writing needs a plot – when reading a story, we want to know *what happens*. This is not the case with a descriptive piece, whose purpose is to capture and convey a mood and atmosphere.

Structuring descriptive writing

It may be helpful to think of descriptive writing like managing a camera, moving around a static scene. This metaphor is useful in several ways, as you can:

- write *panoramically*, taking in the whole scene
- *zoom in* to focus on different parts of the scene
- *track* an individual person or creature across the scene.

However, it is important to remember that a camera only focuses on the visual, and when organising a description it is essential to include other senses. Descriptive writing requires references to sound and often smell and texture too, in order to fully transport the audience to the scene. To develop the metaphor further, while you as a writer may be holding the camera, you want your audience's experience to be fully cinematic, so they forget everything but your description.

There are other ways of structuring a descriptive piece:

- You could choose a time reference, such as dawn, in the first paragraph, and move through the day. This also allows you to show cohesion by opening and closing with the sun rising and setting, for example. This shape may not be possible for some descriptive topics, however.
- You could select a small detail from the scene and follow it throughout the description. For example, you could focus on a person or animal moving around within the setting you are describing, or a leaf blowing across the landscape. This detail serves as a 'hook', leading your reader across and around the scene. This also lends cohesion to your description, but make sure you do not give your person or animal actions that are too 'plot-like'.

Activity 1

Note down some initial ideas for a descriptive piece entitled 'The Garden'. Your writing should include reference to sounds and smells as well as sights in order to create atmosphere for your readers.

When you have some initial ideas for your description, try out at least two different structures in plan form. In what order would you address the different details? Add to your ideas to make the plans more effective if necessary.

Using language features effectively

Descriptive writing should include adjectives and adverbs, along with imagery and references to the senses. However, you need to be careful as all these features can be overused. They should not draw attention to themselves; language features like this should act subtly on the reader, drawing them in and taking them to a different place. If your reader is thinking about the language, they are not thinking about the scene.

Activity 2

Which of these openings is more effective? Why?

> The sun was sluggishly sinking on the horizon, dragging orange and purple the shade of a parrot's wing in its wake. Tiny boats bobbed gently back to the safety of the shoreline, where a few hardy holidaymakers lay stretched out on towels at random intervals.

> Warmth was leaving the beach, just as the boats were leaving the sea to return safely to the shore. The sun seemed to drain the sky of colour as it slowly sank through the layers of orange and purple cloud.

Strong figurative language can transform a piece of descriptive writing, so you should try to include a variety of imagery in your writing. This should contribute to the atmosphere and overall tone of your piece, so think carefully about the connotations of any images you create. For example, in describing 'The Beach', you could choose to create a busy, active scene full of holidaymakers, or a peaceful, tranquil scene. Whichever you choose, your choice of imagery – and the specific comparisons it makes – should support the tone and atmosphere you aim to create.

Look at the following example of a good piece of descriptive writing.

Barely an inch of dry sand is visible. Up to the wet stripe where the sea laps, the entire beach is divided into territories by families intent on fun. From this patchwork of towels, blankets and occasional windbreaks, children surge squealing into the sea, or drag candy-coloured buckets and spades onto the wet sand. The overall effect is chaotic and colourful, like spilling a jumbo box of crayons.

A pair of small children in jewel-bright T-shirts and shorts leave the safety of their parents' windbreak compound. Stepping carefully and respectfully around the towel-territories of others, a turquoise bucket dangles between them, laden with spades and forks. Reaching the band of sodden sand, the pair place the bucket down, turn and wave and unload their tools. Working as one, and with all the concentration of any master architect, the children begin digging a hole. As the discarded sand piles up beside them, birds shriek as they circle overhead.

Beyond the small intent diggers, other children squeal and shriek as they run into the shallows, retreating as the waves hit. The rhythm of this game pulses across the entire beach like a backing track to the afternoon's entertainment: run, splash, squeal, retreat, run, splash, squeal, retreat.

Annotations (right margin):

- clear way of saying the beach is crowded without negative implications
- military/political implications
- careful lexical choices
- comforting connotations
- effective use of alliteration
- cheerful connotations and alternative way of saying 'colourful'
- effective alliteration
- cheerful simile
- alternative way of saying 'colourful' with positive connotations
- reference back to military lexical choices earlier
- better way of describing them carrying the bucket
- rhyme makes phrase effective
- effective description of children's absorption in play
- good to use sound to transition
- adverbial to link paragraphs
- alliteration and assonance tie these verbs together
- strong simile emphasising positive connotations of sound
- use of repeated verbs to underline 'pulse' and 'soundtrack' concept

This description emphasises how busy, loud and chaotic the beach is and creates an atmosphere of happiness associated with the enjoyment of the holidaymakers. The references to colour and the loudness of the noises build this atmosphere.

If you were trying to create a different atmosphere, the style and imagery would also need to change. It is important to think carefully about the atmosphere you want to convey, not just what makes a good image. It needs to be a good image *for that description*. For example, look at this second piece of writing describing 'The Beach'.

opening emphasises tranquillity ——

movement and sound – still stressing calmness of scene ——

engaging idea connoting peace and freshness ——

good idea to include dialogue ——

could perhaps be more subtly expressed, but a sound idea ——

effective description with range of details

> The expanse of pale sand lays flat and undisturbed. Gentle waves lap at the edge of the beach as though freshening it for a new day, the sound carrying across the sandy plains.
>
> 'Look at that,' breathes a woman to her husband. 'It's perfect.'
>
> Their two small children, unable to contain their excitement, run towards the water clutching buckets and spades and begin to dig. Soon the children's breathing and their digging is synchronised to the rhythm of the waves and they feel at one with their surroundings. Meanwhile, their parents have spread out a blanket and are blissfully dozing, hands interlocked, soaking in the sun and the warmth of the sand.

As this example shows, it is possible to exert quite a lot of control over your descriptive writing. You will be given a title and some directions – such as to include different senses, or to focus on atmosphere – but the type of atmosphere will be your choice. The specific details of what is in the scene will usually be within your control, so think carefully before writing. Remember that description is not a story, so you should not have a plot. You can have people, they can be doing things, but those things should essentially be everyday things that do not lead anywhere – so walking onto a beach and lying in the sun is fine, but running from spies or discovering treasure is not!

Activity 3

Draft a description entitled 'The Garden' in two different ways. Write 200–250 words for each description. You should aim to include some of the same details, but use alternative imagery or phrases to create two contrasting atmospheres – for example, one peaceful and the other vibrant.

Final task

Write a descriptive piece entitled 'The Pool'. Focus on describing movement and sound in your writing and think carefully about the structure and atmosphere of your piece. Write between 600 and 900 words.

4.4 Writing critically

What does 'writing critically' mean? What should
be included in critical writing?

How do you write critically?

When you write critically – that is, a review or critical essay – you should:

- evaluate
- make judgments
- offer recommendations.

Activity 1

You are going to be a restaurant critic and write a brief review of your main
meal from yesterday evening. First, read Text 5 below and any examples of
restaurant reviews you can find in your local press.

- Get a feel for the tone and style used in reviews. Think about an
  appropriate tone for your own review. If you had a simple meal at home
  (or a takeaway), either imagine it was a restaurant meal, or think back to
  the last restaurant meal you had. If you ate out, how close to an authentic-
  sounding review can you get?
- Write 2–5 sentences to set the scene, including describing the ambience
  (atmosphere) of the place where you ate. You could include references to
  décor and the staff's attitude.
- Describe the food, in courses if possible. If you ate with others, describe
  what your companions ate and how they felt about it. Remember to
  include comments on texture and presentation/appearance, as well as
  taste. Consider including drinks.
- End with an overall evaluative comment. Would you eat there again?
  Would you advise others to? What kind of person might want to?

Text 5

Don't let the blue spirulina tagliatelle at Mark + Vinny's put you off. No, wait. On second thoughts, DO let the blue
spirulina tagliatelle at Mark and Vinny's put you off.
If you can't cope with the idea of pasta made with anything other than doppio zero flour, eggs and olive oil, then stay
well away.
Chances are you may not be able to cope with spaghettini that is ruby-red with beetroot, bucatini that is black with
charcoal, or an egg yolk made from sweet potato.
Or the atrocious puns on the menu – gnoc, gnoc, gnocchi on heaven's door […] and a catch-cry of "don't be upsetti,
eat some spaghetti".
With a vegan vibe […], Mark + Vinny's has all the things millennials require from a dining experience – #cleaneating
options, […] Insta'bility and no preachy sermons – and I have to say it's a load of fun.

Mark Filipelli and Vince Pizzinga, Aussie Italians who met up in LA, have hit the ground running at this cute, tall-ceilinged but still squeezy 45-seater, where […] pink neon sings Fly Me To the Moon and Little Italy's Sinatra and Dino are in the air.

The menu is full of surprises, and I don't mean sky-blue tagliatelle, I mean – meatballs. Chef Adrian Jankuloski shows off his Icebergs and The Dolphin heritage by hand-chopping [meat…] and mortadella into nonna-style meatballs with a dense tomato sugo ($18); an island of glorious comfort food floating in a meat-free sea.

And right next to a (real) burrata with green tomato jam and basil oil ($20) is a fake mozzarella, all soy and coconut oil, with heirloom tomatoes and basil ($18). It doesn't taste like mozzarella, or tofu, but something nicely in-between. Chickpea hummus is a terrific starter, scooped up with fingers of grilled schiacciata flatbread ($14) […].

That blue tagliatelle ($34) is pliable, silky and surprisingly al dente, with a clean, seaweedy finish. Combining blue swimmer crab, bottarga and crunchy breadcrumbs and pasta made with a nutrient-dense powdered algae is intuitive, although I fear it never really comes together as one.

Then there's an aggressively al dente maccaruni Calabrese ($28), the pasta made by Peppe's in Haberfield, with a chunky […] rib ragu that's more […] rib than ragu. A juicy slab of bitter orange cake with blood orange granita […] makes me happy I didn't go for the deep-fried "no-tella" ravioli.

Weaknesses? The pasta doesn't fly me to the moon. I miss that indivisible fusing together of sauce and pasta, when the starches and sauce emulsify and bond.

I get that this traditional fusing isn't a priority here, but without the sauces coating and being absorbed by the pasta, you're left with more fashion than form.

Strengths? The humour, the warmth […], and the sassy, savvy combo of American red-sauce joint and Surry Hills spritz bar. It just needs a bit more work on the core product, before it can play among the stars.

From goodfood.com., 'Mark and Vinny's review'

Key elements of review writing

The following are typical features of review writing, from movie reviews to plays, books and art shows, video games and music albums. Even reviews of purchases, such as power tools and electrical goods via online stores, will have some of these features:

- opinion
- comparisons to other works in the field
- field-specific lexis
- evaluative comments
- summary and selected details
- recommendations ('if you like…', 'recommended for fans of…')
- rating/score (not always included, depends on context).

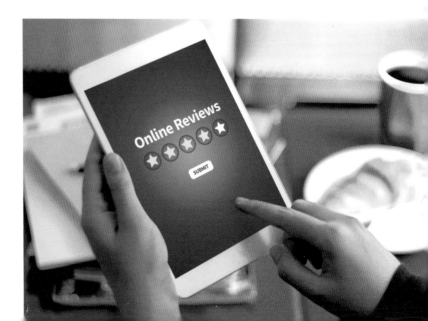

Read Text 6, which is a blogpost discussing the film *Thor: Ragnarok*.

Text 6

Why *Thor: Ragnarok* is my Favourite Avengers Movie Yet (Spoiler-Free)

Firstly, let me contextualise this by explaining that I am an Avengers fan, and have worked my way steadily through all the movies. I've cheered for Iron Man's character development (thank goodness he's no longer an entitled idiot, right?), been there for Captain America's complex inner conflicts, and – best of all – enjoyed the crazy character clashes of the ensemble stories. But Thor – he's always been my favourite. His solo outings, I find, represent the very best aspects of those ensemble movies: action with a healthy dose of humour.

And humour is what the latest Thor film is most generous with. Yes, there is action too – plenty of that, with peril and angst and all of that nail-biting goodness – but its core appeal is definitely the humour. There are laugh-out-loud moments in this movie, but there is also a lightness of touch, a delicacy to the storytelling which makes it a delight and brings that humorous tone even where it isn't explicitly funny.

If, like me, you most enjoy your superhero narratives when they're aware of their over-the-top nature and don't try to take themselves too seriously, I'd suggest you make seeing *Thor: Ragnarok* a priority.

Activity 2

Text 6 is not a straightforward review, but it is a good example of critical writing. Which features of review writing from the list given opposite can you see in the text? In what ways is it different? What makes it fulfil the purpose of critical writing?

Mode makes a difference

Reviewing has become more accessible thanks to the internet. It is no longer only professional critics who write reviews; many people routinely review their purchases and experiences on websites such as Amazon and Trip Advisor in order to help other people. There is also a growing trend in reviewing things such as trades and services. Such reviews demonstrate variable standards of writing, and often contain errors, because they are informal and the writers do not plan or edit their reviews. However, they still include many standard features of review writing.

- They contain evaluative language.
- They make comparisons to similar products/experiences.
- They include a summary.
- They discuss specific details using appropriate lexis.
- They offer recommendations.

Where there are differences, therefore, these are usually related to the mode, audience and form.

Activity 3

Write a brief (150–200 words) review for a website, such as Amazon, of the last media product you purchased, for example the last movie you watched, book you read, video game you played or album you listened to. Make sure that your writing is helpful to others considering buying the same product and use the bullet points opposite for ideas on what to include.

There has also been a rise in reviewing as a hobby or on a semi-professional basis. Blog and vlog (video blog) reviewing has grown considerably over the past decade, and some bloggers now make a career out of their writing.

Activity 4

Find a vlog review of a product you are interested in. It should be no more than six minutes long and discuss a single product that the vlog creator has actually used. Comment on how this spoken review compares to written reviews by following the steps below:

- Transcribe the vlog, using the conventions of a transcript (no standard punctuation, timed pauses, underlining for emphasis, non-verbal communication in brackets and italics).
- Note the overall structure that the vlogger follows. Annotate your transcript to show the different parts of the review (e.g. summary, details, recommendations).
- Note the language used in the vlog – how is it the same as and/or different to written reviews? Again, annotate your transcript to show the key features and any significant differences you notice.
- Note how language is used because of being spoken. Does the vlogger repeat ideas to help the audience take them in? What kind of lexis and grammar does the vlogger use? Are there any other linguistic features worth noting?
- Note how language is used because of the vlog format. How does the vlogger relate to their audience? Are there things worth noting pragmatically which appear to be about building and retaining an audience?

Now script a vlog of your own, reviewing an entertainment product such as a book, movie, album or video game that you know well.

Audience is key

An awareness of audience is essential in good critical writing. Making recommendations is one of the key elements of a review, and that of course requires an understanding of the audience. But more than this, a reviewer needs a clear awareness of and an appropriate address to the audience. This should also be reflected in the position the writer takes in the text. In Text 6, for example, the writer uses the phrase 'If, like me'. This invites the audience to be with her, but also acknowledges that they may not be, thus encompassing any potential reader.

Now read this review of an album.

Text 7

Review: Vance Joy Nation of Two

Vance Joy's second album, Nation of Two, is sure to please fans of his first by sticking to the breezy acoustic pop sound established on his 2014 album Dream Your Life Away.

Cheery finger-picking guitar backing and delicate vocals combine to create a folky feel in songs like 'Take Your Time', while more fun-pop vibes in 'Saturday Sun' will have many tapping their feet. For those who enjoyed his first album, there will be no disappointments here, as Joy has not strayed in style or sound.

The album has an overarching concept, following the ups and downs of a couple, which is perhaps the reason some of the lyrics being rather blandly over-sentimental, but this is arguably a question of taste. Nonetheless, the emotional content of the lyrics is well suited to Joy's warm and mellow vocal tones.

The album as a whole is likely to be enjoyed by fans of Joy's first and will almost certainly spawn some radio hits and chart success.

Activity 5

How might you use lexical analysis to discuss the writer's relationship to the audience in Text 7?

If you were reviewing an album/playlist, what features would help you to address an audience of your peers effectively? You should assume that your target audience is people from your area, of roughly the same age as you, who like the same sort of music, read similar magazines and use the same social media accounts/websites as you.

Choice of lexis is important in the creation of an evaluative text. Adjectives and adjective phrases that demonstrate judgment or imply assessment of the item being reviewed against others in the field are an important part of this. Key lexical choices in critical writing include items such as:

* comparative and superlative adjectives and adverbs: 'sharper visual effects than…', 'the wittiest dialogue'
* adverbs of degree: 'well', 'very'
* comment clauses: 'in my opinion', 'as far as I'm concerned'
* conditional clauses: 'if you enjoyed…', 'if you're a fan of…'.

Activity 6

Write a short review of an album or playlist you know well, following a similar structure to the review above.

* Paragraph 1: brief overview (single sentence)
* Paragraph 2: compare to similar or previous album/playlist, referring to specifics

- Paragraph 3: pick out some highlights, aiming to show the album's range, then focus on a more technical detail, such as vocals, an instrument or production
- Paragraph 4: sum up and make recommendations. What kind of album/playlist is this? Who is it for?

Organising your content

The structure you choose to follow will depend largely on the context and the product or experience you are reviewing, but it is possible to describe a broad structure as follows:

overview → summary → details → recommendations

Begin with a very brief overview, followed by an expanded summary to contextualise the product more clearly by comparing it to others. Details belong in the middle of the review, and this is where most of your evaluative detail should appear. Conclude with your recommendations about who the product would suit.

This broad structure allows for variation according to the specific context, while offering flexibility depending on what you are reviewing and where (and for whom) you are reviewing it.

Activity 7

Copy and complete the following table to compare a range of products following the structure outlined above.

	A book you read recently	A game you played or watched (video, board or sports)	An electronics item (e.g. phone, laptop, watch)	A snack food or a beauty item
One-sentence overview				
Broader summary				
Detail 1				
Detail 2				
Detail 3				
Recommendation(s)				

Final task

Write a pair of reviews of the last movie you watched that you can remember well. One should be a positive review and the other a negative one. Each review should be 300–350 words. Take care to use language effectively – in both reviews – to convey the appropriate views to the reader without writing in an exaggerated or unrealistic manner.

4.5 Writing discursively

What is discursive writing? What are the features
of discursive and argument writing?

What is discursive and argument writing?

Discursive writing discusses an issue. Argument writing, on the other hand,
presents an argument. The key difference between the two is balance and
direction: a piece of discursive writing does not need to offer a single, clear
opinion.

Both discursive and argument functions may be found in a range of forms
and can be used in writing for either reading or listening audiences.

Activity 1

Copy and complete the table below to provide examples of texts for a range
of contexts. Aim to include multiple examples in some boxes.

	Discursive	Argument
Newspaper or magazine article		opinion column
Letter	letter to a newspaper	
Script for TV or radio		advertisement
Leaflet		
Speech	debate	

Although there is a wide range of text types to be considered here, there are a
few key features to bear in mind when writing texts of this nature. It is important
to set out your argument clearly. Language features such as precise lexis, clear
conjunctions and careful syntax all help with clarity in discursive writing.

Rhetorical features are also very useful in both argument and discursive
texts because they can strengthen an argument by helping to make writing
more persuasive. The table overleaf shows some of the most common
rhetorical features you can use. Other language features such as metaphor,
hyperbole and anecdote are also commonly used in this kind of writing.

Feature	Explanation	Example
anaphora	repetition of a word or phrase at the beginning of successive clauses	And if I could only get ten people to listen, if I could only persuade a handful to hear my story.
antithesis	the placing together of opposites, or near opposites, usually phrased similarly to emphasise the contrast	Do not reject my ideas because you cannot accept me as a woman; try to accept my ideas because you should not simply reject me as a woman.
distinction	definition or elaboration of terms explicitly	Eating meat is wrong, by which I mean it is morally inappropriate.
hypophora	asking and then answering a question	And what do you think she did next? She did what any woman in that situation would do…
polysyndeton	listing ideas using an excess of conjunctions	It is crucial to avoid not only laziness but also greed and hypocrisy and sheer stupidity.

Read Text 8 below, which is an extract from a book by an investigative reporter.

Text 8

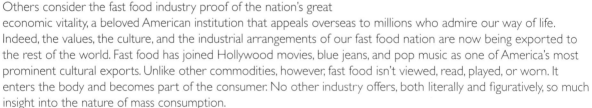

Elitists have always looked down at fast food, criticizing how it tastes and regarding it as another tacky manifestation of American popular culture. The aesthetics of fast food are of much less concern to me than its impact upon the lives of ordinary Americans, both as workers and consumers. Most of all, I am concerned about its impact on the nation's children. Fast food is heavily marketed to children and prepared by people who are barely older than children. This is an industry that both feeds and feeds off the young. During the two years spent researching this book, I ate an enormous amount of fast food. Most of it tasted pretty good. That is one of the main reasons people buy fast food; it has been carefully designed to taste good. It's also inexpensive and convenient. But the value meals, two-for-one deals, and free refills of soda give a distorted sense of how much fast food actually costs. The real price never appears on the menu.

The sociologist George Ritzer has attacked the fast food industry for celebrating a narrow measure of efficiency over every other human value, calling the triumph of McDonald's "the irrationality of rationality." Others consider the fast food industry proof of the nation's great economic vitality, a beloved American institution that appeals overseas to millions who admire our way of life. Indeed, the values, the culture, and the industrial arrangements of our fast food nation are now being exported to the rest of the world. Fast food has joined Hollywood movies, blue jeans, and pop music as one of America's most prominent cultural exports. Unlike other commodities, however, fast food isn't viewed, read, played, or worn. It enters the body and becomes part of the consumer. No other industry offers, both literally and figuratively, so much insight into the nature of mass consumption.

Hundreds of millions of people buy fast food every day without giving it much thought, unaware of the subtle and not so subtle ramifications of their purchases. They rarely consider where this food came from, how it was made, what it is doing to the community around them. They just grab their tray off the counter, find a table, take a seat, unwrap the paper, and dig in. The whole experience is transitory and soon forgotten. I've written this book out of a belief that people should know what lies behind the shiny, happy surface of every fast food transaction. They should know what really lurks between those sesame-seed buns. As the old saying goes: You are what you eat.

Eric Schlosser, from *Fast Food Nation*

Activity 2

Choose three sentences form Text 8 that you find particularly powerful or effective. What made them work for you?

Structuring discursive writing

To make it clear for your reader where your argument will go (a position you should state in your introduction), it is important to choose a clear, logical structure. Planning is therefore essential. So too are the links between the different sections of your work. A well-placed 'as argued above…' and an 'as previously proven by…' can make all the difference to a piece of discursive writing. The equivalent in journalistic writing is returning to an anecdote or metaphor at the end of the text to give a circular and well-polished feel to an article. These cohesive touches refine and improve a text.

See Unit 2.1 for more detail on connectives and discourse markers for logical connections.

In formal discursive writing such as essays, you can use a dialectical structure. This is broadly as follows:

- Introduction (thesis): the main idea is introduced – you give an overview of the topic.
- Argument: one view on the idea is explained – you present (usually) the view you agree with.
- Objection (antithesis): an opposing view on the idea is explained – you present a counter-argument.
- Response: an answer specifically to the objection is explained – you deal with the objection, rather than repeating the original argument.
- Conclusion (synthesis): a new position is reached – you show how the ideas combine to produce a new understanding.

In more informal discursive writing, such as in newspaper articles, counter-arguments are used less obtrusively than in true philosophical dialectics. For example, you might introduce a counter-argument simply to show that you are aware of it and to enable you to make your response – but you would be unlikely to explain it fully, as you would in a truly dialectic essay. For example:

> I know there are those who would say that schools should not use their resources to provide meals for poorer students, but I would argue that any other intervention with someone who is hungry is a waste.

Activity 3

Plan a discursive essay on the issues surrounding the fast-food industry, using one of these tasks:

- Discuss the ways in which the fast-food industry is contributing to a health crisis.
- 'The fast food industry preys on the poor.' Discuss.

At this stage, gather ideas by noting:

- your initial thoughts and views
- possible arguments and counter-arguments relating to the title you have chosen.

Key term

topic sentence: the sentence in a paragraph that states the main topic of that paragraph; the topic sentence is often (but not always) the first in the paragraph

Topic sentences are a good way to help structure your ideas in discursive or argument writing. A topic sentence is often the first sentence in each paragraph, and clearly states the main topic for that paragraph.

Read Text 9, which is the opening of a discursive essay entitled 'Does media cause isolation?'

Text 9

Social media is a new phenomenon that has exploded into popular use. The majority of adults and young adults in the developed world have at least one social media account, many having multiple accounts which they are checking constantly. Although it may at first appear oxymoronic to ask if 'social' media can be isolating, this is in fact the reality for some.

Clearly, social media are social. The intention behind the software and most users is to connect – to make connections with others, to find commonality, to share. Often, this has been highly successful, with many people feeling that some forms of social media have allowed them to find others who share their niche interests, their isolating health conditions or their unusual passions. Used this way, social media is the opposite of isolating.

On the other hand, we all have times when social media makes us feel inferior. Times when we look at everyone else's Instagram feed and forget that reality is not like that for them either, that what they are sharing is not the full picture but a cropped and filtered version of their life that they have chosen to share. Comparing that glossy Insta-perfect life to your own unfiltered version can feel isolating and depressing. It must be so much worse for people who are dealing with anything as dark as cyberbullies or trolls.

Activity 4

For each paragraph in Text 9, identify the topic sentence. Give reasons for your choice.

Proving your point

When writing discursively, you also need to provide evidence for your claims. There are various ways of doing this:

- Expert opinion – including the views of named experts in the field
- Examples, including case studies of individuals and statistics to show a wider application
- Anecdotal evidence – a personal story about the writer or a person known to them.

Each of these kinds of evidence can be persuasive, but not all are appropriate in every type of discursive writing. For example, anecdotal evidence is commonly used in newspaper articles, but is less useful in formal discursive essays because its personal tone contrasts too strongly with the necessary formality.

In your assessment, you may need to make up statistics or expert opinions. If you do so, make sure that any invented material is plausible.

Activity 5

Copy and complete the table below by inventing a range of evidence to support your views on the topics outlined. Some have been suggested as a starting point.

	Expert opinion	Example	Anecdote
Are youth prisons the solution to youth crime?		Case study of Alex who went to prison for a minor crime, befriended gang members in prison and committed worse crimes on leaving.	
Should meat be banned from the school cafeteria?			
Should we choose school subjects to study?	Dr Drew: 'students are not equipped to make life-changing choices as young teenagers. They are too easily distracted by what their friends say, what the media says. The brain is not yet flexible enough to hold sufficient information at 13 or even 15.'		

Activity 6

Text 9 would benefit from some evidence. What could you add in and where?

Different modes

Political speeches are often discursive, aiming to clearly and fully outline an argument for their audience. If you look again at the speeches by Roosevelt and Obama in Unit 4.1, you will notice features such as logical connections and a concern for evidence and reasoning. At the same time, they have additional features reflecting the fact that their audience is listening rather than reading.

Activity 7

a) Reread the speeches, on pages 88 and 89. Which features seem to relate to their spoken nature? How do the speakers keep their listeners' attention?
b) Which features of rhetoric from the table on page 108 or from your wider knowledge of rhetoric can you identify?
c) Based on your findings, how would you characterise the features of discursive speech? Summarise the ways the texts seek to present their ideas to their audience.

You may also need to consider discursive techniques in other spoken texts, such as podcasts and audio tours. In an audio tour (often used at historical sites and museums), a visitor has a device with headphones; as they walk around, they press a numbered button to hear relevant information at each location of the site. Writing audio tours requires careful structuring and a clear sense of explanation and logic, as you are effectively bringing a guide book to life for listeners.

For more information on mode, see Unit 3.1.

Activity 8

Script a self-directed audio tour for your school/college aimed at prospective future students and their families.

- Write each segment with walking instructions to the next location, so that the visitor will listen to the information at each point and then know how to reach the next.
- Begin with your school's/college's hall or meeting place (wherever large addresses to students/parents would normally take place), and number each piece of information.
- Include a range of key places and provide visitors with a mix of information, official and unofficial, so that it is both helpful and lightly entertaining.

For example:

> 1: You should now be standing in the hall. Face the stage. This is where most school assemblies take place, and also large events such as performances and prize-givings. You will have assemblies about once every two weeks with your year group or house – don't worry, they're not too boring. For performances, we alternate annually between a play and musical. This year, we did 'Oliver!', which was brilliant, so next year it will be a play. On your left, you will see a portrait of our founder Dr Dawson. We are very proud of this school's long history, and to your right, the windows look out onto the sports fields. Now, if you could please turn completely around to face the other way, you need to leave through the doors behind you. (pause 3 secs) Thank you. Now turn left and go up the stairs. Take the first door on the right up there into the science lab.

Structure and key features

Form dictates the structure of any text, and discursive and argument texts can take several different forms. As such, there is no 'one size fits all' outline. Planning is the most helpful step in ensuring that you have a structure that works. The activity below uses the form of an article – which is like an informal essay – to illustrate points about structure.

Activity 9

Carry out a brief investigation into some opinion articles in a quality news source. You will need a physical copy of news sources to do this (ideally two, but one will work). Use the articles in the 'opinion' or 'comment' section. Copy and complete the table below (you will need more columns, but do total/average all your findings).

	Article 1	Article 2	Total/Average
Mean number of sentences per paragraph			
Anecdote used and in which paragraphs			
Mean number of lines per paragraph			
Total number of first-person singular pronouns (I/me/my)			(mean per article)
Total number of first-person plural pronouns (us/our/we)			(mean per article)
Total number of first-person pronouns			(mean per article)
Total number of second-person pronouns (you/your)			(mean per article)

Extension: You might also notice patterns in the use of metaphor, intertextual references or other shared resources. Feel free to add rows to your table to comment on these also.

Looking at the overall shape of the articles you have been studying, you may notice some similarities in their organisation. When writing articles, a good basic structure might be:

* Introduce the key idea, perhaps with an anecdote, a metaphor or a reference.
* Expand by introducing and quickly despatching a counter-argument.
* Provide a clear set of explanations and/or developments, usually with lots of illustration (and perhaps touching on that initial anecdote/metaphor/reference to ground it).
* Finish with a strong conclusion, ideally returning to your opening anecdote/metaphor/reference.

You should reference a structure like this in your planning. For example:

> Opinion article plan: 'music should have certificates like films and video games'
>
> - Anecdote – friend's 14-year-old son listening to music full of inappropriate references and language that would not be allowed in a film for his age – shocked me.
> - Counter-argument: hard to control due to radio/ streaming, although radio does censor.
> - Videos also inappropriate, various strands of inappropriateness – all linked to different social problems (attitudes to women, violence, attitudes to money/work/ crime), mention friend's son again.
> - Close with image of friend's son and other young men – what about influence on less nice boys than him?

Activity 10

Explore some possible structures by planning responses to each of the six writing briefs below. Note that these are all quite varied in context so require different approaches.

Make each plan clear in terms of the content you would include and make sure you consider the overall structure required for the text form you are writing.

Write a letter requesting support for a charitable event.	Mobile phones should be banned in schools. Write a response to this statement.	Write an opinion article on gaming (any opinion).
Bringing food from home has been banned at your school or college. Write to the management to complain.	Write the text of a speech for a student ambassador to give in assembly 'Our Topic of The Week' (you choose).	Write the script for a 90-second internet video advertisement for a retro video game being launched as an app.

Final task

Write an article for your school/college magazine aimed at students' families on how you have seen technology change in your lifetime. You should choose one or two developments to focus on in some detail and you could choose to also discuss how things could progress in the future. You may express your opinions on the issues.

Remember to plan your ideas first and to ensure that you address the audience appropriately. You may want to refer back to your work in Activity 9 first for ideas on article writing.

4.6 Writing reflectively

What are the features of successful reflective writing?

Why write a reflection?

As part of your assessment, you may be required to write a reflection on a text you have written, in order to further demonstrate your understanding of writing skills and analysis. You may also be asked to compare your writing to another text. Reflective writing allows you to show that you are writing *consciously*. In producing a reflective commentary on your own writing, you are demonstrating awareness of the following:

- adapting language to audience and purpose
- selecting language according to form, mode and genre
- choosing language precisely for effect and meaning.

Activity I

Refer back to your work for the film review in the final task in Unit 4.3. The task was to write a pair of reviews for the same movie, one positive and one negative. Imagine that a student had begun their negative review with the statement:

> 'Blade Runner 2049' is the most self-indulgent, slow-moving film I've sat through in years.

In a piece of reflective writing on the review, the student might then write:

> I started my negative review with a clear declarative to show how much I disliked the film.

The student has used the first person, but they have not selected the best features about their opening sentence. What could they have written to show a better understanding of the requirements of a reflective commentary?

As with all analytical work, the trick with reflective writing is not simply to show as many linguistic features as possible, but to use those labels with purpose. It is far more helpful to analyse one feature in depth than it is to list four or five without any reference to meaning or context. In the example in the activity above, the student was correct that it was a declarative sentence, but that fact did not really add anything to their point – it being declarative is not why or how the sentence displays dislike of the film.

Now look at this example of an extract from a student response which successfully groups features together to create a reasonable analysis.

clear overview of features ———

precise label ———

bit broad here ———

still a bit vague ———

exact language features ———

I used evaluative language, including the superlative 'most self-indulgent' to show the strength of my feelings about 'Blade Runner 2049'. I then continued this negativity with the adjective 'slow-moving' and the verb phrase 'sat through'. The combination of these in the declarative sentence makes immediately clear to the reader that I resent having spent time on this film.

clear explanation ———

Activity 2

Look at your answer to the film review task. Choose the five best features and explain why you used them and/or their effect, using a sentence (or more) for each feature. You may give more than one example for each feature if you want to show a pattern.

Selecting features

When reflecting on your writing, you will not have space to describe everything, so it is important to be selective. Get into the habit of quickly deciding which are the most interesting and important features. Again, as with analytical writing (of which this is a type), it is not about listing everything, or working from top to bottom in a slavish manner. Show intelligence in the selection of features you write about. Try to avoid choosing those that will lead to you repeating yourself in the explanation. For example, explaining everything in terms of audience will result in a weak reflective commentary.

Look at this extract from a task and the reflection that follows. The student was asked to write to their parliamentary representative complaining about local transport provision.

Dear Ms Kendall

I am writing to complain about the provision of buses in my area of the city. They are not regular into the evenings and are often running late even first thing in the morning. How can we expect people to use public transport when it is not reliable? People cannot be expected to give up their cars and reduce their carbon footprint when the buses on offer might not get them to work on time!

Reflection:

I have used formal, high-register lexis such as 'provision' because my audience is a government representative, so she is a highly educated woman. My sentences are varied in function, e.g. the interrogative 'how can we… reliable?' because I need to attract the attention of my audience who is a busy woman. I have kept a focus on issues around the environment and people going to work because this is likely to meet the needs of my audience.

Activity 3

What other explanations could this student have used to avoid constantly talking about audience? Consider other contextual factors such as form, purpose and mode as well as intended effect and meaning.

Even students who otherwise write well often find it difficult to create a good reflective commentary, so it is a good idea to get some practice at reflecting on and analysing your own work.

Activity 4

Choose a piece of writing that you are proud of. Copy and complete the table below in order to help you reflect on it effectively.

Phrase you feel is effective (Quote a phrase from your writing.)	Language technique (Choose a label that you can apply to the quotation.)	Contextual factor (What aspect of context most influenced this choice of language?)	Intended effect (What did you want to achieve with these words? Why are they there? How do they work?)

Choosing a structure

Having identified some of the things that make your text work, you next need to arrange these points into a coherent structure. Ask yourself the following questions:

- Are these points similar or related, or do they show a range across language levels and context? If they are too similar, do you need to replace one or more? Could you cluster them together to make one point about a pattern of language use? Can you change the labels you have used or the contextual factor you have linked to on one of them?
- Do they fall into a natural order (e.g. according to different language levels or contextual factors or effects) or does it make sense to take them in text order?

To give overall shape to a piece of reflective writing, think about its most important features and highlight these in the introduction and conclusion. You might also find that it makes sense to use these sections to suggest an overall theme, although this does not always apply.

Reflective writing is similar to analytical writing, so structural concerns are the same. It is important to use an introduction and conclusion. You will also want to make sure that you cover context and different language features.

Activity 5

Using your points from Activity 4, write the reflection on your piece of writing. You will need to think about and add an introduction and a conclusion.

Reflecting on different kinds of writing

You may be asked to reflect on all kinds of writing except for the analysis of texts, so make sure that you use a variety of sources when practising this skill. With creative writing, there is usually less to say about audience and purpose, but often there are more features and effects to discuss. With transactional forms of writing, it is the other way around.

Activity 6

Read these sentences from a range of reflective writing. Copy and complete the table by writing the correct form in the left-hand column. Choose from the list below the table.

	I used the simile 'like cannon firing' to emphasise the volume and ensure that the sound carried connotations of danger and fear to contribute to the tense atmosphere.
	My choice of inclusive pronoun with 'our school' was intended to evoke a sense of responsibility in my audience and provoke a strong reaction.
	I chose to use imperative sentences as headings throughout, as this is common for the form, but also it helps the advisory purpose and directs the audience, making it clear what I want them to do.
	I felt that the verb 'slipped' was effective in showing how Chloe left the room, as it showed her shame.
	I included jargon such as 'fold', together with a following imperative on how to do that, to enable the audience to follow the instructions no matter their level of expertise.

voiceover	narrative	leaflet	letter	descriptive

Final task

Write a descriptive piece called 'The Forest'. In your writing, aim to create a clear sense of atmosphere, using no more than 400 words. Then write a reflective commentary of 200–250 words, explaining how your choices helped you address the brief.

Key term

monologue: a long speech given by a character in a film or play

End-of-chapter task

It's end-of-year show time at your school or college! Pick one of the following tasks (or do several/all of them for additional practice) and follow it up with a 250-word reflection, explaining how your choices helped you address the task:

- Write the script for a two-minute dramatic **monologue** showing a character at a turning point in his/her life.
- Write the script for a radio advertisement for your local radio station to persuade the community to come to your school/college variety performance.
- Write a school or college magazine feature on the star of the show.
- Write the opening of a story entitled *The Show*.
- Write a description of curtain-up on opening night.
- Write an opinion piece on the culture of school and college performances.

Chapter 5

Language change

loweth the fyxth
he noble and woz-
e kyng Arthur.

uncelot and fyz Lyonell
e courte foz to feke auen-
z Lyonell lefte fyz Lau-
 was taken. Caplm.j.

None after that the
noble & wozthy kyng
Arthur was comen

tes of the roude table
refozted vnto p kyng

knyghtes / Whiche encre
mes and wozthyp that t
theyz felowes in prowesse
 that was well proued o

This chapter marks the shift from AS to A Level work.
First, it introduces the idea of working with data,
explaining how to use data analysis with a range of
linguistic concepts that will be familiar from your AS
Level work. The remaining units deal with the topic
of language change, exploring a range of content and
ideas. The chapter concludes with a unit that gives
some examples of topic-related data. This practice in
working with data is helpful when looking at trends
within society or when dealing with questions about
how language has changed over time.

On this course, language change is considered across
the periods of Early Modern English to Contemporary
English (from around the year 1500 to the present
day), so this chapter only includes data from this
period. You will explore the key features of language from this
time and consider the contextual influences on change,
theories and models of change, and attitudes towards it.

Key concepts introduced in this chapter are *change* and
diversity, which you will consider by always looking at
language in its *context*. Here, change in linguistic terms
means how the English language itself has changed over
time. Diversity in English is considered in global terms.
So, for this topic you will need to consider the concepts
in broad terms, encompassing the entire English-
speaking community.

fauour aboue all other k
certaynly he loued the qu

5.1 Working with data

What kind of data do you need to understand for English Language? How do you work with English Language data?

Data in language study

When you explore language by looking at data, you are investigating *trends* within language use, rather than exploring *specific choices* made by speakers or writers. Data is used for **quantitative analysis**, making claims that are supported by a substantial amount of evidence, although this is often combined with **qualitative analysis** to go into more detail. This approach represents a move into the more advanced linguistic work required at A Level.

Many aspects of language can be explored quantitatively. Data presented in charts and graphs allow linguists to explore many different questions. For example:

- Do men or women ask more questions in interactional conversations?
- Are there differences in the way teenaged and 20- to 25-year-old university students talk?
- Do people speak to older people the same way they speak to small children?

Questions like this require the collection of spoken-language data, which would involve a large recording project followed by transcription. After this, researchers would comb through the data to find examples of particular features in order to generate the numerical comparative data required. Such data can be presented in a range of ways.

Key terms

quantitative analysis: methods of analysis concerned with statistics and numerical assessments of data

qualitative analysis: (in language) methods of analysis primarily concerned with the qualities of language used

Case study: **Classroom data**

In a lesson with a class of 17–18-year-olds, data was collected from students as they worked in groups. This does not represent the entire class time, as only part of the lesson was dedicated to group working time. Note that students 1–6 are male and 7–12 are female (student numbers are on the *x*-axis of the charts that follow). Students worked mostly in pairs or threes, with classmates of their choice, so they were comfortable in their chosen groups.

The charts below show the data collected.

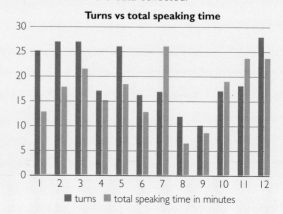

Turns vs total speaking time

■ turns ■ total speaking time in minutes

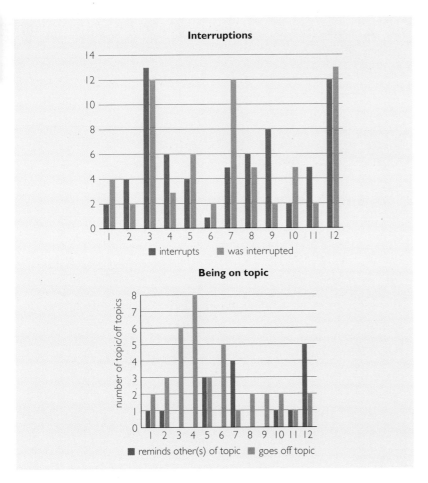

Bar graphs are clearly very useful for displaying linguistic data. However, to make broader claims, you need to look at averages and group data. With a small group like this, individuals can make a big difference to results. You can see this in the examples of bar and whisker charts below. This type of chart is good for showing the spread and concentration of results.

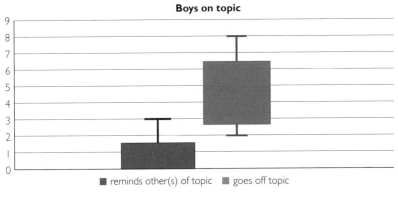

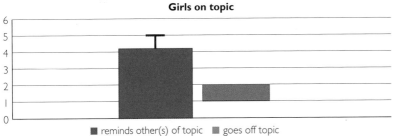

Activity 1

Which of the following conclusions could you reasonably draw from the data in the charts?

- The male students went off topic more than the female students.
- Female students spoke more than male students.
- There was not a significant difference between male and female students in terms of going off topic.
- The students who interrupted others most often were also the ones who got interrupted the most.
- There was no clear link between number of turns and total speaking time.

Corpus linguistics

Corpus linguistics is a relatively new branch of linguistic study, made possible by the use of computers to support working with language. Various corpora are available to explore online, all of which provide slightly different kinds of data. For example, the British National Corpus (BNC) represents 100 million words of data, 90% of which is written and 10% spoken. This data was gathered from a wide range of sources in the late 20th century. The benefit of large online corpora is their size, but one drawback is that they date quickly because it takes time to gather the material and make it available in digital format.

Key term

corpus: (plural corpora) a large and structured set of texts, usually stored electronically

Activity 2

Other than the BNC, what corpora of English language can you find online? Can you access any for the English spoken in your country?

Key term

collocate search: a search conducted in a corpus of language to find the words that occur most commonly on either side of a search term (e.g. for 'majority', 'vast' would be a left-hand collocate and 'rule' a right-hand collocate)

You can perform several types of search with a corpus. One of the most useful is a **collocate search**. The image below shows a BNC search for 'diet' using the open-access Intellitext service. It shows words occurring most commonly immediately before the word 'diet' in the data. Do not worry at this point about the column headings, or the other data in the table – just focus on the collocates.

Collocations of diet

Collocation	Count	F1	F2 ▲	LL	MI	T
diet ~~ calorie-controlled	5	3768	5	25.73	14.85	2.24
diet ~~ weight-reducing	4	3768	5	19.34	14.53	2
diet ~~ WNAS	7	3768	14	31.18	13.85	2.65
diet ~~ sugar-free	4	3768	22	15.37	12.39	2
diet ~~ wholefood	4	3768	25	15.09	12.21	2
diet ~~ high-protein	4	3768	26	15.01	12.15	2
diet ~~ weight-loss	6	3768	39	22.51	12.15	2.45
diet ~~ vegan	11	3768	49	43.57	12.69	3.32
diet ~~ fibre-rich	5	3768	58	17.22	11.31	2.24
diet ~~ low-calorie	10	3768	60	37.96	12.26	3.16
diet ~~ fromage_frais	4	3768	60	13.24	10.94	2
diet ~~ high-fibre	16	3768	67	63.95	12.78	4
diet ~~ polymeric	9	3768	72	32.76	11.85	3
diet ~~ F-Plan	7	3768	81	24.12	11.32	2.64
diet ~~ well-balanced	11	3768	99	39.35	11.68	3.32

<< first   < prev   **1**   2   3   4   5   6   7   next >   last >>

Concordance
Parallel Table
Frequency Comparison
Affix Main Table
Affix Forms Table
Frequency Comparison
Empty
KeywordsCond Table
KeywordsTable
KeywordsFreq

Having found a list like this one, it is then possible to view samples from the data, showing the context of each example, as shown below. This is particularly useful in identifying exactly where your results have come from.

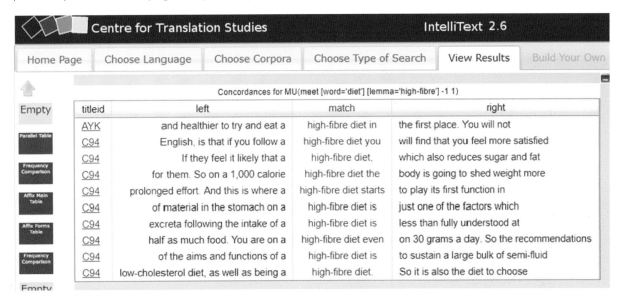

In the example above, almost all the 'high-fibre' hits are from the same text in the database, identified as C94 in the left-hand column. Seeing the data in context like this, even in short strings, also gives an idea of the typical representation of concepts. For example, in reference to diet, the initial page of results opposite shows that 'high-fibre' was the top result, closely followed by 'vegan' and 'well-balanced'. These top three all represent diet in relation to health. However, most of the lower-ranking results link diet to weight loss, so it is clear that in most discourse around diet, health was the main concern.

Activity 3

Find the British National Corpus. Do a search using Intellitext for collocates of one of the following words, or choose a word of your own that you think either might be interesting in terms of representation, or might show changes since the 1990s.

- 'environment'
- 'skirt'
- 'carbon'
- 'music'

You can reorder the list by clicking on the column titles, so if you click on the word 'count', you will get the results in rank order. Then clicking on the results themselves will bring up the text extracts (as in the 'high-fibre' example above).

Extension: This service offers other corpora with more recent data. If you want to look further, click on the 'choose corpora' tab and look up the same word in a different corpus.

N-grams

Linguistic data can also be presented and explored using *n*-grams. This is a way of searching a corpus for a specific item – a phoneme, a group of graphemes, a word or a phrase – and creating a line graph of the results. One example of this online uses Google Books as its corpus. Put in a search word, and the Google Ngram Viewer creates a graph showing that word's frequency over time. This tool is particularly useful for showing changes in the frequency of word use in written texts over time. Another useful feature of the Google N-gram Viewer is that you can compare up to three search terms in a graph.

Look at the *n*-gram below for the word 'proper'. It was decreasing in usage from 1800, but incorporated a new meaning as a slang word in the late 20th century. This can be seen in the slight uptick at the end of the graph. Google N-gram Viewer only allows searches up to 2008 at the moment, due to practical issues with getting data entered into Google Books, so that is why the search ends there.

N-grams can also be used to compare words and phrases. This *n*-gram compares the use of three related terms – 'internet', 'multimedia' and 'cyber' – since 1960.

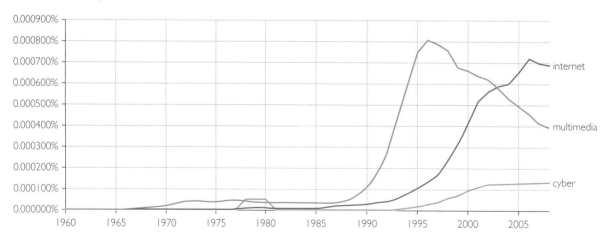

Final task

Investigate a person's online behaviour in context – this could be a celebrity or someone you know personally. Collect two days' worth of tweets and replies (or equivalent from another social media outlet) and analyse it quantitatively using numerical data in charts. What exactly you look at/for is up to you, but you may wish to consider the following:

- Pragmatics: Can you categorise the person's output by function/ what they seem to be trying to achieve with it? Follow this up by analysing how they use language to do these things.
- Context: Who does their audience seem to be? How do they appeal to them? (Apply all relevant language methods in following this up.)
- Do they address different people in different ways (e.g. do they use language differently when addressing men and women in direct replies)?

5.2 Early Modern English

What is Early Modern English? What makes Early Modern English distinctive?

When was Early Modern English spoken?

Over the course of history, different types of English have been spoken and written at different times. For example, linguists refer to the language spoken by the Anglo-Saxons in England from around AD 500 to roughly 1066 as 'Old English'. However, although we can talk about different periods and draw up timelines, it is important to remember that there are no fixed parameters for linguistic labels – people did not go to sleep at the end of the year 1599 speaking Middle English and wake up at the beginning of 1600 speaking Early Modern English!

These labels (like much linguistic description) are applied retrospectively to help explain something that happened naturally over a period of time and in order to discuss it as a social phenomenon. The transitions between these periods are gradual and subject to a combination of factors. Even the most concrete of dates – 1066, when the Normans defeated the English at the Battle of Hastings – did not lead to the overnight adoption of Norman French as the spoken language of most people in England. However, it did become the administrative language, and the event was, of course, followed by great (but gradual) linguistic change.

1066 Changes in governance begin with the Norman Conquest of England. Norman French becomes language of upper classes and English is a spoken-only language for part of this period
1385 English replaces Latin in schools
1473 First book printed in English by Caxton
1476 Caxton prints Chaucer's *The Canterbury Tales* (composed late 14th century)

Old English (AD 500–1066)

Middle English (1066–1500)

Begins with Angles, Saxons and Jutes conquering native Celts in Britain
AD 878 Danelaw established: northern England is under Danish rule; southern England under the Anglo-Saxons
c.1000 *Beowulf* (Old English epic poem) written down

Language in context

Whatever aspect of language you are studying, there is one key concept that you must keep returning to: context. Language does not exist in a vacuum; it is always affected by the world around it. In turn, language affects the world around it.

Activity I

The table below contains two lists of words, which entered the English language in the centuries indicated. Compare the two datasets. With reference to the timeline below, what links can you make between the words and the context of their entering the language? It may help to cluster them into smaller groups within each list. For example, what Native American words can you identify?

16th century	20th and 21st centuries
buffalo	blog
calculate	earworm
canoe	espresso
catastrophe	fuselage
combat	garage
demonstrate	gene
genteel	Google (verb)
hereditary	infotainment
horrid	IQ
omen	microaggression
potato	neo-cortex
radius	reflexology
renegade	taco
split	Tumblr
squadron	vegan

1806 Webster's A *Compendious Dictionary of the English Language* published
1828 Webster's *An American Dictionary of the English Language* published
mid-19th century English well-established throughout colonial settlements
1922 BBC founded
1928 First edition of the *Oxford English Dictionary*
1960s Social revolution in many countries (e.g. **1968** student revolution in France, hippie movements in UK/USA)
1990 Internet invented

Early Modern English (1500–1800) ———————————— **Late Modern English (1800–present*)**

1530s The Reformation (establishment of the Protestant Church)
1536 Act of Union makes English the official language of Wales
1558–1603 Reign of Elizabeth I
1576 First attempt at colonisation by the British (Frobisher Bay, Canada)
1590–1611 Shakespeare's writing period (plays and sonnets)
1611 The King James Bible created – an English translation of the Christian Bible

1755 Dr Samuel Johnson's English Dictionary published in England
1760–1840 Industrial Revolution
1776 American colonies win independence and form the first English-speaking country not ruled by Britain
1788 British penal colony established in Australia

* The most recent part of Late Modern English – the language used in the 21st century – is referred to as 'Contemporary English'.

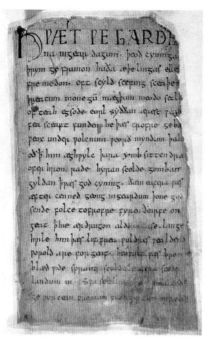

Old English

Case study: **The PIDC model**

The PIDC model was created by language professor Jean Aitchison to describe the process by which a new word or phrase enters a language. It is sometimes called the 'four-stage model'. In order for a word to enter a language:

1. There must be the **P**OTENTIAL for the word in the language. For example, someone has invented something, and it needs a name, or there is a new social trend which we (the users of the language) would like to describe.
2. The new term undergoes **I**MPLEMENTATION. At this point, the appropriate word/phrase begins to be used. Occasionally, there is a short period where two possibilities exist and one quickly dies away as more people choose to use the other (perhaps due to ease of articulation, or the formulation being cleverer and more pleasing).
3. The word/phrase undergoes **D**IFFUSION – it spreads beyond the original group of users into wider use.
4. The term is eventually validated through **C**ODIFICATION – it is entered into a dictionary or similarly made an official part of the language.

These images are pages from *Beowulf*, *The Canterbury Tales* and *Macbeth*. You can see that there are many differences between Old, Middle and Early Modern English. You will not study any pre-Modern texts, but it can be useful to have a general sense of what came before Early Modern English (and when) – and to understand why Early Modern English should never be referred to as 'Old'!

Middle English

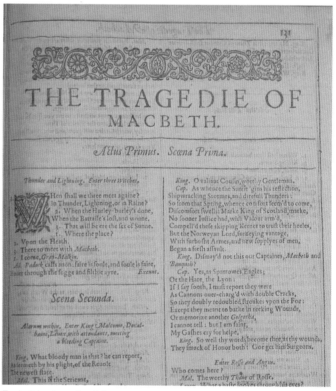

Early Modern English

Activity 2

How much of each text is familiar to you? You may need to use different criteria when assessing your familiarity with each one. For example:

- Do you know all the letters?
- Can you recognise any words?
- Do you know what all the words in a line mean?

Features of text in the Early Modern period

Under Norman French rule, English had been seen as the language of the lower classes. At the start of the Early Modern period, therefore, it was only just beginning to be recognised as a 'worthy' language for writing. English began to break free of the tendency to use lots of different endings, as **inflections**, for example. However, spelling was not standardised – there was no 'correct' way to spell any word. The idea of consistent spelling did not evolve until the Late Modern Period. In Early Modern English, people used spellings that reflected their pronunciation of a word. For example, an *n*-gram looking at past-tense inflections could compare something like 'walk'd', 'walked' and 'walkt', as the plosive sound of this **morpheme** was often rendered with a 't'. Despite this, it is possible to identify patterns of difference to contemporary spelling.

Read the text below, an extract from the explorer Richard Hakluyt's book *The Principal Navigations, Voiages, Traffiques and Discoueries of the English Nation* (written 1589–1600).

Taking things further

Try to find a recording of each of the texts above spoken with its original pronunciation (it does not need to be the section reproduced here). Listen to the sounds of each version of English. David and Ben Crystal have some videos about Shakespearean pronunciation online, and there are many useful recordings of 'The Miller's Tale' and *Beowulf*.

Key terms

inflection: a form or change of form that distinguishes different grammatical forms of the same lexical unit (e.g. the ending '-s' to distinguish certain plural forms from their singular forms)

morpheme: the smallest unit of grammatical meaning (e.g. 's' – a marker of plurality, 'dis' – a negative prefix)

Text 1

VII. A relation of the first voyage and discouerie of the Isle Ramea, made for Monsieur de La Court Pre Ravillon and Grand Pre, with the ship called the Bonauenture, to kill and make Traine oyle of the beasts called the Morses with great teeth, which we haue perfourmed by Gods helpe this yeere 1591.

For the performance of our said voyage, we departed from S. Malo with the fleete that went for Canada, and kept companie with the ships called The Soudil and the Charles halfe the way, and then lost them, a violent wind arising at Northwest, which separated vs.

After which we had faire wether, and came to the coast of Cape Rase, and had no further knowledge thereof, because the winde was at the Southwest but a scarce gale: and we came to the sounding Southwest of the Isles of S. Peter about 10. leagues, where we found 20. fathoms water, and we sayled Northwest one quarter of the North, and came within 12. leagues of Cape de Rey.

The next day being the 6. of May 1591. we were come to Cape de Rey, and saw a ship Southwest of vs, and stayed there that night.

The next day being the seuenth of the sayd moneth, we came to the Isles of Aponas, where we put foorth our boat, because we had not past 8. leagues to our hauen, which we kenned very clearly, although the coasts lay very low: and because the night approched, and the wind grew very high, we sought not to seeke our port, because it is very hard to find it when the wind is lofty, because of the shoalds that are about it.

Richard Hakluyt, from *The Principal Navigations, Voiages, Traffiques and Discoueries of the English Nation*

Activity 3

Look at the text above and the image from *Macbeth* on page 130. What observations can you make about the features of Early Modern English? Use the headings below to organise your ideas:

- Print conventions and letter formation
- Spelling (including patterns of letters used in place of modern letters)
- Grammar/syntax (including word order and sentence formation).

How does the text show evidence of ways in which the English language has changed? Choose three examples of patterns or features that you notice and try to explain at least one of them in relation to social, historical, political or technological changes over time.

For example, if you were writing about the *Macbeth* image, you might note that the graphological feature of the decorative border at the top of the page shows changes in the technology of printing over time, as it appears to be a woodcut image. This border is similar to older illuminated texts and is quite complex but would be the same pattern used in different printed texts. In older manuscripts, however, the illuminations would have been hand-produced.

Note that Text 1 was written near the start of the Early Modern period and many 'typical' features of Early Modern English, regarded as non-standard in writing today, disappeared over this period. Later texts of the period may show many more similarities to Late Modern English than this one does, particularly in their use of spelling.

An English Renaissance

The Early Modern period coincides with what is often called the English Renaissance – an era characterised by a revival of interest in the arts and sciences. People were fascinated by science, especially astronomy and mathematics. This period marked the advent of printing, as well as a rise in popularity of English literature and theatre. There was also a great deal of religious upheaval in Britain and across Europe.

One of the key linguistic events of the period is known as the 'Inkhorn controversy' (so-called because some people regarded the influx of new words as unnecessary snobbery). Many of the new discoveries in science and mathematics had come about through the study and subsequent development of the work of ancient Greek philosophers and mathematicians. As a result, scientists used Greek and Latin names for their discoveries rather than using English or English-sounding words. This mass **borrowing** from Latin in particular was made easier because English had already absorbed a lot of French words in earlier centuries (for example, 'government', 'soldier'). Some Inkhorn terms were direct or lightly anglicised loan words (words adopted directly from another language), such as 'equilibrium' and 'specimen', while others were formed by the **affixation** of Latin or Greek morphemes. It is still the case that many scientific words in English are of Greek or Latin **derivation**. 'Inkhorn' was a sarcastic name given to these terms, based on the assumption that the scientists coming up with them would have fancy inkwells for their quills made of horn. Using this name for them shows a belief that they are pretentious.

Key terms

borrowing: the adoption of a new word directly from another language
affixation: the creation of a new word by adding a suffix or prefix to an existing one
derivation: the act of creating new words from existing words; the origin of a word

Activity 4

Try to explain the attitudes in the 'Inkhorn controversy'. Wherever possible, make links to equivalent contemporary language use.

The move towards standardisation

The Early Modern period is generally regarded as the time when written English was standardised – when a particular set of rules was arrived at. Of course, not all English speakers (or a particular group of English speakers) sat down and agreed on this set of rules. Rather, over time, one existing form of English became recognised as the 'standard' form. Several factors influenced this:

- geographical centrality: the regional dialect spoken in and around the powerful triangle of London, Cambridge and Oxford
- status and education: the dialect's association with the two universities of Cambridge and Oxford, and with government and the law courts in London
- the rise of printing: producing written material for a mass audience meant that a wider audience needed to be able to access it than previously.

By the middle of the Early Modern period, around 1650, most printed texts were written in a way that more closely resembles Contemporary English, having lost features such as:

- terminal e (e.g. 'paine')
- doubled consonants (e.g. 'stopp')
- instability between 'u' and 'v' (e.g. 'trauaile')
- flexibility between 'I', 'y' and 'ie' (e.g. 'worthie', 'if')
- long 's' (e.g. in 'praise')
- ligature (e.g. in 'first').

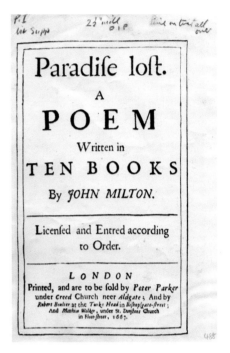

Punctuation had become more regularised, and apostrophes were used for possession as well as for omission. By the end of the period, it was also less common to find a word spelled in different ways within a text.

This process of standardisation was slow, spreading gradually across the country from London, beginning with the educated classes. It is not unusual to find a handwritten letter from the late 18th century that appears unaffected by standardisation, while printed texts from the mid 16th century may appear much more 'standard'. As with all language work, it is important to consider the context of such texts in order to explain why that may be the case.

Printing was introduced in England at the very start of the Early Modern period. William Caxton introduced the printing press to England from Germany and published Chaucer's *Canterbury Tales*, amongst other works, in 1476. But standardisation is sometimes wrongly described as taking place when Samuel Johnson published the first true English dictionary in 1755. There had been earlier dictionaries in English, but they had only listed 'difficult' words: Johnson's was the first to try to include all kinds of words.

Throughout the 17th and 18th centuries, many books on grammar were published. These often borrowed rules from Latin, which was seen as a superior language to English. This was due to factors such as a lingering snobbery that associated English with the spoken language of the lower classes and Latin with a classical education and religious texts. It resulted in rules that do not really work with English structures, but which some people still repeat today. For example:

Abb. 747. Handdruckpresse von Caxton aus dem Jahre 1474.

- **Do not use double negatives:** In fact, double negatives have been used since Old English times and do not, as people imply, tend to lead to misunderstanding. A person saying 'I didn't do nothing' would never be misunderstood as meaning they did something, although we would see this as informal speech and not Standard English.
- **Never split an infinitive:** It is not possible to split a Latin infinitive because it is a single word, so although this rule is often cited, it does not fit well with English, where the infinitive is two words: 'to eat', 'to walk'. 'To boldly go' (as made famous in *Star Trek*) is wrong according to this rule, but it is more powerful than 'to go boldly'.

Key terms

prescriptive: an approach to language that seeks to prescribe how it should be used

descriptive: an approach to language that seeks to describe how people actually use it

- **Never end on a preposition:** Observing this rule rigidly can lead to very convoluted 'in which' sentences. For example, attempting to avoid saying 'This is the box to put the buttons in' results in 'This is the box in which to put the buttons'.

These traditional **prescriptive** grammars are still favoured by many people. However, contemporary linguists tend to take a more **descriptive** approach towards the language – often to the annoyance of contemporary prescriptivists.

Activity 5

Look back at Text 1. How is the grammar different from the grammar you might find in a similar contemporary text? Think about:

- how sentences are constructed
- how sentences and clauses are linked
- how punctuation is used
- how verb tenses and aspects are used.

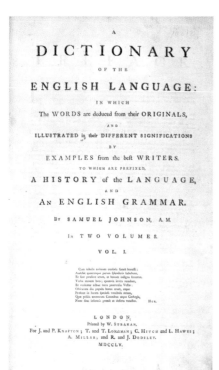

Religious upheaval and its effect on text and language

The religious Reformation began in Europe in the 16th century and led to the establishment of Protestantism as an alternative to the Catholic Church. In the British Isles, one consequence of the Reformation was the formation of the Church of England. In terms of language, the Reformation is significant, as it was through this movement that the Bible was translated into English. Although there had been earlier translations, they were often incomplete and were regarded as secret, unofficial texts that had to be hidden from the authorities. The King James Bible, commissioned and authorised by King James I of England and translated by a team of biblical scholars, is an important text. This complete translation of the Bible has had a lasting effect on the idioms of English.

Around the same time, Shakespeare was including many words and phrases in his plays that are still in common use today. He did not necessarily invent all of them (although he may have done) but his version is often the earliest written record of them that we have, or the record that lexicographers looked to for examples.

Activity 6

Which of these sayings do you know/use? What possible reasons can you give for these particular texts being so linguistically and culturally influential? Why and how have they stood the test of time?

From the King James Bible	From Shakespeare's plays
a fly in the ointment	jealousy is the green-eyed monster
the powers that be	refuse to budge an inch
a leopard doesn't change its spots	wild goose chase
filthy lucre	band of brothers
no peace for the wicked	set my teeth on edge
the blind leading the blind	heart of gold
go from strength to strength	wear your heart on your sleeve
it's a sign of the times	vanish into thin air

The impact of empire, exploration and trade

English is often described as a 'mongrel' language, because throughout its entire history it has borrowed from other languages. This has resulted in great flexibility and nuance in the English vocabulary. The Early Modern period added to this tradition through borrowing and adopting words into English from regions that England colonised or traded with. These areas include the Americas, India, Australia, China and the Arabic states, and loan words from this time were often concepts or inventions that were indigenous to those countries, or wildlife or plants that came from those places.

> In an assessment, you will not be expected to know or to work out the etymology of all words. You may want to discuss patterns in vocabulary and talk about what seems likely, but you do not need to identify when and from where a word entered English.

Activity 7

Work out where these words originated. Consider their likely origins in terms of place and/or original language. Check your ideas in a good dictionary, an etymological dictionary or online.

- tobacco
- canoe
- maize
- guru
- henna
- chocolate
- lychee

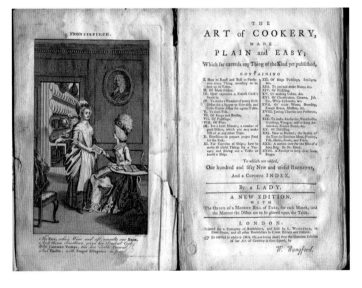

Final task

Read Text 2 below, which is an extract from a recipe book published in 1747. Write a short essay outlining the key historical features of this text. You should consider:

- typical features of the Early Modern period
- aspects of standardisation
- how the text has been affected by its context
- anything else you feel is worth commenting on.

Text 2

I Believe I have attempted a branch of Cookery, which nobody has yet thought worth their while to write upon: but as I have both seen, and found by experience, that the generality of servants are greatly wanting in that point, therefore I have taken upon me to instruct them in the best manner I am capable; and, I dare say, that every servant who can but read will be capable of making a tolerably good cook, and those who have the least notion of Cookery cannot miss of being very good ones.

If I have not wrote in the high polite style, I hope I shall be forgiven; for my intention is to instruct the lower sort, and therefore must treat them in their own way… So as in many other things in cookery, the great cooks have such a high way of expressing themselves, that the poor girls are at a loss to know what they mean.

Hannah Glasse, from *The Art of Cookery Plain and Easy*

5.3 Late Modern English

How has the English language changed since 1800? How is it continuing to change in the contemporary period?

Features of 19th-century texts

The 19th century is linked with the expansion of the British Empire through exploration and colonisation. During this period, many new words were introduced into English through contact with other cultures. A standard form of English had been established by this point and it was no longer acceptable to spell a word according to one's own phonological assumptions. However, language use in this period still seems old-fashioned to us. Texts from this period may contain **archaisms**. Sentence structures are often dense, long and meandering. Contemporary writing has a clear preference for shorter sentences in general, with occasional very short sentences and tighter control over punctuation. In 19th-century works, the use of conjunctions and punctuation such as semicolons and commas set within very long sentences can feel very unvaried to a modern reader.

Global factors that influenced language change are discussed in Chapter 7.

It is worth noting that a key reason for differences between historical texts and similar contemporary texts is the concept of **informalisation**. This theory, suggested by Sharon Goodman and based on Norman Fairclough's work, stems from the idea that as society has generally become less formal over time, so has language. For example, dress codes and etiquette have become more relaxed in a range of situations and this is reflected in language. You can identify informalisation when discussing either older texts – which may feel more formal than their contemporary counterparts – or modern ones, where informal language can be cited as an example of change over time.

Read Text 3, which is an extract from an account by the famous explorer Dr David Livingstone, describing his travels along the Zambezi River and its tributaries. It was published in 1894.

Key terms

archaism: a word that has fallen out of use entirely

informalisation: the idea that language, in line with society, has become more informal over time

Text 3

The first twenty miles of the Kongoné are enclosed in mangrove jungle; some of the trees are ornamented with orchilla weed, which appears never to have been gathered. Huge ferns, palm bushes, and occasionally wild date-palms peer out in the forest, which consists of different species of mangroves; the bunches of bright yellow, though scarcely edible fruit, contrasting prettily with the graceful green leaves. In some spots the Milola, an umbrageous hibiscus, with large yellowish flowers, grows in masses along the bank. Its bark is made into cordage, and is especially valuable for the manufacture of ropes attached to harpoons for killing the hippopotamus. The Pandanus or screw-palm, from which sugar bags are made in the Mauritius, also appears, and on coming out of the canal into the Zambesi many are so tall as in the distance to remind us of the steeples of our native land, and make us relish the remark of an old sailor, "that but one thing was wanting to complete the picture, and that was a 'grog-shop near the church.'" We find also a few guava and lime-trees growing wild, but the natives claim the crops. The dark woods resound with the lively and exultant song of the kinghunter (Halcyon striolata), as he sits perched on high among the trees. As the steamer moves on through the winding channel, a pretty little heron or bright kingfisher darts out in alarm from the edge of the bank, flies on ahead a short distance, and settles quietly down to be again frightened off in a few seconds as we approach. The magnificent fishhawk (Halietus vocifer) sits on the top of a mangrove-tree, digesting his morning meal of fresh fish, and is clearly unwilling to stir until the imminence of the danger compels him at last to spread his great wings for flight. The glossy ibis, acute of ear to a remarkable degree, hears from afar the unwonted sound of the paddles, and, springing from the mud where his family has been quietly feasting, is off, screaming out his loud, harsh, and defiant Ha! ha! ha! long before the danger is near.

David Livingstone, from *A Popular Account of Dr Livingstone's Expedition to the Zambezi and its Tributaries: and the Discovery of Lakes Shirwa and Nyassa 1858–1864*

Activity 1

a) Look up any unfamiliar words in a dictionary and determine which, if any, are archaic.

b) Comment on the usage of sentences in this extract by selecting a typical example to analyse in some detail.

c) How would you characterise the tone of this text? Select some textual evidence to help you. Do you think modern travel writing would be similar in tone, or different? How/why?

d) Text 3 is taken from a book entitled *A Popular Account of Dr Livingstone's Expedition to the Zambezi and its Tributaries*. Who do you think Livingstone's intended audience was? How do you think his language fits his audience and purpose?

Bringing words into English

With the expansion of the English-speaking world, English also acquired a great deal of vocabulary from other cultures that it came into contact with. There are two reasons why a loan word might be successfully integrated into English:

- The word and the item it denotes are both being brought into British culture from the other language and culture – this is the case with tobacco, for example, which was a new discovery at the time. This is a *functional borrowing* – we need the word as without it, we cannot label the item.

Taking things further

With so many English words being lifted from other languages, it is interesting to look at how English deals with other languages' rules, and to think about how this has (or has not) changed over time. For example, in British English, the degree of anglicisation of the pronunciation of French borrowings is quite variable. Words like 'ballet' retain their silent 't' ending and the 'ch' sound in words like 'charlatan' is soft like 'sh', while 'restaurant' may lack the nasal consonant at the end for many speakers. In grammatical terms, foreign borrowings usually align to English rules: one cappuccino, two cappuccinos, or one panini, two paninis, when the Italian is one panino, two panini.

Why might this be? Consider the theories of change and factors such as prestige and standardisation, as well as the status of English in a global context.

- We have a word for the item already, but we like the foreign word better. Often the loan word in this case seems to offer something more precise, but certainly has more prestige – this is the case with all the coffee-related borrowing and adaptations in the late 20th and early 21st centuries (espresso, cappuccino, latte and into frappuccino, mochalatte, and so on). These are social borrowings – we do not need the word (we could have continued to use variations on coffee: black coffee, white coffee, frothy coffee, coffee with foam, and so on).

> **Key term**
>
> **lexical gap:** space in the language for a new word to come in

In both these cases, a **lexical gap** has to exist for the new word to fit into, in order for it to last. This gap might exist literally – we did not know what to call the tobacco plant before anyone told us – or it might be a perceived gap: that is, we believe we need fancy new names for fancy new coffees (how could they possibly just be 'coffee'?), but the gap must be accepted by enough speakers of the language for a new word to be accepted. This is the same as the 'potential' stage of the PIDC model (see page 138). When new words come into and fall out of use very quickly, sometimes it is because there was never really the space for them in the first place.

Change is constant

Language change is intimately connected to social change. This means that language is continually changing. English has adapted and adopted new words throughout history, and it continues to do so due to a variety of driving forces:

- society
- science and technology
- politics and international relations
- arts and culture
- media and entertainment
- youth culture.

Activity 2

All the words below have come into the English language since 2000. For each word, decide which of the driving forces listed above is most likely to be the source or cause of this new lexical item. How might each one have entered English?

- selfie
- podcast
- lit
- dieselpunk
- bougie
- Chinglish

For each driving force, come up with at least one example of your own. Consider the variety of English spoken in your country.

Because the process of language change is gradual, we do not always notice it as it happens, but rather at key points. For example, when dictionaries release updates, there is a flurry of news articles about which words or meanings have been added. New words are not always slang, as people often assume. Many will become core vocabulary. **Neologisms** (new words) may be acquired lexically, semantically or grammatically via a range of processes.

> **Key term**
>
> **neologism:** a new word or expression in a language

Lexical processes

New words can be formed from existing words. This group of processes includes the simplest ways of forming neologisms and, consequently, many new words are acquired this way.

Process	Explanation	Example
blending/telescoping	two words being combined; one or both words are incomplete	Brexit
compounding	joining two whole words together	laptop
acronymisation	initial letters of a series of words which are together said as a word	NASA
initialism	initial letters of a series of words, pronounced by saying the letter names	FBI
borrowing	word taken from another language or dialect	bare
backformation	word created from a longer existing one that seems to be derived from it	enthuse

Blends are particularly popular for words from social phenomena and from fashion, while technology has used many acronyms and initialisms to label gadgets. Borrowing may happen due to immigration/cultural contact (for example, 'bare' from Jamaican dialect being used by urban British English speakers), or due to fashion, such as 'latte' and the many Italian-inspired coffee labels in English.

Semantic processes

At a basic level, we can talk about a semantic shift, in which a word simply changes meaning. There are, however, more specific ways in which to describe and define semantic changes resulting in new usages.

Process	Explanation	Example
semantic shift	changing a meaning or adding a new meaning	mouse (for computer)
broadening	expanding a word's meaning to refer to a greater range of items or to include additional meanings	literally
narrowing	reducing a word's meaning to refer to a smaller range of meaning than previously	meat (used to mean 'food')
pejoration	shifting a word's meaning from positive to negative, or adding a secondary negative meaning, possibly in slang	cowboy (e.g. 'cowboy builder')
amelioration	shifting a word's meaning from negative to positive, or adding a secondary positive meaning, possibly in slang	sick

Semantic changes are particularly common in youth dialect, where it may be an act of rebellion to use a word differently to its 'real' meaning. These changes are often the most dramatic and the least easy to explain, such as using the word 'sick' to mean 'good'. More linked meaning changes, which work metaphorically or analogically, are more likely to be found in language used online or to define social trends.

Grammatical processes

Grammatical processes create new words, either by adding morphemes to existing words or by changing the word class of existing words. The latter – a conversion, or functional shift – is becoming more common, and is something that many people resist, particularly while a reasonable standard alternative exists. For example, since 2008 commentators in the Olympic Games have referred to athletes as having 'medalled' and 'podiumed', which many people object to as clumsy and inelegant forms. They argue that saying 'won a medal', for example, does not require many more syllables to say.

Process	Explanation	Example
conversion/ functional shift	using a word in a new grammatical class, e.g. a noun used as a verb	Google (as a verb)
affixation	forming a word by adding a suffix or prefix	Snowgate, microclimate
prefixation	forming a word by adding a prefix	e-meet
suffixation	forming a word by adding a suffix	bookaholic

Word of the Year

Each year, different organisations select a Word of the Year – some by popular vote, some by usage, some to reflect the zeitgeist of the year. The Word of the Year does not have to have been coined during the year in question, but it must have become *prominent* during that year. These words can be used to exemplify the point about language change and context.

Activity 3

This is the shortlist for the Collins Dictionaries 2017 Word of the Year:

- fake news (n) – this was the winner as the Word of the Year
- antifa (n)
- corbynmania (n)
- cuffing season (n)
- echo chamber (n)
- fidget spinner (n)
- genderfluid (adj)
- gig economy (n)
- insta (adj)
- unicorn (n)

Look up the meaning of any word(s) you are unsure of. Identify a process of formation for each word or phrase, as far as you can. Consider the context that led to each word being important enough to be selected as Word of the Year. Which driving force(s) of change seem to be relevant?

Extension: Look online for a discussion about any Word of the Year that you find interesting (you could look at Oxford's or Merriam-Webster's, for example). What did people say about these choices? What kinds of attitudes to language change are shown in these discussions?

Activity 4

Come up with your own examples of new words and phrases in English. What words have you noticed people using recently? What changes in meaning have you seen in the past year or two?

- Make a list of as many as you can think of in five minutes – just write down everything, without censoring yourself or overthinking it.
- Then, try to group them according to the different driving forces at work.

- Finally, apply formation process labels from the tables above. Do you have more blends than acronyms? Have you thought of a lot of examples of semantic shift? Note down any patterns that you notice.

When analysing any Contemporary English text, it is useful to be able to comment on the processes that have produced any interesting neologisms. Depending on the text, you may also be able to comment on patterns – for example, a lot of acronyms or many words coming from the field of fashion that have been created through blending. This is a key aspect of analysing a text in context for modern texts.

Technology and the speed of change

People perceive change as happening extremely quickly now due to the internet. However, although the spread of new words and meanings is certainly helped by such global links, change has always happened at a rate that has felt too fast for some!

The image below shows the opening to Jonathan Swift's 'A Proposal for Correcting, Improving and Ascertaining the English Tongue', published in 1712. In it, Swift claims that the language develops more problems than improvements every day and argues that it needs to be 'fixed' – by which he means stopped in its course, rather than mended (although of course that secondary connotation is not accidental).

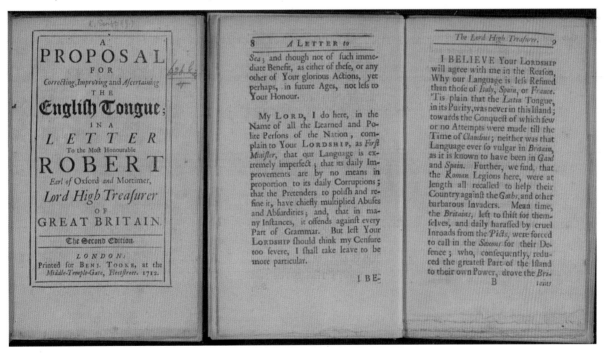

Activity 5

How does Swift's text show the position of language change in 1712? Consider:

- graphology: how the text is laid out (try to link to printing technology)
- orthography: spelling, capitalisation and letter production conventions
- pragmatics: address terms and register in relation to context.

Technology is a driving force for change. It affects language in three main ways:

- Words for technological devices and tech-related phenomena are required as new inventions are made (e.g. 'laptop', 'USB').
- There are words and phrases used online but not really in spoken or written language – or words and phrases used in a specific way online that differs from their use in the real world (e.g. 'lol', '#').
- These new words, and others relating to different topics, are spread throughout the world using technology. Some are absorbed in spoken and written forms in other contexts (e.g. people now sometimes say 'hashtag _____' ironically to call attention to something).

Activity 6

Sort these words and phrases using the first two categories above – those used to label technology and its world, and those used to communicate online. Which ones fall into both categories? Can you add your own examples?

- #catsofinsta
- DM (verb)
- email
- forum
- modem
- retweet
- Tumblr
- URL

Read Text 4, which is an article about older people and technology.

Text 4

From Silver Surfers to Social Seniors – half of older people now have a smartphone and are on social media

By Jonathan Owen, June 28, 2017

Planners of forthcoming public sector campaigns might take note of the findings of a new Ofcom report, which details the rise of the 'social senior'.

Older people are increasingly adopting tablets and social media accounts, according to Ofcom.

Silver surfers have evolved into social seniors, with a surge in older people embracing the digital age, according to the report.

New research by Britain's communications regulator reveals how older people are using smartphones and tablets in record numbers, driven by factors such as keeping in touch with family and friends.

There has been a steep rise in the proportion of over-75s using tablets, from 15 per cent in 2015 to 27 per cent in 2016, and the number of people in this age group with smartphones has tripled, from five to 15 per cent, during this time.

And 51 per cent of those aged 65–74 now have tablets, compared to 39 per cent in 2015, with smartphone use having doubled among this age range in recent years – from 20 per cent in 2013 to 39 per cent last year.

A growing proportion of both of these age groups are also using smart TVs and streaming media players.

The findings, from Ofcom's annual Adults' Media Use and Attitudes report, released this month, also reveal that almost half (48 per cent) of internet users aged 65–74 now have a social media profile – up from less than a third (28 per cent) in 2012.

During this time, the proportion of over-75s on social media has more than doubled – from 19 to 41 per cent.

Facebook is the most popular social network for senior citizens, cited by 87 per cent of pensioners who are on social media.

In contrast, just six per cent choose to be on WhatsApp and only one per cent opt for Instagram.

Almost half (48 per cent) of 65 to 74-year-olds now have social media accounts – up from less than a third (28 per cent) in 2012. During this time, the proportion of over-75s with social media accounts has rocketed from 13 to 41 per cent.

Yet, while a record number of pensioners are going digital, they spend less time online than the younger generation.

Over-65s spend 15 hours online each week, compared to 32 hours among 16–24s.

But some older internet users lack confidence when using the internet, with one in five describing themselves as "not confident" online – far higher than the seven per cent average.

Commenting on the report, Alison Preston, head of media literacy at Ofcom, said: "The UK's older generation is beginning to embrace smart technology, and using it to keep in touch with friends and family. But some older people lack confidence online, or struggle to navigate search results. Many are new to the internet, so we'd encourage people to help older friends or family who need support getting connected."

From *PR Week*, 28 June 2017

Activity 7

Identify the technology-related vocabulary in Text 4 and classify the formation process used to create it.

Taking things further

Analyse the representation of older people in Text 4. How are they presented? What audience positioning is used? Consider the dangers of suggesting that texts about technology are only for 'young people' as an audience in analytical work.

To remind yourself about audience positioning, look back at Unit 3.2.

New lexis in the field of technology often arrives through lexical processes or using semantic shifts. These are often chosen via an analogical or metaphorical link between the original meaning and the new, technology-related meaning: 'mouse', 'virus', 'web'.

There is also a tradition of word creation using symbols and letter substitution. This began in the early days of the internet, when such a code (or 'antilanguage') was known as L33t or leetspeak. In L33t, numbers and other symbols are used to replace letters to obscure meanings, such as the 3s for 'e's in the name of 'leet' itself. A few tendencies from L33t have persisted into contemporary gamer language. For example:

- using 'z' to make plurals (e.g. 'gamez')
- the suffix '-age' (e.g. 'ownage')
- zeros for 'oo' sounds (e.g. 'n00b' and 'd00d')
- retaining typos (e.g. 'pwn/ed' for 'own/ed', 'teh' for 'the').

Activity 8

What are your own experiences of language and technology?

a) Are you aware of words that you use on social media which you do not use in written or spoken language?

b) Are there words and phrases that you first learned online that have transferred into your 'real' life?

c) In which contexts are 'online' language words and phrases appropriate – for example, are there contexts where you would/would not use online language? Who would/would not understand you? Why?

d) What attitudes to online/social media-derived language are you aware of in the world? Why do you think this exists? To what extent do you think it is to do with the language itself and how far is it an attitude towards social media?

Politics and social change

As well as technology, social change and politics are key drivers of contemporary change. Society changes all the time, and what is acceptable or what needs to be discussed also changes. Key areas that have led to many new words and phrases over the past century are as follows:

- movements concerned with social justice, such as feminism and civil rights
- environmentalism
- shifting powers due to the world wars and the Cold War
- increase in leisure time and rise of the entertainment industries
- changes in fashion and beauty ideals
- increase in world travel.

One area where politics and the social world often connect is the topic of political correctness. This has had an impact in many areas, including gender, race and disability, and it is an important area to discuss appropriately. You need to watch out for PC myths. These are stories reported in the media about phrases that you 'aren't allowed' to say any more. These can be dangerous, as they lead to outraged responses of 'PC has gone too far', and a backlash of people wanting to use terms that real PC language has replaced.

Final task

Choose two different social/political areas of language change, either from the list below or from your own ideas. These may be internationally relevant within English, or have impact only within your own country. Research words and phrases that have entered the language because of these areas. Did you find any examples that were unfamiliar to you and that have since fallen out of use?

- gender roles and feminism
- environmentalism
- conflict and war
- interest in diet and healthy eating
- television

5.4 Ideas about language change

What are the key theories about language change?
What attitudes to language change exist?

The 'why' of change

There are two main theories about why language changes:

- functional theory
- random fluctuation.

However, these should not be seen as opposing schools of thought. Rather, they are different reasons for different changes appearing in the language.

According to functional theory, language changes to suit the needs of its users. This fits well with other concepts, such as lexical gaps, and clearly applies to words coined to name new inventions ('laptop'), new social trends ('commuting') and fashions ('jeggings'). Cultural transmission is a related concept. In this theory, language is transmitted via culture from generation to generation and change is like evolution: only that which is useful will survive.

The concept of random fluctuation argues that changes in language are like changes in fashion – random and unpredictable. This theory is impossible to support as a general argument for why language changes, because many changes are clearly logical and sensible. But there is an overall randomness to social borrowing, and some semantic changes in slang (such as which words are chosen to change meaning – why is 'sick' **ameliorated**, for example). There are also some isolated examples of truly random incidents that have led to new words, such as the gamerspeak example of 'pwned', which originated from a mistyping of 'owned' because o and p are next to each other on the keyboard.

Substratum theory, which explains how language changes through contact between languages, or between dialects, is a different example of a random series of events leading to language change. The classic example for this is the New York pronunciation of 'coffee' ('caw-fee'), which US linguist William Labov (1927-) noted as having derived from the New York Jewish community's **hypercorrect** pronunciation. (The randomness is not in the hypercorrection itself, but in the unexplained adoption of a minority pronunciation.) More contemporary examples of substratum theory in practice are likely to occur online or through mass media. An example of this is the increase in US forms such as 'gotten' being used in UK English through people hearing them in US TV and film.

Key terms

amelioration: when a word takes on a more positive connotation over a period of time

hypercorrection: using a non-standard form of language (usually phonetic or grammar) that the speaker mistakenly believes to be the prestige form (e.g. 'between you and I')

Activity 1

Copy and complete the following table, adding three more words from your own variety of English. You should try to explain:

- the driving force that caused the word to exist
- who currently uses the word (e.g. is it youth dialect only or is it in wider use? Is it only in your country or your part of the country, or is it international?)
- what theories you can link it to from those discussed so far (also consider where in the PIDC model the word is).

Word	Force that caused the word to exist	Current state of spread	Link to relevant theory/ies
selfie	fashion/social change	wide use, international	codified – has been a Word of the Year
millennial			

The 'how' of change

As well as theories about *why* language changes, there are also theories about *how* language changes. At the simplest level, the ideas about how it changes are the formation processes discussed earlier in this chapter – the concepts of derivation and etymology that describe how a word or phrase has been constructed. At a more conceptual level, however, the 'how' of change is about how these changes pass from person to person, how it takes hold within the language and, eventually, how it sticks (or fails to stick) and becomes permanent.

There are two key models of how language spreads: the wave model and the S-curve model. Once again, these should not be seen as competing theories, but as models that may suit different specific changes and could therefore be used together to explain different elements.

Wave model of language change

Proposed by C. J. Bailey in 1973, this states that language users closer to the centre of a change will be more affected by it. This idea of 'closer' can be interpreted geographically, temporally or socially – that is, if a new word is implemented in urban youth culture in a particular city, a teenager in the next city is 'closer' to it than an adult in the same city. The wave idea is a metaphor. If you drop a pebble into a still pool, the waves are bigger at the centre, and flatten out the further away from the original pebble you get.

S-curve model of language change

The S-curve model, proposed by Chen in 1968, states that a new word will initially experience a fairly steady uptake, followed by a rapid increase in the number of new users picking it up. Then, after a while, the number of people adopting it will flatten out again as everyone who is going to take it on will have done so. It gets its name because the rate of uptake looks like an S when plotted on a graph.

S-shaped curve - slow beginning, rapid centre, slow ending

The S-curve model of language change

Activity 2

Look again at the words you chose for Activity 1. How could you apply wave and S-curve models to them? Whereabouts in the process are these words, do you think?

There is one more metaphor that may be useful when considering language change. It was first used by the British linguist David Crystal, who said that language was like the tide. When the tide goes out, it leaves some things behind on the beach, then it comes in and some of these things are taken away again while new ones are left behind. Language change is like this, with new words and phrases constantly being coined. Some remain and become long-term parts of the language, but others are short-lived, and it is not

always possible to predict which will be which. Crystal also says that language change is like the tide due to its inevitability.

How is language change discussed in everyday life?

As noted, one of the main times when language change is discussed publicly is when Word of the Year announcements are made. The media usually report on them, and often people discuss how relevant (or not) they feel the words are. Some even express disgust that an institution such as a dictionary could support what they believe to be slang or not 'proper' words.

The problem here arises largely from a conceptual clash between what people believe the dictionary stands for and how dictionaries really work these days. This clash centres on the opposing approaches to language of prescriptivism and descriptivism:

- A prescriptivist approach to language is to tell people how to use it: to prescribe what is correct.
- A descriptivist approach to language is to explain how language is used: to describe how it is.

Dictionaries get caught in the middle of this, because we use them as tools to guide our language use and because they were prescriptivist in their early days. We tend to see them as the place to check 'correct' or 'standard' usage and spelling, and many people believe that they should only contain language of a certain standard. Of course, the full version of each dictionary (the multi-volume version) contains every word.

People are often shocked when new words which they regard as frivolous are entered into dictionaries, as this seems to legitimise such words in a way that those people consider unnecessary. They may even see it as a sign that the language is being spoilt. Dictionaries are generally considered to serve a prescriptivist purpose, and some people are disappointed when dictionaries 'allow in' modern words which are not formal enough, or not standard enough for people's expectations of that role.

In reality, the deciding factor on whether or not a word is added to a dictionary is frequency of use. Some dictionaries are updated annually, others several times a year, but they all have lexicographers constantly working on checking and cross-referencing usage. To qualify for addition to the dictionary, a word must be used in different contexts, published and broadcast (so it can be verified), clearly with the same intended meaning. Dictionary compilers watch for the word over a period of time, as any word can be popular for a week and then drop out of use. As well as new words, lexicographers also add new meanings or usages to existing words. So, despite most people's perception of a dictionary as prescriptivist, in fact the way dictionaries operate today is entirely descriptivist.

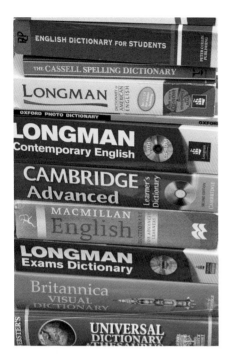

Further Reading

The main dictionary brands all have interesting blogs that are worth looking at for information about individual word histories, how they do their lexicographic work and links to world events. Try those below, or search for your local dictionary to see if they have one too:

- Merriam-Webster
- Collins Dictionaries
- Macmillan Dictionaries
- Oxford Dictionaries.

Activity 3

Look at these comments taken from an article about contenders for 2017's Oxford Dictionaries Word of the Year (won by 'youthquake'). What position does each comment take? What overall attitudes to language are revealed here? (Note: B is in direct response to A; C is separate.)

> **A:** I wonder if my lack of familiarity with any of the words is a good thing or not, I suspect it is.

> **B:** I'm sure it is. I haven't come across any of these words, useful though they are. The most annoying phrase in constant use at the moment is 'fit for purpose'. Apart from being illiterate, it implies the user is too busy or expert to use real English.

> **C:** Expression of the year – 'Oxford Dictionary' – a group of words randomly mashed together to appear modern & cool but in fact are very dated & uncool. Use: 'Broflake, I don't want your Unicorn Latte. It's so very Oxford Dictionary.'

Prescriptivism has focused on different things at different times. It is reasonable to argue that the process of standardisation was helped by prescriptivism. Various factors led to the particular variety of English being selected to be the standard, including the centrality of the geographical region it was associated with, its links with education and prestige, and its association with printing via Caxton.

The 18th century, however, is regarded as the key period of standardisation, and there were many pressures on the language to standardise even more formally at that time. Jonathan Swift's treatise in Unit 5.3 (see page 141) argued for an Academy of English, just as the French had (and still have) the Académie Française to police their language.

In the extract from Samuel Johnson's introduction to his dictionary, shown on the right, his prescriptivist intentions are made clear.

Activity 4

Identify Johnson's claims about his intentions for his dictionary – what were his goals? What does this text have to say about concepts of language: standardisation, prescriptivism and change?

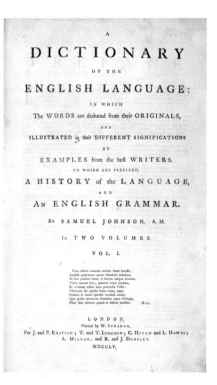

A

DICTIONARY

OF THE

ENGLISH LANGUAGE:

IN WHICH

The WORDS are deduced from their ORIGINALS,

AND

ILLUSTRATED in their DIFFERENT SIGNIFICATIONS

BY

EXAMPLES from the best WRITERS.

TO WHICH ARE PREFIXED,

A HISTORY of the LANGUAGE,

AND

AN ENGLISH GRAMMAR.

BY SAMUEL JOHNSON, A.M.

IN TWO VOLUMES.

VOL. I.

LONDON,

Printed by W. STRAHAN,

For J. and P. KNAPTON; T. and T. LONGMAN; C. HITCH and L. HAWES; A. MILLAR; and R. and J. DODSLEY.

MDCCLV.

Final task

The two car advertisements on these pages are from 1910 and 1962. Which concepts about language change are most useful to you in exploring them and why? What can you tell about the contexts the advertisements were produced in from their language? Explain your findings with detailed reference to linguistic features.

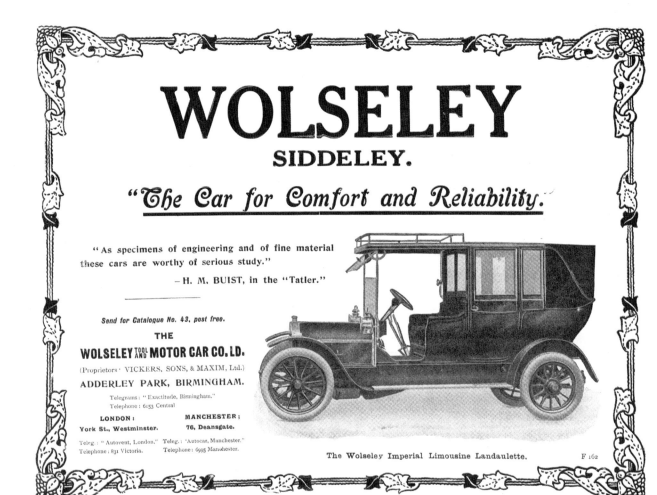

WOLSELEY
SIDDELEY.

"The Car for Comfort and Reliability."

"As specimens of engineering and of fine material these cars are worthy of serious study."

– H. M. BUIST, in the "Tatler."

Send for Catalogue No. 43, post free.

THE
WOLSELEY TOOL AND MOTOR CAR CO. LD.

(Proprietors: VICKERS, SONS, & MAXIM, Ltd.)

ADDERLEY PARK, BIRMINGHAM.

Telegrams: "Exactitude, Birmingham,"
Telephone: 6153 Central

LONDON:	MANCHESTER;
York St., Westminster.	76, Deansgate.
Teleg.: "Autovent, London."	Teleg.: 'Autocar, Manchester."
Telephone: 831 Victoria.	Telephone: 6995 Manchester.

The Wolseley Imperial Limousine Landaulette.   F 162

FIRST-CLASS LUXURY VALUE... WOLSELEY 16/60

W215

One of the most popular cars in the Wolseley series, the 16/60 combines lively performance, safety, roominess and luxury, all for a modest outlay. The 16/60 is little more than 14 ft. 6 in. long and therefore well suited to in-town work; at the same time there are all the requisite features for comfortable long-distance motoring. With the introduction of the 1622 c.c. O.H.V. engine, with its improved low-speed torque, Wolseley is now able to offer fully automatic transmission on the 16/60. The specification includes real leather, pile carpets, polished woodwork and lavish interior appointments. The luggage boot has a capacity of 19 cu. ft. Altogether, you buy wisely when you buy a Wolseley 16/60.

BUY WISELY —BUY WOLSELEY

TWELVE MONTHS' WARRANTY and backed by BMC service

From £680 plus £256.0.3 P.T.
With Automatic Transmission, from £748 plus £281.10.3 P.T.

WOLSELEY—A LUXURIOUS WAY OF MOTORING

WOLSELEY MOTORS LIMITED, COWLEY, OXFORD.
London Showrooms: 12 Berkeley Street, W.1. Overseas Business: Nuffield Exports Ltd., Oxford and 41-46 Piccadilly, London W.1

5.5 Working with language change data

How do people research language change?

How do people research language change over time?

To compare across time, you need to track particular linguistic features, and you need to do that on as large a scale – but within as tightly controlled a dataset – as possible. For example, you would want a lot of texts, but you would not necessarily want a lot of different *kinds* of texts. You might carry out a pilot study within one type of text and then, having established some patterns, check those findings in a larger and more varied dataset.

Activity 1

Why would it not work to just compare a text from 1600 and one from 1700 and declare 'this is how language changed in the 17th century'?

Nowadays, it is possible to use computational linguistics. This means that once you have assembled your texts – your core data – you can input them into your program and then search for what you want, producing *n*-grams and tables of collocates, depending on what you are looking for.

Case study: CLiC Dickens project

This project has built a corpus of Dickens's work, alongside several other corpora of other novels and children's literature from the 19th century. A web app allows you to search the corpora for collocates as usual, but you can also search for words appearing in suspensions – phrases positioned between two pieces of dialogue such as 'she said, taking both his hands'. These are useful for body language and therefore attitude.

Activity 2

Visit the CLiC Dickens website and select 'concordance' in the main menu. Carry out a few searches to familiarise yourself with the app. A sample table of the first few lines of data is shown below – the result of a concordance search in both C19 reference corpus and Dickens corpus for 'sea'.

to think that you live in an island with the	sea	a-rolling and a-bowling right round you. Guster is busy
stormy days of its youth time on the wild salt	sea.	A comfortable little cabin for the use of the fowlers in
The days passed: the yacht was rigged and fitted for	sea;	a cruise was arranged to the west coast – and Midwinter

| specks of sail that glinted in the sunlight far at | sea. | A face habitually suppressed and quieted, was still lighted |
| see there!' As the stranger spoke, he pointed to the | sea. | A far cry died away upon its surface; the last |

Once you are confident with the controls, search for any noun, adjective or verb that you think will give you interesting results. Read through the results to spot any patterns.

- First, look at meanings – what representations are being created or how is whatever you searched for being used?
- Second, think about change – what differences to Contemporary English can you see? Think about syntax and punctuation as well as words and meanings (as far as you can with the snippets you are given).

Using a synonym list with a text helps you to see how a text may be using words in a different way than those words are used now, or have been used since.

Reread Text 3 in Unit 5.3 (page 137) in conjunction with this synonym list.

ornamented	decorated, adorned, festooned
cordage	twine, yarn, line
exultant	triumphant, joyful, celebratory
compels	forces, obliges, requires
unwonted	unusual, atypical, unexpected

Activity 3

What can you tell from this data in combination with the Livingstone text? How does this help you to further understand the text as an exemplar of language change?

How do people research contemporary change?

When researching change happening in the moment, the most useful factor to consider is frequency of use. The internet has made this much easier, as it is now possible to examine where and how words are being used and what they mean in context, and to look at broadcast media from other countries. In effect, you can use a search engine as your corpus search tool. For example, if you wanted to see how the word 'literally' was being used, to track the extent to which it is used with a figurative meaning ('I literally died') as opposed to its older literal one ('I literally could not hear you, please repeat that'), you could search for 'literally' and see what comes up.

Activity 4

What problems might you have with the method outlined above for investigating usage of the word 'literally'? How could you refine your search to help you obtain 'cleaner' data to examine how people use the word in casual situations?

How can you test theories on change?

To look at how and whether different change theories apply to various changes in language, you need to examine the rate of change and the extent of changes. This can be difficult, as change often occurs in spoken language, and records are usually confined to written language. However, written data can still tell us a lot. Dictionaries usually record the earliest published or written usage of a word as its origin date, so this is a standard method.

N-grams are useful for looking at the incidence of a word or phrase in a corpus, which can tell us about spread.

Activity 5

Look at the Google n-gram below, which tracks the incidence of three terms related to environmentalism in the Google Books corpus between 1960 and 2000. What can you tell from this graph? Which theory/ies of language change might help you to interpret it and how do they add to your comments?

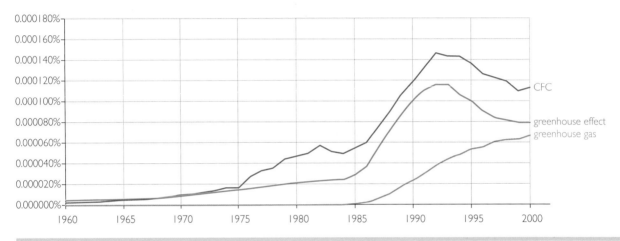

How do people research attitudes towards change?

Researching attitudes can be difficult – if you ask people directly, they are not always clear and honest with you. Surveys and opinion polls have been used in the past to ascertain people's views on different features of language, but it can be difficult to write good questions for these.

Activity 6

Which of the following two sets of questions is better? Why?

Question set 1

Rate these words and phrases 1–5, where 1 = very good and 5 = very bad. Also indicate whether you use the word or not.

- selfie
- emoji
- yolo
- dench
- whatevs

Question set 2

Pick one or more comments for each of these words and phrases, choosing from:

I use this word often

I use this word sometimes

I occasionally use this word

I would never use this word

I love this word

I like this word

I hate this word

People who say this are_____

- selfie
- emoji
- yolo
- dench
- whatevs

Final task

Choose a topic in language change and design a research project. What kind of data would you need? How/where would you get it? What kind of features would you look at? What are you hoping to find out?

You will not actually be doing the research, so do feel free to design something you may not physically be able to do. You could choose one of the topics below, or come up with an idea of your own.

- How has the representation of women changed in magazines from 1850 to 2000?
- How much has travel writing changed from Victorian explorers' writing to travel blogs?
- What attitudes do different groups of people have to language change coming from technology?

End-of-chapter task

Analyse text A, which is a review of the Apple HomePod from February 2018, using the data provided in Texts B and C to help you. How does taking it all together help you to understand language change?

Text A

Apple HomePod review: **Superb sound, so-so smart speaker**

OUR VERDICT

With the HomePod, we're really reviewing two things at once: a premium speaker and a smart home hub. In the former category, the HomePod is excellent, with amazing sound and incredibly intuitive set-up. But in the latter Siri is only middling in its implementation, and the fact that you're not able to break out of the Apple ecosystem for many key functions also rankles.

FOR
- Amazing sound quality
- Siri voice accuracy is high
- Attractive, understated design

AGAINST
- Siri is limited
- No Bluetooth streaming
- Apple Music subscription needed for a worthwhile experience

Apple's devices have evolved hugely over the last 15 years or so, changing the brand from the rebooted upstart that gave us the iPod to the consumer tech powerhouse of today.

The HomePod takes the name of that iconic portable device, but a decade and a half on we're faced with the same question posed by previous Apple gadgets: how much of a premium should you pay for owning a device that fits seamlessly into the Apple ecosystem?

Let's not forget that the HomePod is a late entry to the smart speaker game, but that's standard operating procedure for the Cupertino-based brand: let the rest of the industry stride ahead with a new form factor, identify the issues and then offer something that 'just works'… and generally for a higher price than the competition.

That's what's happened with the HomePod, although not in quite the same way as before. There's no denying that the sound quality of Apple's speaker is top-notch, but in a marketplace where Amazon has such an entrenched smart speaker/voice assistant ecosystem and Google isn't far behind, can a great-sounding-but-imperfect device be worth buying?

From techradar, 11 July 2018

Text B

An *n*-gram of the words device, speaker and brand from the Google Books corpus searching 1600–2000.

Text C

Collocations list for 'Apple' and 'ecosystem'.

Apple (right-hand collocates, or words that follow 'apple')	Ecosystem (left-hand collocates, or words that precede 'ecosystem')
tree	marine
juice	forest
pie	our
orchard	fragile
cart	global

Chapter 6

Child language acquisition

As long as someone speaks to them, all developmentally normal children learn to talk – and in startlingly similar ways. This remarkable process is the subject of this chapter. It first discusses typical development and the stages and patterns of children's speech, before examining theories that have been formed to explain this phenomenon. The last unit shows you how research into child language is carried out and offers examples of child language data to explore for analysis. This is helpful when looking at, for example, the extent to which children's use of syntax is similar to that of adults within a language community. A key concept introduced in this chapter is *change*, which, as before, you will consider in association with *context*. With the topic of child language acquisition, change in linguistic terms means how an individual's use of language changes as competence grows from early childhood. In these terms, then, you will be considering a *personal* element of change.

6.1 Learning to talk

What features are typical of children's speech when they are starting to talk? How much variation is there in the features of children's speech?

Ages and stages

Within the parameters of 'normal' development, there is a wide variation in what children should be doing at different ages in terms of language. However, the *order* of events in children's **acquisition** of language is fairly standard, so it is possible to talk about stages in a fixed way.

It is fascinating to note that children around the world, speaking different languages, follow the same pattern. This supports the idea that language acquisition is a key human trait for which we are all equipped in a particular way. When a child is learning two languages at once, progress though these stages may be slower, as they are effectively processing more material in the form of both vocabulary and grammar rules. However, the stages are followed in the same way. Bilingual children tend to treat both native languages as one big language initially, and it can be some time before they learn to separate them. They may find this easier if the two languages are distinguished by context – for example, if each parent speaks a different language, or if one language is only spoken inside the home and the other outside it.

Babies make various noises before they start to say proper words. These follow a clearly defined path, as children gradually gain control over the muscles in their mouth and face, and learn that they can produce sound in a deliberate way. The earliest noises are biological sounds such as crying (which they continue to do once they can speak). Speech-related sounds follow the pattern below:

- Cooing seems to be the earliest deliberate noise; this is largely vowel-based.
- Vocal play develops out of cooing, and expands into longer sounds with some intonation variation.
- Babbling introduces hard consonants. There are two kinds: **reduplicated** babbling (the classic 'gaga', 'baba', 'dada', 'mama', in which a consonant–vowel combination is repeated) and **variegated babbling** (where different consonant–vowel combinations are combined such as 'baga', 'maba').
- **Melodic utterance** overlaps with babbling. It may include some babbling sounds and perhaps even the odd word (or **proto-word**). At this stage, babies use realistic-sounding intonation without actually speaking in sentences, as though they are 'singing' speech.

Key terms

acquisition: a native language is described as acquired rather than learned to highlight the naturalness of this process, and its apparent effortlessness

reduplication: repetition of a sound or syllable in a word

variegated babbling: early speech consisting of different consonant-vowel combinations

melodic utterance: the use of realistic-sounding intonation without speaking in actual sentences

proto-word: an early form of a word, not pronounced as an adult would, but recognisable by the child's caregivers to have a specific meaning due to its consistent use

The table below outlines the key stages in child language acquisition from the time of the first word.

Stage	What happens?
holophrastic stage (one-word stage)	The child speaks in single-word utterances, known as **holophrases**. Words used holophrastically require interpretation by caregivers. They are usually clear in context and their interpretation is based on other cues, such as intonation.
two-word stage	The child combines words into two-word utterances, which follow standard syntax – e.g. if a noun follows a verb ('eat apple'), it is being used as an object not a subject.
telegraphic stage	The child combines three or more words at times into proto-sentences, which have a **telegraphic** quality because only lexical words (nouns, main verbs, adjectives and adverbs) will be present: 'Daddy go get ball'.
post-telegraphic	The child begins to add some of the function words into their utterances, but they are not yet producing the full adult versions reliably: 'I am eating banana. Is you like banana?'

When describing what stage a child has reached, it is important to take a holistic view and to look at the most advanced utterance in the data. For example, you should not place a child in the one-word stage if the data shows they are sometimes using telegraphic utterances. (You can probably speak fluent English, but you will sometimes produce one-word utterances!)

> **Key terms**
>
> **holophrase:** a single word carrying the meaning of an entire utterance or sentence (e.g. 'juice' to mean 'I want juice' or 'give me juice')
>
> **telegraphic:** describing an utterance typified by the missing out of function words such as auxiliary verbs, determiners, conjunctions and prepositions

Activity 1

Identify the possible meanings of the holophrases below. Create mind maps like the example given, or write lists of the possible meanings. Using just that one word, imagine what a one-year-old child might intend to say. Are there any that do not work as holophrases?

- milk
- teddy
- no
- bye-bye

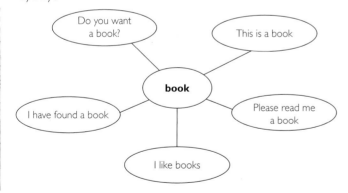

Phonetic development

Activity 2

If a child mispronounces a word or even applies its own idiosyncratic label to something, but people around the child know what it means, is that a word? What makes something 'count' as a word?

The table below shows the typical phonological features of children's speech.

Feature	Meaning	Example
consonant cluster reduction	removing part of a consonant cluster to make a sound easier to pronounce (a form of simplification)	*tuck* for *truck*
unstressed syllable deletion	not pronouncing an unstressed syllable (often the first in English)	*nana* for *banana*
assimilation	copying a sound across from another part of the word/ interference from one part of the word	*gog* for *dog*
substitution	swapping one sound for another (a form of simplification)	*fink* for *think*
reduplication	repeating a word or syllable	*choo-choo* for *train*
addition	adding a sound, usually a vowel, to the end of the word	*horsey* for *horse*
final consonant deletion	not pronouncing the final consonant	*ca* for *cat*

Taking things further

When learning to read and write, children are asked to link phonemes to graphemes (letters). This is actually a highly artificial process – and very difficult to do, given that Standard English has 44 phonemes (some dialects have a different number), and the alphabet has 26 letters. In addition, we often spell the same sound with different combinations of letters due to the many different ways that words have come into English. The best way to teach reading is a subject of much debate, but at the time of writing, phonics-based tuition is favoured in many English-speaking countries.

Key term

velar: a sound produced using the back of the tongue against the velum, or soft palate (e.g. g/k)

When considering phonological features, it is important to think in terms of sounds rather than letters. For example, if a child says 'tink' for 'think' (as many accents do), it is not consonant cluster reduction, because we do not pronounce the 't' and the 'h' as a cluster. They form a single fricative sound, which is being *substituted* with the plosive 't' sound (which is easier to say).

Children produce vowel sounds first, then the plosive and nasal consonants in babbling. The ones produced at the front of the mouth usually come before those produced towards the back. This is often a feature of substitutions – sounds from further back in the mouth will be replaced with easier, more forward sounds (known as fronting). The last sounds to be mastered are a group of consonants called the approximants: 'r', 'w' and the hard, consonantal 'y'.

For more information on phonology, see Unit 3.5.

Activity 3

Look at these examples of children's pronunciation. Which of the features in the table above does each one show? Try to give as much detail and explanation as you can. The first one has been done as an example.

- *ba* (bag) – deletion of the final consonant, which is the **velar** plosive 'g'
- *baggy* (bag)
- *chick-chick* (chicken)
- *fower* (flower)
- *kicken* (chicken)
- *puter* (computer)
- *wed* (red)

Add three examples of your own, explaining the feature and phonetic detail involved.

Early words and meanings

There are also patterns in the type of words and meanings children acquire early on. For example, most children's early vocabulary is largely made up of nouns. This may be because of the way parents and other caregivers tend to play with babies and toddlers by showing them objects and naming them, saying things like 'What's this? This is a…'. A phenomenon known as the 'naming spurt' has been observed that occurs at around 18 months (although such averages can vary considerably). During this phase, many new nouns are acquired as the child seeks to label the objects and people around them.

There is, however, some variation within this overall pattern. Developmental psychologist Katherine Nelson classified the word types within children's early vocabularies. She found that the first 50 words spoken by children tended to fall into four categories (presented here in order according to how frequently they appear in most vocabularies).

Naming	Action	Modifying	Social
words used to label objects and people: 'mama', 'ball', 'car'	words used to elicit or describe an action: 'give', 'go', 'bath'	words used to add description or comment: 'no', 'nice', 'good'	words with a social or personal function: 'bye-bye', 'hi', 'thank you'

Nelson identified two different types of children by their vocabularies:

- 'Referential' children had a vocabulary that was made up of at least 50 per cent naming words – they used their language to refer to things, to describe the world around them
- 'Expressive' children were those with a higher proportion of social and modifying words.

It is interesting to note that even where there are similarities in early vocabularies – perhaps most children in a study are referential – it is still possible to identify context-driven differences. These can emerge right from the start. For example, urban children's vocabularies are more likely to include words such as 'park' and 'bus', whereas children living in a coastal setting may be more familiar with nouns like 'shell' and 'rockpool'.

Activity 4

a) Do you know what any of your first words were? Is there a story linked to it, or can you explain it by your specific context? What about the first words of other family members?

b) With reference to the concepts in this section, and any ideas of your own, explain the following two scenarios:
- 'book' being a child's first word
- 'mama' (or equivalent) being the most common first word.

Experimentation with semantics

Key terms

referent: the item or concept that a word refers to

over-extension: stretching the limits of a word's definition by applying it to extra items

mismatch: when people or things are put together that would not normally be associated

While children are developing their early vocabularies, they also have to learn what words mean. It may seem surprising, but in most cases the link between a word and the thing or concept it refers to (its **referent**) is actually quite arbitrary (except in the case of onomatopoeia). Children may therefore make mistakes in how they use words, applying a word incorrectly while they work out what the correct referent for the word is. For example:

> Child says 'bottle' while pointing to her empty bottle. The mother understands that she would like her bottle refilling. 'Would you like me to fill your bottle?' replies the mother and goes to get more water. It is only later, when they are out and the child points to a river and says 'bottle', that the mother understands that the child thinks 'bottle' is the word for 'water'.

The example above shows semantic **over-extension**: the word has been applied to an incorrect referent. In this case, it is a type of over-extension known as a **mismatch**. There is a reason the child thinks 'bottle' means 'water' – it does make sense in context, but only if you know that the child usually has water in her bottle and has therefore associated the two things. The table below explains the different types of extension errors that children can make.

Term	Definition	Example
categorical over-extension	a hyponym is promoted to a hypernym (this is the most common type of over-extension)	'apple' is used for all fruit
analogical over-extension	two items are associated because of a quality they share (an analogy)	'cat' is used for a soft blanket
mismatch over-extension	a physical connection between two items causes an association (this is the least common)	'doll' is used for the doll's pushchair
under-extension	a word is used for too few referents – this treats a common noun (a label for a type of thing) as though it were a proper noun (a unique label)	'shoes' is only applied to the child's own shoes, they do not know what to call anyone else's shoes

To remind yourself about hyponyms and hypernyms in semantic fields, reread Unit 3.4.

British linguist Jean Aitchison described the process of learning meaning, using a three-stage model:

- **Labelling:** The child learns the names of objects, processes and ideas.
- **Packaging:** The child tests out and learns the limits of the labels (this is where over- and under-extensions might occur).
- **Networks:** The child begins to understand the connections between things and realises that objects belong to categories – they would recognise that there is such a thing as 'fruit' and that 'pineapple' and 'banana' both belong to that category while 'carrot' belongs elsewhere.

Activity 5

The examples below are all drawn from the language of a 20-month-old child. Comment on each example, noting the lexical and semantic features of her language (e.g. Nelson's categories, any extensions or any application of Aitchison):

- First ten words/phrases of the day: 'hello', 'get up', 'play', 'draw', 'that one', 'no', 'horsey' (referring to a toy), 'juice', 'toast', 'allgone'.
- She uses 'horsey' to describe a cuddly toy horse but cannot label a picture of a horse in a book.
- She identifies juice, milk and her mother's coffee as 'juice'.

[handwritten margin notes: similar extension / categorical extension]

For example:

> The data suggests that this 20-month-old child is more of an expressive child than a referential one following Nelson's categories, as only 30 per cent of the data is made up of nouns, plus the pronoun phrase 'that one' being also arguably referential. However, this is a limited sample and it is possible that she produces more referential utterances later in the day.

clear identification using Nelson's categories

precise analysis of the data using grammatical labels

evaluative approach to the data

opportunity here to discuss context

As well as this trial-and-error experimentation, children may also display creativity with lexis and semantics, where they clearly link known ideas from words to other words, or use the words they have to make the meaning they want. An example would be a three-year-old, in the absence of a suitable adverb, demanding that his father pushes him 'fast and fast and fast' at the playground.

Interestingly, research has shown that children do seem to know they are not using the correct word. Leslie Rescorla, who identified the different kinds of extension, tested children who had been overextending words by showing them pictures of things they had been mislabelling. So, for example a child who had been calling all four-legged animals 'cats' would be shown a horse and a cow as well and asked to point to the cat. The fact that they could do so showed that they did not actually think the horse was a cat; they were just choosing the best word available.

Early grammar and syntax

There are several ways of examining children's grammatical development. Some of the main areas of study include:

- **Key word classes in early vocabularies:** These are largely lexical words such as nouns, with functional words filling in the gaps from the post-telegraphic stage.
- **Word order and syntax of early utterances:** Word order almost always follows the standard adult word order as soon as words are being combined.
- **Application of suffixes:** Both Cruttenden and Brown reach similar conclusions about the stages children go through in applying grammatical items such as suffixes or inflections (see below).
- **Formation of specific constructions:** How questions and negatives are formed, in particular, have been explored (see below).

Right, wrong, right

Two interesting pieces of research into children's application of grammatical terms reach similar conclusions. Both studies found that children initially seem to acquire irregular grammar correctly, then they will suddenly start getting it wrong before eventually getting it right again.

For example, a child may initially seem to know the irregular plural 'men', but then may inexplicably start saying 'mans' or even 'mens' instead before settling back into using 'men' correctly and routinely. Around the same time, they may also be making mistakes with other irregular plurals, but they will not necessarily work them all out at once. Each irregular word seems to have its own timeline, probably based on the frequency with which the child hears it. Although this may seem like regression, it is actually all a process of progress.

This is linked to nativist theory and the idea of the Language Acquisition Device (LAD), which is discussed in Unit 6.2.

Alan Cruttenden (1974) described these stages, while Roger Brown (1925–1997) presented a graph showing children's competence in any particular irregular form over time as a U-shape (they start out seeming competent, then dip, then regain competence).

The dip in the middle can be alarming to parents, because their child had previously produced the word correctly. However, experimentation with inflections is a clear sign of working with language creatively and intelligently. In some cases, children even effectively apply inflectional changes twice. So, in the examples shown in the chart below, the plural 'childrens' shows the standard 's' inflection added to the full plural form, which has already been made plural by the addition of 'ren'. Similarly, 'wented' shows application of the standard '-ed' past tense inflection to the already past tense verb 'went'. The child is therefore showing awareness of the past form of 'to go' but has created a virtuous error in unnecessarily adding the ending. Similar doubling of grammatical forms happens with examples like the comparative 'more better', while children work out the rules about which words use 'more' and which '-er'.

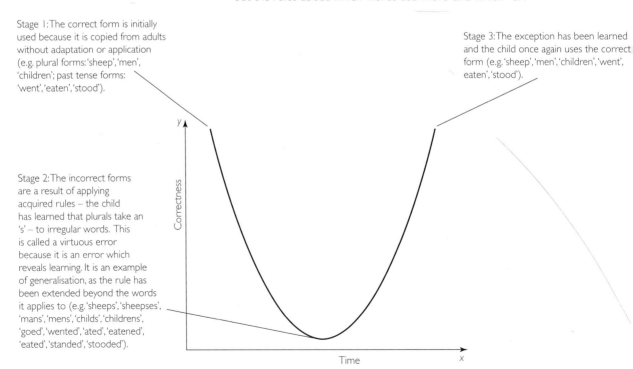

Stage 1: The correct form is initially used because it is copied from adults without adaptation or application (e.g. plural forms: 'sheep', 'men', 'children'; past tense forms: 'went', 'eaten', 'stood').

Stage 3: The exception has been learned and the child once again uses the correct form (e.g. 'sheep', 'men', 'children', 'went', eaten', 'stood').

Stage 2: The incorrect forms are a result of applying acquired rules – the child has learned that plurals take an 's' – to irregular words. This is called a virtuous error because it is an error which reveals learning. It is an example of generalisation, as the rule has been extended beyond the words it applies to (e.g. 'sheeps', 'sheepses', 'mans', 'mens', 'childs', 'childrens', 'goed', 'wented', 'ated', 'eatened', 'eated', 'standed', 'stooded').

Correctness

Time

Activity 6

Comment on the virtuous errors below. What exactly is the child doing? Give as much detail as you can.

- *I standed on it.*
- *She tookened it from me.*
- *Look at my feets!*

[handwritten annotation: Irregular verb conj...]

Constructing negatives and questions

It is worth looking at how questions and negatives are constructed in Standard English in order to understand the complexity of what children have to grasp. Because these are complex constructions, children master them gradually, in clearly discernible stages. The example below shows how questions and negatives are created in Standard English.

How questions are created:

> You want to go shopping:
>
> Do you want to go shopping?
>
> When do you want to go shopping?
>
> You are going shopping:
>
> Are you going shopping?
>
> Will you be going shopping later?

'dummy' auxiliary verb inserted purely for the purpose of making a question

'wh-' word added plus dummy do ('wh' words = 'when', 'where', 'what', 'why', 'who', 'how')

subject and verb inverted – this is only possible with the primary verbs ('to be' and 'to have') and the modal auxiliaries, otherwise a dummy 'do' is needed

modal auxiliary added, causing existing auxiliary to change to infinitive form 'be'

How negatives are created:

> I want to go shopping – I don't want to go shopping.
>
> I wanted to go shopping – I didn't want to go shopping.
>
> I'm going shopping – I'm not going shopping.

'dummy' auxiliary verb inserted contracted with 'not' to make the negative

the dummy auxiliary (like all auxiliaries) carries the tense and the main verb reverts to base form

'not' inserted – again this is only possible with primary and auxiliary verbs; 'not' can be contracted with most modal verbs: 'won't', 'can't', and with 'have' ('haven't') but only contracts with 'be' in some non-standard English dialects ('ain't')

Here are the stages of what children do:

Negatives	Reliance on 'no' and 'not' at start of utterance – 'not have bath'	"Don't and can't' acquired and negatives begin to appear between subject and verb	More forms appear (e.g. in different tenses); most forms accurately used

Questions	Rising intonation at the end of the utterance marks a question	'Wh-' words at start of utterance, no change in word order	'Wh-' word plus auxiliaries, no inversion; yes/no questions are inverted	'Wh-' questions and simple yes/no questions full adult version with dummy auxiliary	Modal auxiliaries added

Even in the early stages of speech, children handle quite sophisticated constructions, so it is important to always describe what they are *able* to do rather than just identifying errors. For example, a child saying 'me no want bed' is already positioning the negative 'no' between the subject and verb, which can be seen as the second stage of negatives acquisition. Even this obviously telegraphic and immature utterance demonstrates implicit understanding of some rules of grammar, as it communicates successfully through its syntax.

Activity 7

Comment on the following examples of children's sentences. What can you say about their use of grammar? Feel free to add in any other comments that occur to you (for example, about stage, lexis, semantics).

- *You want play my room?* (said to a cousin, indicating upstairs)
- *You not take it.*
- *No dinner. Allgone.*
- *Did you did get the ball down?*

Early pragmatics

Children start developing an understanding of what they can achieve through language at birth. Nelson's work considers pragmatics, as she classifies language according to its purposes or functions. There are two more key studies that approach children's language similarly, carried out by Brown and Michael Halliday.

Brown

Brown's research into children at the two-word stage found that words were combined in a multitude of ways. He ascribed different function labels to these words to try to explain what children were trying to achieve with their two-word utterances. He also demonstrated that children's language use could be subtle and multi-faceted, even with just two words at a time. Brown's classifications are outlined in the following table.

Classification	Definition	Example
agent	someone who does something	*Daddy* (in 'Daddy go')
action	a thing someone does	*go* (in 'Daddy go')
affected	the object of an action	*apple* (in 'eat apple')
entity	a person or thing being commented on rather than doing something	*teddy* (in 'Teddy nice')
location	a place	*here* (in 'Mummy here')
possessor	someone owning something	*my* (in 'my ball')
possessed	a thing being owned	*ball* (in 'my ball')
nomination	an indicator or something being named	*this* (in 'this ball')
recurrence	a request or statement of repetition	*more* (in 'more juice')
negation	a denial of something	*no* (in 'no bed')

For example, the utterance 'Mummy sit' is clearly an example of agent + action. It may be intended as a command or as a description, but this would be clear from the context (and probably by accompanying body language). 'Sit chair' on the other hand is action + affected (or, arguably, location).

Halliday

Another useful approach is Halliday's list of the functions of children's language, which also serves to demonstrate that children are using language with some sophistication from the start. According to Halliday, children are able to use a range of these functions even when speaking holophrastically, although a couple of the functions do not appear in their language until a little later.

Function	Use	Example
instrumental	to fulfil a need	*Juice please*
regulatory	to control others	*Mummy sit*
interactional	to develop relationships	*I love you*
personal	to express opinions, emotions and identity	*I like that one*
representational/ informative	to provide and request information	*What's that?*
heuristic	to discover and explore	*Why is the sky blue?*
imaginative	to pretend, imagine and narrate	*I'm a caterpillar*

Activity 8

Classify the following two-word utterances according to Brown's labels and Halliday's functions. Could any of them fit more than one category?

* *teddy eat*
* *doll chair*
* *get ball*
* *no apple*
* *more milk*
* *Mama allgone*
* *love teddy*
* *mine book*

Final task

Read the transcription overleaf of a conversation between four family members. Charlotte (19) and Freya (14) are sisters. Adam (6 years 7 months) and Zoe (3 years 5 months) are their cousins and are visiting Charlotte and Freya at their home. Charlotte has just come back from work.

Identify and list the features of children's language that are interesting in this transcription. What can they do at this point? How are they using language here?

Text 1

Charlotte:	what did you do today ↗ (7) what did you have for lunch ↗
Zoe:	um (.) we had toast and beans and egg
Charlotte:	OH was that for breakfast ↘
Zoe:	yeah
	//
Charlotte:	ah was it good ↗
Adam:	we saw cinderella
Charlotte:	(2) DID you ↗ (1) you saw cinderella (1) WOW
Adam:	i think tomorrow theres going to be a boy one
Charlotte:	oh dyou reckon (.) right (.) you let me know
Zoe:	i think theres a be a girl one
Charlotte:	oh you think therell be a girl one ↗
Zoe:	no white (.) no white up there a box [indicates box of princess books]
Charlotte:	boxes (1) could be any of them (.) rapunzel
Zoe:	or cinderella
Charlotte:	or cinderella
Zoe:	belle
Charlotte:	oh (.) thatd be nice wouldnt it ↗
Zoe:	mmm
	//
Charlotte:	what did you have for your lunch
	//
Zoe:	is this
Freya:	cold pizza and buffet
	//
Zoe:	i play with it (1) dey go up dere [indicates shelf]
Charlotte:	they do go up there (1) but you can't go up there though (.) youre too little

Transcription key

(1) = pause in seconds
(.) = micro-pause
underlined = stressed sound/syllable(s)
// = speech overlap
[italics] = paralinguistic features
[UPPER CASE] = words spoken with increased volume
↗ = upward intonation
↘ = downward intonation

6.2 Theories of language acquisition

How have theorists sought to explain children's linguistic development? What ideas exist about what is happening as children acquire language?

Key theories

Theorists have been discussing how children learn to speak for decades. There are four key approaches to child language acquisition, which largely build on one another.

The initial ideas, now termed behaviourism, came out of the field of psychology in the 1950s. Some of the basic ideas of behaviourism were refuted by the development of nativist theory shortly afterwards. Cognitivism is another psychology-based theory, rooted in what children are biologically capable of. Lastly, interactionalism was conceived especially to interact with nativism. Other than nativism specifically critiquing behaviourism, these four schools of thought should not be seen as opposing theories; rather, each offers an explanation of part of the puzzle that is language acquisition.

Behaviourism

The earliest theory about how children develop language is associated with the behaviourist psychologist B. F. Skinner. He had been experimenting with rats and pigeons, and found that they could learn to behave in particular ways (such as finding the way through a maze or operating a button to open a door) through a system of punishment and reward (reinforcement). He theorised that human behaviours were similar, and specifically stated that this is how children learn language. They imitate what their parents say and receive **reinforcement** that is either **negative** (correction or disapproval, rather than punishment) or **positive** (praise or parental excitement at their achievement).

> ### Key terms
> **negative reinforcement:** a response is strengthened by stopping or avoiding a negative outcome such as correction or disapproval
> **positive reinforcement:** a response is strengthened when a favorable outcome occurs, such as praise

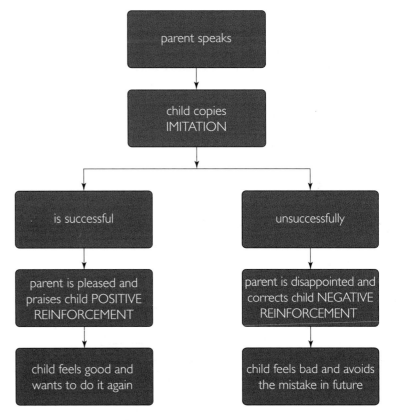

Skinner's ideas are now considered too simplistic to adequately explain something as complex as language. They are also at odds with the idea that language is acquired rather than learned. Children do not consciously seek to learn to speak, and people are not aiming to *teach* children to speak – the process happens naturally, like babies growing or gradually gaining more fine motor control. However, there clearly is an element of imitating parents/early caregivers, and Skinner's theories, being the first concepts in initial language acquisition, set the stage for others that followed.

Activity 1

What aspects of children's language might be associated with copying? Which of the following do you think are most likely to be acquired by imitation rather than by another process? Do any of these examples fit with Skinner's model of imitation and reinforcement?

- using politeness tokens (e.g. saying 'please' and 'thank you')
- having an accent
- the networking stage of meaning acquisition
- getting word order mostly right
- matching adult intonation from the melodic utterance stage
- experimenting with inflections

The main problem with the theory of behaviourism is that it fails to take account of children's creativity and their application of rules in acquisition. It would be far more time-consuming to learn language if we had to copy every bit of it, and children actually learn to speak relatively quickly. Most have their first word at about one year old, and can produce sentences that strangers can understand at around four years old. That rapid development cannot be explained by the rote learning process implied by Skinner. Also, children say things that are clearly not copied, such as in the case of virtuous errors. A toddler saying 'I eated my dinner all up' is unlikely to be imitating an adult; rather they appear to have taken apart what they have heard and re-formed it to construct new meanings. That is a much more active process than the one suggested by Skinner, and it is not supported by his thesis.

Nativism

US linguist Noam Chomsky explained where the difficulties lay in Skinner's theory of child language acquisition. He noted particularly:

Noam Chomsky, b. 1928

- what he called the 'poverty of the stimulus' – that what children hear from their caregivers is not necessarily the whole of their native language
- that the immediacy of input, behaviour and reinforcement is not a simple and straightforward relationship with language, as it would be with a rat pressing a button and receiving a food reward
- that children (and in fact, all people) combine words to produce new utterances regularly, which cannot be explained by imitation
- that virtuous errors imply that children are aware, on some level, of rules that they are generalising to all words in a group (e.g. plural endings applied to all nouns), before fine-tuning this by learning the exceptions.

In the 1960s, Chomsky theorised that language is a human-specific trait. Animals may communicate, but their systems of doing so are nowhere near as flexible or as complex as human language. Therefore, he stated, our brains are specially adapted and developed to enable us to accomplish this feat. Chomsky came up with the idea of the Language Acquisition Device (LAD), located somewhere in the brain, which processes the language we hear (the input) and works out what the rules must be, to enable us to combine words and make the appropriate generalisations. When a baby's brain is exposed to two (or more) languages at once, it sorts out multiple sets of rules simultaneously, figuring out the patterns in the language, such as word order (e.g. nouns preceding or following adjectives, verbs following or preceding subjects) and endings (e.g. plurals, tenses, possessive rules).

Activity 2

Analyse each of the examples below in relation to the ideas of Skinner and Chomsky.

- 'I saw some sheeps'
- 'want sweeties' – 'what do you say?' – 'want sweeties please'

An analysis of the child's utterance 'I falled over' can be seen overleaf.

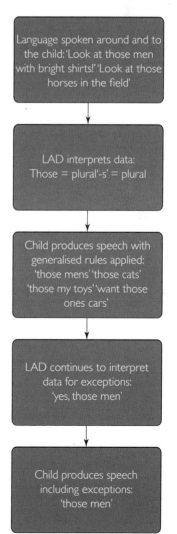

Language spoken around and to the child: 'Look at those men with bright shirts!' 'Look at those horses in the field'

↓

LAD interprets data: Those = plural '-s' = plural

↓

Child produces speech with generalised rules applied: 'those mens' 'those cats' 'those my toys' 'want those ones cars'

↓

LAD continues to interpret data for exceptions: 'yes, those men'

↓

Child produces speech including exceptions: 'those men'

This virtuous error calls Skinner's views on imitation and reinforcement into question, as the child would not have heard any adult use the non-standard past tense form 'falled'. However, this generalisation of the usual inflection to an irregular verb supports Chomsky's idea of the LAD, as it shows the child clearly applying rules, as they are unlikely to have heard this form. This very unlikeliness shows that it is probably the child's own process of deduction that has led to the production of this form, demonstrating an active acquisition process rather than the passive imitation suggested by the behaviourist model.

Case study: **Feral children**

Occasionally, a case comes to light of a child growing up without the normal input of adult caregivers. Such children are known as 'feral', and they provide some insight for scientists (in a range of fields) into the 'natural' state of children existing outside of civilisation. Whether and how such a child has learned language has obviously been a subject of great interest to researchers in the field. They have discovered that:

- input in the form of heard language is essential for the development of language
- this input is needed early in the child's life
- there is a critical period for language (that is, if we don't develop it by a certain time, it is not possible), which closes at early puberty.

Children experiencing a prolonged feral period (or neglect and isolation) lasting into puberty have been able to learn to reproduce isolated words with meaning, but have not been able to acquire grammar and construct their own sentences. However, children found at an earlier stage in their development, and therefore exposed to language during the critical period, have eventually been able to acquire language.

Further reading

Key examples of feral/isolated children for further research include:

- Victor of Aveyron (late 18th-century France)
- Genie (born 1957 in California)
- Oxana Malaya (born 1983 in Ukraine).

Cognitivism: Piaget

The cognitive approach to child language acquisition was associated initially with the Swiss psychologist Jean Piaget. Cognitivism assumes that children must have an intellectual (or cognitive) understanding of a concept before they can use language associated with it. The naming spurt that coincides with the timing of children's development of the concept of **object permanence** lends support to this theory. It is best explained as an understanding of the 'thingness' of things – the idea that something exists even when you cannot see it. A test for object permanence is to cover some toys with a blanket and then bring a child into the room. You show the child a toy in your hand and walk the toy under the blanket, keeping the child's attention on it. But then you bring out a different toy. If the child is surprised (that is, if they were expecting the first toy), they understand object permanence, and if they are not surprised then they do not yet grasp this concept.

> ## Activity 3
>
> How are object permanence and the naming spurt related? Why is the similarity in their timing considered to support cognitive theory?

However, it is possible for children to use words in a semantically empty way, which shows a lack of understanding of the concept behind it. In addition, as we have already seen, children sometimes use under-extensions, which can also reveal a lack of cognitive understanding. For example, a child may learn 'blue coat' as a label that separates a particular coat from others, but they may not actually know the (abstract and fairly demanding) concept of 'blue' yet. Another child might appear to be using the word 'shoes' correctly, but then turn out to only apply it to their own shoes. These examples show that there are some limitations to any claim that children need to cognitively fully understand words before using them. It is, of course a process, and children apply trial and error, using some words incorrectly at first.

Piaget's stages of cognitive development (1936):

Sensorimotor: 0–2 years: child co-ordinates senses and motor control; language used for demands; object permanence developed.

Preoperational: 2–7 years: child begins to think symbolically, uses imagination and intuition but not abstract thought; uses syntax and grammar to fill out language.

Concrete operational: 7–11 years: child can use concepts for concrete situations, e.g. time, space, quantity; still not possible as separate, abstract notions.

Formal operations: 11+ years: child is able to think theoretically, in the abstract, hypothetically and counterfactually; concepts can be transferred from one domain to another.

Cognitivism: Vygotsky

Lev Vygotsky was another cognitive theorist who, in 1978, emphasised the social element of learning, considering how the people around the child will support them in their acquisition of language. He referred to the importance of a '**more knowledgeable other**' who may be a parent, sibling or any person with more understanding than the child in context – the term is flexible, who can model language for the child, and who will usually instinctively operate within what he called the '**zone of proximal development**'. This means they instinctively work a little bit ahead of the child, not using language that is completely out of their reach, but instead showing them the 'next step'. There is little point correcting a child's speech from 'dere de sheeps' to 'look at the sheep in the field over there.' – instead, most caregivers will naturally praise the child and say, 'yes there are the sheep!', emphasising the invariable plural and modelling the correct pronunciation of the fricatives. These ideas are similar to some of those found in social interactionalism.

Key terms

object permanence: the understanding that objects exist always, even when not in view

more knowledgeable other: (MKO) an individual who models and guides language for a child

zone of proximal development: the space in which the MKO instinctively works, just ahead of where the child is currently capable

Social interactionalism

Conceptualised by Jerome Bruner around 1976, social interactionalism is the most recent of the 'big' theories. Bruner worked mostly in response to Chomsky's nativism, which he felt did not take enough account of the child's environment. He therefore came up with the idea of the Language

Acquisition Support System, or LASS, claiming that the LAD needs a LASS to make it work correctly. The LASS is, in essence, the people around the child. Bruner felt that the idea of 'input' did not go far enough in describing what parents, caregivers, family members and others provide for the child in terms of a linguistic environment. A large part of his work went into exploring the particular ways people speak when addressing children, describing the features of that kind of talk and discussing its functions.

Activity 4

The particular way people speak to children (and sometimes to older people, disabled people and animals) has been given various names over time. Currently 'child-directed speech' (CDS) is favoured, and is the term we use in this book. What do you think have been the problems with the following labels used in the past?

- 'fatherese'
- 'motherese'
- 'parentese'
- 'caretaker language'
- 'baby talk'

The features of child-directed speech are outlined in the following table.

Feature	Explanation	Example
turn-taking games	used even before speech but part of learning turn-taking rules	*peek-a-boo*
exaggerated intonation	the pitch changes within a turn from high to low are more dramatic than usual speech	
exaggerated mouth movements	thought to make it easier for a baby to focus on	
avoidance of pronouns	names are used instead (because pronouns have different meanings dependent on context)	*Daddy's just going in the kitchen now* (instead of *I'm just…*)
simple lexis – avoidance of specific terms or jargon	broad labels used at first with specifics introduced later	*Look at that birdie* (They can learn it's a parakeet later!)
reduplications	repetitions of simplified syllables	*Choo-choo, ba-ba, nana*
vowel additions	softened endings by adding a vowel sound	*horsey, toesies*
reformulation	when a child makes a mistake, the adult offers the correct version without explicit correction	*'sheeps' 'That's right, **sheep**'* rather than *'no, we say sheep, not sheeps'*
interrogatives	used to encourage interaction, often quite repetitive in form	*what's that/who's that*
repeated sentence frames	particularly when introducing or reinforcing new vocabulary/ concepts	*That's a horse/elephant…* *Look at the sheep/owl…* *Point to the tiger/giraffe…*

put on flash cards

Read the following text, which is a transcription of a bedtime reading conversation between a mother and daughter (Freya). Freya is two years and five months old.

Text 2

Mother:	you ready for stories now ↗
Freya:	yep
Mother:	what are ya doing ↗
Freya:	its trousers
Mother:	yep (.) which book are you having first ↗
Freya:	that one
Mother:	this one (.) ok (.) come here to mummy then ↘ (2) right this is called scratch and sniff food (.) which smell do you prefer ↘ whats this ↗
Freya:	its nana
Mother:	its a banana yes (.) can you smell it ↗ (4) nice fruity smell ↘ (1) whats that ↗
Freya:	its pizza
Mother:	dyou like pizza ↗
Freya:	i did eat it
Mother:	did ↗ you
Freya:	mm
Mother:	whats this ↗
Freya:	onange
Mother:	oranges (.) thats right (.) can you smell them ↗ (1) dyou like oranges ↗
Freya:	yeah
Mother:	yeah (3) ah (1) whats that ↗
Freya:	cocklut
Mother:	what is it ↗
Freya:	its cocklut
Mother:	chocolate (.) thats right (.) what kind of chocolate do you like ↗
Freya:	mm I like them
Mother:	you like them do you
Freya:	yeah {unintelligible – tries to say 'chocolate} is down there
Mother:	downstairs (.) its downstairs (1) yeah (.) we havent got any chocolate upstairs ↘ have ↗ we (6) sthat a nice smell
	//
Freya:	yeah
Mother:	good (.) what about this one ↗
Freya:	this one nice dawbries
Mother:	strawberries (.) thats right (1) and wha whats this ↗ (3) theres some strawberries (1) theres a strawberry (.) tart (1.5) and whats this ↗ (2)
Freya:	sambuh
Mother:	what is it ↗
Freya:	samp
Mother:	isnt it ice cream ↗
Freya:	its amb (1) not samidge (.) peam
Mother:	its ice cream (.) thats right (2) allgone {closing book}

Transcription key

(1) = pause in seconds	[*italics*] = paralinguistic features
(.) = micro-pause	[UPPER CASE] = words spoken with increased volume
<u>underlined</u> = stressed sound/syllable(s)	↗ = upward intonation
// = speech overlap	↘ = downward intonation

Activity 5

Comment on the transcription on the previous page. You should think about how the mother uses features of child-directed speech, as well as how the child is using language at this point in her development.

Talking about theories

In writing about the theories of acquisition, it is useful to see them as building on one another, rather than being definitively opposed to one another. You should therefore see your discussion of child language data as an opportunity to explore which aspects of the theories are most helpful or can be most easily discarded.

For example, in looking at the exchange between Freya and her mother, you could note the following:

The mother repeats the interrogative 'what's this' multiple times in the data, creating a familiar structure for the child to follow and clearly teaching turn-taking. This is supportive of Bruner's model of child-directed speech, showing that this child has a good Language Acquisition Support System, which enables her Language Acquisition Device to function. This can be seen from her effective use of word order such as 'I did eat them', using an auxiliary verb to support the main verb of 'eat', although not fully successfully. The mother operates carefully within the Zone of Proximal Development (as posited by Vygotsky) by only asking the child questions which she believes are possible for her to answer, building her confidence in speech and making it possible for her to participate in conversation.

Final task

Consider the following questions and write a paragraph or two to explain your thoughts.

a) Why might it be unhelpful to reduce the theories down to 'nature versus nurture'?

b) In what ways are Bruner's interactionalism and Vygotsky's cognitivism related?

c) How would you explain the LAD? Can you think of (or find) an analogy or metaphor to help you?

d) What other reasons might there be for feral children finding it difficult to acquire language, even if found within the critical period?

6.3 Working with child language data

How do people study child language? What can you tell from a transcription?

Studying children

Learning how children use language is more ethically sensitive than many other areas of linguistic study. Researchers need permission from parents (as children are not able to give it for themselves), but it is also crucial that children are not put in situations that make them uncomfortable. Also, from a 'purity of the data' standpoint, observer's paradox – the idea that the observer can change the language being collected – can be particularly acute with children because they are so curious.

Some tips for gaining usable data from children include the following.

- Create a party atmosphere for any experiment set up, for example by decorating with balloons and offering snacks (this advice comes from William Labov).
- Alternatively, record children in their normal, everyday environment with no changes to routine.
- Use the smallest, most unobtrusive recording equipment possible to avoid notice.
- Involve children's usual caregivers so that there are no extra adults present.
- Think about variables if you are setting up an experiment – how close are the children in age? Do you have a balanced gender mix? Are they all one ethnicity or is it balanced?

There are several different ways of looking at child language data, and once collected it can often be used in multiple ways. Broadly speaking, studies tend to either have a linguistic focus or a social focus: to be looking primarily at or for particular linguistic features or to be trying to find out something about a particular (type of) child(ren).

Some aspects that might be explored in various studies are outlined in the table below.

Linguistic	Social
How do children form questions? How do children of different ages get people to do what they want? How do children use labelling while resolving over-extensions? How do children develop fricative sounds?	Do four-year-old old boys and girls use language differently? Is there a difference in the language of children of different social classes over the first five years? How does X's language develop from six months to three years?

Activity 1

What other questions might you have as a researcher into first language acquisition? Try to form three sound research questions, of which at least one is linguistic (feature-focused) and one is social (child-centred). You could include the following types of study:

- Comparative (comparing children or groups of children, e.g. age groups or social groups such as genders, ethnicities).
- Longitudinal (examining the development of one or a small number of children over time).
- Experimental (setting up an artificial scenario or using test questions/prompts to elicit the kind of language you want — with children this can easily be role play or a game).

This is a Wug.

Now there is another one.

There are two of them.

There are two _____.

Specific focus studies: the wug test

In 1958, Jean Berko Gleason designed the 'wug test', which is still used today to test children's acquisition of inflections. She created a series of nonsense words, including 'wug' (an invented creature) and a series of cards, which she used to test children at different ages. The experimenter uses prompts like: 'This is a wug. Now there are two of them. There are two…'. If the child says 'wugs', then they have learned the standard '-s' plural inflection. The test also includes the nonsense verb 'to rick' which is tested in the progressive 'here is a man who knows how to rick. He is…' and the verb 'zib': 'What would you call someone whose job is to zib? He has to do it every day.'

The wug test is generally seen as strong evidence for the existence of the LAD, as children are able to supply at least some of the inflections even in the relatively early stages.

Activity 2

Why does the wug test use nonsense words? What would happen if they were real words?

Activity 3

How might you find out how children use labelling, including over-extensions? How would you set up an experiment? Think carefully about how you would:

- design an experiment to capture children's specific over-extensions
- invite children who use over-extensions
- measure whether children still use over-extensions over time.

It might help to think of some specific possible extensions and think through how they could be tested.

Case study: **Deb Roy's Human Speechome Project**

MIT professor Deb Roy has recorded the first three years of his son's life, using 11 ceiling cameras and 14 microphones installed in the family home, to try to map language acquisition. This ambitious project grew out of his work in engineering, in which he was teaching robots to speak and wanted to understand human language development in order to simulate it more accurately. The project resulted in a massive amount of data, which is being processed and transcribed to create a unique corpus of language.

Activity 4

Look at this dataset of an 18-month-old's vocabulary (ignoring pronunciation). What could you do with it? Try clustering the data in different ways and think about:

* what you can tell from it as it stands
* what else you would like to know about the dataset.

again	bye	flower	mummy	shoes
baby	car	get	nice	sit
back (preposition)	cat	gone	owl	spider
bag	catch	hair	Panda (from Maisy Mouse)	star
balloon	cheese	hat	Pat (Postman)	stuck
band (as in hair)	colour (verb)	head	play	teddy
bang	daddy	hot	please	teeth
bear	dog	juice	Pooh (Winnie the)	that
bed	door	look	poor	tickle
bird	duck	Maisy (mouse)	pretty	Tigger (from Winnie-the-Pooh)
book	eyes	more	Roo (from Winnie-the-Pooh)	Tom (cousin)

Final task

Read the transcription overleaf of data recorded in a room where six-year-old Adam is setting up a game with 14-year-old Freya, while three-year-old Zoe is looking at a children's magazine with her mother, Rachel. Freya's mother Beth is also present.

Section C: Exploring A Level language topics

Text 3

Freya:	ok (.) so thats if youre playing with all the cards (1) we're just going to be playing with (.)
Adam:	what are the wed[1] ones ↗
Freya:	[to Beth] what do you think ↗ (.) it says for young players who cant read (.) he <u>can</u> read but zoe might come over and play and it is a bit quick ↗
	//
Beth:	yeah its a bit quick and you dont want to leave her out if she wants to join in again ↘
Freya:	right (.) so we'll just do the blue ones again ↘ (1) ok
Adam:	ok (.) i like the blue ones (.) i could find them (.) i was good at that wasnt i ↗
Freya:	yes you were (.) but we are a good winner as well as a good loser arent we ↗ (.) like mummy says (1) so we get them out here
Rachel:	ooh look it says write your name here (.) dyou want to write your name there ↗ (2) right (.) thats enough colours
Zoe:	do need have (.) do need have all dem
Rachel:	are we gonna write your name here ↗ (.) [follows text with finger] write your name (.) here ↘ (2) dyou want to write your name ↗ (1) so what letter comes first
Zoe:	a zuh
Rachel:	right (.) a zuh (.) you do it
Zoe:	im too littuh
Rachel:	you can do a zuh ↘
Zoe:	i <u>cant</u> (.) no ↘
Rachel:	alright ↘ [writes] zuh (.) and what comes next ↗
Zoe:	uh oh
Rachel:	oh (.) then what
Zoe:	<u>eh</u>
Rachel:	good girl (.) are you going to colour in anna or elsa ↗
Zoe:	anna
Rachel:	so you need the pink colours and i need the blue colours ↘ (3) those are elsa colours
Zoe:	dis ones not elsa
Rachel:	no
Zoe:	no
Rachel:	actually this ones more of an anna colour

Notes:

[1] Adam's way of saying 'red'

a) In this transcription, what evidence can you find to support any of the acquisition theories you have read?

b) Is there any evidence in this transcription that would help you to criticise any of the theories you have encountered, that is, to point out potential gaps or shortcomings?

c) Which features of children's speech in this transcription stand out to you?

d) Which features of speech directed towards children in this transcription stand out to you?

Transcription key

(1) = pause in seconds
(.) = micro-pause
<u>underlined</u> = stressed sound/syllable(s)
// = speech overlap
[italics] = paralinguistic features
[UPPER CASE] = words spoken with increased volume
↗ = upward intonation
↘ = downward intonation

End-of-chapter task

If you could explore any aspect of children's language further, what would it be and how would you go about it? Design a research brief, explaining:

- what the focus of your research would be (e.g. children's use of questions)
- how you would get the data (e.g. observation of paired play with toys)
- how you would reduce observer's paradox and make your research ethical
- which aspects of language you would single out for study
- how you would control variables (e.g. use same-sex pairs, study 3 sets of 10 pairs of the same age – age 2.5, 3 and 4)
- if you have a hypothesis/what you might expect to find.

Chapter 7

English in the world

Since the Early Modern period, the English language has spread across the globe. This chapter begins by exploring the ways in which English can be considered a 'global language'. It then investigates how English varies around the world, before looking at the attitudes people have held – and continue to hold – towards these issues of English as a global language and its variation. The final unit explains how these ideas are discussed and explored in both linguistics and the wider world today.

Key concepts to be considered in this chapter are *diversity* in terms of global diversity specifically, and also *change*, with particular reference to how English has developed around the world. As always, both ideas need considering in *context* – as language can only fully be made sense of in its context. For this chapter, there are a range of different contexts to consider, with the broad global context forming a key background to the specific local contexts of each country that uses English.

7.1 English as a global language

What does being a 'global language' mean? How has English become a global language?

What do we mean when we say English is a 'global language'?

English is accepted without question as a global language for a range of reasons. It is not that English has the largest number of speakers in the world – Mandarin Chinese would be *the* global language if that was the case. However, Mandarin is not classed as a 'global' language because, despite its large number of speakers, they are largely concentrated in a single location – China. English, on the other hand, is:

- the native or first language of a large number of people across several countries
- an official language of several countries, including world powers such as the USA
- a second language required in contexts such as education and business in many countries
- a popular choice as a foreign or additional language for many speakers around the world
- a recognised business language and used as a **lingua franca** in international meetings
- one of the official languages of the United Nations
- the official language of shipping and air traffic control
- one of the official languages of space
- dominant on the internet
- used in popular media such as Hollywood films and much commercial music.

There are various labels for a language's status within a country or household, all of which have picked up a range of connotations over time.

> **Key term**
>
> **lingua franca:** a language used to communicate that is not the native language of either speaker in the interaction

Status	Meaning
native	the language(s) a person speaks from birth; also sometimes known as 'mother' or 'home' language
near-native	a description of competency used to indicate a high level of skill and fluency in a language
second language	a language learned later than from birth ('additional' or 'other' tend to be preferred terms now, as these do not presuppose only one pre-existing language)
foreign language	any non-native language (negative connotations may be read into this, though)
official language	language accorded a formal status (e.g. English and French are the official languages in Canada, so both are used in official documents and are found on road signs)

Activity I

Find out the following:

a) Approximately how many people speak English as a native or near-native language?
b) How many people are estimated to be learning English as an additional language?
c) The names of ten countries across at least three continents where English has official status.
d) The status of English in your own country.

The spread of English

As you probably discovered from Activity 1, the places where English is a first language or has official status tend to be countries which were part of the British Empire or the Commonwealth. The history of global English, then, is inextricably linked with Britain's colonial past.

The construction of the colonial empire began in the late 16th century, under Queen Elizabeth I. At this time, people from England travelled to other countries and claimed them in England's name. These lands were ruled by England, and later Britain, for varying lengths of time, as different places gained independence (usually through war) at different times. Part of the colonial project was to impose the English language on the country, as it was assumed that everything British was superior to everything foreign.

In the post-colonial world, many people in former colonies (now members of the Commonwealth) regard English as a symbol of British rule. However, the language is usually too strongly embedded to be abandoned. In some of these places, people – often those descended from white British settlers rather than from indigenous peoples – may be **monolingual** English speakers, so they have no other language to revert to. In other places, where people retained their original language alongside English, the situation is more complex.

> **Key term**
>
> **monolingual:** describing someone who only speaks one language

Activity 2

Copy and complete the table below to clarify the situation in the countries mentioned. If you are living in a different Commonwealth country, add it and research its information.

Country	Date of British colonisation	Date of independence	Other official language(s)	Other language(s) commonly spoken
USA		1776	11	Eng Spa
Canada				
Jamaica				
India		1947		
Pakistan		1947		
Australia	1005			
New Zealand				
Botswana				
Nigeria				
Malaysia				

The topic of English in the world has strong links to that of language change (see Chapter 5). As English leaves the shores of Britain it becomes 'global English', but the same processes of language change apply – so be aware that some of the theoretical and conceptual material from the language change topic also apply to this one.

Babel and the idea of different languages

According to the book of Genesis in the Bible, the people decided to build a tower to reach heaven. This was not acceptable to God, so he destroyed the tower, scattered the people and made them all speak different languages, so that they could never communicate and organise themselves so efficiently again. This tower is known as the tower of Babel, and the story is used to explain why there are so many different languages in the world.

The word 'babel' is used in a range of language-related products and ideas today to draw on those connotations. One branch of linguistics, known as comparative philology, has been concerned with tracing languages' roots back and looking at language families, to find connections between different languages. For example, many words in Germanic languages that begin with fricative 'v' or 'f' ('vater'/'father') have equivalents in Romance languages which begin with plosive 'p' ('padre'/'père'). This enormous undertaking which began in the 16th century and was developed considerably in the 19th century by the famous brothers Grimm, gives us the tree model of language change. This model presents most world languages as growing out of the ancestral language of proto-Indo-European. Part of that tree is shown below.

Further reading

A beautiful version representing the relationships between languages as a tree can be seen online, drawn by Minna Sundberg. Try to find the full-page version that also has maps showing the spread of different languages.

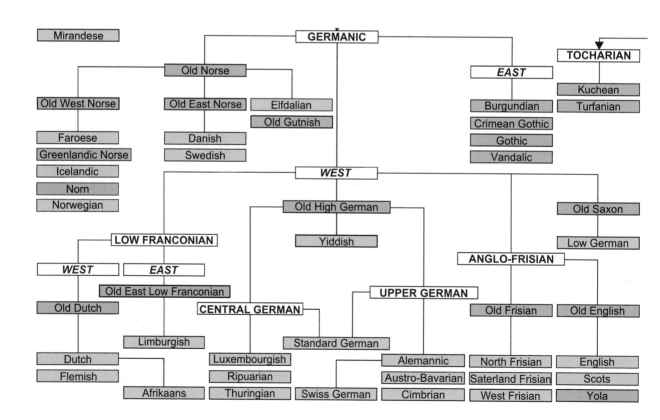

Activity 3

Investigate the following to familiarise yourself with the tree.

a) Indo-European split into various language families such as Romance. Name three more examples.
b) For two of the families you identified, name at least one language within that family.
c) As well as relationships between languages, what else does this image help to make clear?
d) To which families does English belong?

The tree model can also be used to show how a specific language changes over time – for example, how Old English changed into Middle English and then Modern English, as considered in Chapter 5.

English and imperialism

While discussing his poem about the teaching of history in the Caribbean, 'Checking Out Me History', John Agard explained that the history book used in the West Indies opened with the sentence 'The history of the West Indies starts in 1492 with Columbus's discovery of America'. This Eurocentric presentation is symptomatic of the formation of many attitudes to language in countries affected by British imperialism – particularly in locations such as the Indian sub-continent, the Caribbean and the parts of Africa that came under British rule.

Standard English, associated with the ruling power for so long, was taught as the 'correct' form of language, and the version needed in order to advance and acquire well-paid and well-respected jobs. While people may have spoken other varieties of English at home – or indeed other languages altogether – Standard English was accepted as the prestige norm and the necessary form to learn. Speaking it made someone sound educated, so families were in favour of their children learning it at school in order to access equality of opportunity, even if they spoke differently at home. This situation continues in places such as Nigeria, where 'home' varieties like **Pidgin** are becoming more accepted in contexts such as the workplace, while Standard English is still regarded as beneficial for communicating outside the local community, for example in wider business.

> **Key terms**
>
> **pidgin:** a form of speech created when people who do not share a language communicate
> **Pidgin:** a language spoken across West and Central Africa, e.g. in Nigeria, Ghana and Equatorial Guinea.

Activity 4

What is your relationship to language? Answer the following questions.

a) Which language(s) and dialects do you speak?
b) How did you come to learn each language that you know? (e.g. at home/school)
c) If you speak different languages, do you have different purposes or contexts for each one? What are these?

English's current global power

History is not the only reason for English's current global hold, however. Its power is also linked to the large and significant industries of technology and media – both of which have a great deal of influence over our lives – and to the perception of English as an important language of both business and academia.

Read Text 1 below, which is an article from a Malaysian newspaper website about English language proficiency.

Text 1

The Learning Challenge
By Mushtak Parker

In Malaysia, English language proficiency is a hot topic, as evidenced by postings on social media and in newspaper articles by, among others, Permaisuri Johor Raja Zarith Sofiah Sultan Idris Shah and Umno Youth deputy chief Khairul Azwan Harun, both passionate and pragmatic in their support of boosting the level of English proficiency among Malaysian students.

I must confess to having frontline experience in this area having lectured, for some 14 years, groups of Malaysian civil servants – both federal and state – who were attending three-month courses in London aimed at "broadening their horizons" by exposing them inter alia to inter-faith dialogue, workings of the global financial system, Islamic finance, counselling, Islamic political movements and English language proficiency.

I have also taught courses at universities and colleges in London over the years where a number of my postgraduate students were from Malaysia.

My experience vindicated the concern of thinking Malaysians that English language proficiency of many school students, university students including postgraduates, and some sections of the civil service, is seriously lacking. Malaysian politicians, bureaucrats, regulators and industry leaders I have engaged with recently concur. Unfortunately, progress has been frustratingly slow.

There are thousands of Malaysians who excel in English and who have made their mark in politics, business, finance, education, medicine, the law and other fields. I am reminded of Datuk Yunus Rais, the much-revered founder and principal of Sels College in Covent Garden, an English language school of a gem and "with the right heart" established in 1975 and accredited by the British Council, which was responsible for the English language proficiency of a generation of foreign students.

Language nationalism seems to be rooted in the politics of identity, which in Malaysia with its multicultural composition can be an irritant, especially this side of the 14th General Election. This is a non-argument, for no one is suggesting demoting Bahasa Malaysia, which, for the majority of Malaysians, is or should always be the main compulsory language, with English (or French, Arabic or Mandarin) as a compulsory second language.

The fact that many young Malaysians (including Malays) cannot speak Bahasa is not a result of promoting English language proficiency. I know students from Pakistani, Afghan and Arab descent in London who can hardly speak their native tongues — Urdu, Pashto and Arabic – and whose colloquial English is ordinary but who are incapable of understanding their English textbooks in maths, science and history.

Changing such a **Luddite** mindset in language nationalism has to begin at the core of a reinvigorated National Education Policy that is willing to make English a compulsory second language – cool instead of poyo (uncool).

Failing this could compromise the very education experience and expense of those Malaysians studying abroad who cannot fully benefit from the lectures and tutorials because of their lack of English proficiency; or hold back the life and earnings potential of the next generations of Malaysians; or obfuscate Prime Minister Datuk Seri Najib Razak's Transformasi Nasional 2050 initiative in transforming Malaysia into a higher income, productivity-driven and knowledge-based economy.

From *New Straits Times*, 10 October 2017

Glossary:
Luddite: someone who is antitechnology
(taken from the name of a historical group who opposed progress in the industrial period and smashed machinery)

Activity 5

Assess the main arguments offered in Text 1 for learning English.

a) According to the article, why should people learn English?
b) What does the writer recommend Malaysia do to improve the learning of English?
c) What problems does the article highlight with the current state of English in Malaysia?
d) What does it imply people think is an issue with learning English, although the writer does not agree?

English and business

A key reason for English's current power in the world is its value as a business language, and for global cooperation in endeavours such as scientific progress and academia. For a long time, English has been used as a lingua franca to ease communication between those who usually speak other languages. This adds to the value that English holds in people's minds, as it enables access to education, ideas and trades on a global scale.

The cost of having a global language

An inevitable result of the existence of a 'global language' is that there is a negative effect on minority languages – sometimes to the extent of causing 'language death'. This occurs when there are no native speakers remaining for a language or dialect. A language might be revived or preserved by enthusiasts, but if everyone who speaks the language learned it as an additional language, it is officially 'dead'. Children must grow up learning a language as their first native tongue in order for it to be considered 'living'; this may be one of two or three native languages being learned simultaneously.

According to British linguist David Crystal, approximately 50 per cent of the world's 6,000 languages are likely to die out over the course of the 21st century. The Endangered Languages Project, run by the Alliance for Linguistic Diversity, is gathering data online in order to try and capture information about some of these minority languages before it is too late. The website shows where the world's most vulnerable languages are spoken and holds audio material recording data from these languages. Those most at risk of being lost are those that are spoken but not used for writing, so projects such as this are important for recording material while it is still possible. The loss of a language can represent the loss of a culture, a way of thinking and a history.

Taking things further

Eighty per cent of the languages spoken across Africa have no written form, in comparison to 50 per cent of languages globally. Why might this be the case? What are some differences between oral culture and written culture? How might this affect the study and recording of a language?

Final task

Consider these reasons for English's status as a global language. For each one, identify how it has helped to make English important globally. Which do you think have contributed most to the current high status of English globally? Decide on a rank order for them, or sort them.

- English is one of the official and working languages of the UN.
- English is one of the official languages of space.
- English is the language of shipping and air traffic control.
- English's use as a lingua franca.
- The number of countries where English is an official language.
- The popularity of English in foreign language learning.
- The power of Hollywood.
- The relative power/status of the countries where English is spoken.
- The use of English for much academic and scientific writing.
- The use of English on the internet.
- The view of English as important for business.

7.2 Global variation in English

How varied is the use of English around the world?

Classifications of different Englishes

Most countries with English as their official language have a clear historical relationship with the UK through the British Empire or the Commonwealth. The process of gaining independence – whether diplomatically negotiated or won through war – has often resulted in complex relationships that may also have a bearing on the status of English in these countries.

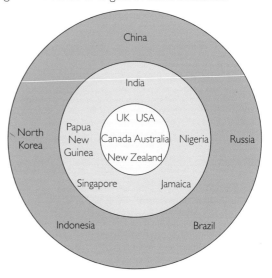

This diagram shows Braj Kachru's 'Circles of English' model. The varieties used in the different circles, and the attitudes to English within the three circles, are quite different.

The inner circle

The inner circle includes countries in which English is a primary first language and the main official language, such as the UK, Australia and the USA. This circle can be seen as *norm-providing*: these are the varieties of English that establish what is seen as 'standard' or 'correct'. For many speakers in these countries, English is their native and often their only language. This leads to a confidence in its use in which English's status can be taken for granted.

The outer circle

The outer circle is made up of countries where English has an official status but may not be the first language for many members of the population – for example, Jamaica, Bangladesh and Kenya. The outer circle is seen as *norm-developing*, in that speakers in these countries adopt, adapt and develop their own norms in terms of how the language is used, often through policy. As English is often experienced as 'official' and 'useful' to most people in these countries, but is not necessarily their native language, there is a tendency to be more aware of language issues, such as the implications of choice of language/variety. English is inherently bound up in a colonial legacy in many of these places and is not the language of 'home' or 'community'.

The expanding circle

The expanding circle represents places where a large or increasing number of people are learning English as a foreign language, including South Korea, Indonesia and the Netherlands. The expanding circle is seen as *norm-dependent*, as speakers in this context look to native speakers to see how to use English: they are entirely dependent on the norms set in the inner (and sometimes outer) circles. In the expanding circle, English is often less problematic than in the outer, as it is free of colonial associations and people are usually *choosing* to learn it for business or travel purposes rather than *having to* in order to access education and careers. Their associations with English are usually positive, therefore, as the relationship is a transactional one – the language is learned for a clear reason. There may be frustrations associated with learning a new language, but they do not experience the emotional issues that inner-circle speakers often have to negotiate.

Activity I

Consider your own use of English.

a) How would you label the variety you use and which of the circles does it belong in?

b) To what extent do you think your own use of English has been influenced by the English used in other countries?

c) Research Kachru's circles model. Can you find recent figures for the number of speakers in each circle?

Now look at McArthur's circle model of world Englishes.

McArthur's circle model of world Englishes, shown on the previous page, approaches the description and definition of global English in a different way. Where Kachru clusters and defines Englishes by type, according broadly to how English entered and is used in a particular country, McArthur simply gives each geographical region its own section of the circle. This avoids the hierarchical nature of Kachru's inner vs outer presentation, instead creating that kind of relationship between standard and non-standard varieties within each location, although there is a difference between 'standard' and 'standard(ising)' varieties. However, this also prevents the model from providing any comparative information about any of these Englishes, apart from where they might be found.

Activity 2

What do you think 'World Standard English' in the centre represents? What variety of English is it likely to be closest to? Where might you see/hear it? For which speakers would it be most familiar? Would everyone/anyone need to learn it as a separate dialect in order to communicate transnationally?

Case study: **US English**

North America was colonised by English-speaking settlers in the 17th century, and declared its independence from England in 1776. US English is generally considered to be less varied than the English of Britain, due perhaps to its relatively rapid spread across America from only a few originating British dialects. (While British English has been developing in isolated pockets all over the UK for many centuries, English speakers have only been in the USA for about four centuries.) Many of the lexical differences between US and UK varieties are due to language change since the Early Modern period – British English has simply changed in different areas to US English.

One of the key differences between US and UK Englishes is in spelling, and this is due to Noah Webster's spelling reform, which he proposed in 1828. Many of Webster's suggested changes were to simplify some of the oddities of English spelling, such as removing 'u's from '-our' words like 'flavour/flavor' and swapping some soft 'c's for 's's as in 'defense/defence'. These have become classic uncertainties for other countries – do they follow US or UK standards? Spellcheck systems in computer software often default to a US setting, which further confuses the issue in the UK, and in Canada, which tends to follow UK spelling.

However, there are also grammatical differences between US and UK varieties of English, such as the use of prepositions following some verbs, e.g. 'write' as in to write a letter or email. UK English requires a 'to' following the verb: 'I will write to you every week', but US English does not: 'I will write you every week'. Tense choices used to express having completed an action, and therefore not needing to do it again, are also different in the two countries:

* UK: I've already eaten, thank you.
* US: I ate already, thank you.

In the UK, the present **perfective** would be used to show that the action has been completed and is having an effect on the present, whereas in the US version, the simple past tense can be used. Again, due to the influence of US voices in the media, the US version now sounds more familiar to a UK ear than it did even just a few years ago.

Key term

perfective: a non-finite verb form used to create a perfect tense; in regular verbs the form is the same as the simple past ('I walked', 'I have walked') but in irregular verbs it is usually different ('I was', 'I have been')

Activity 3

Find out some details about Webster's reforms of English. You will probably already be familiar with some of the differences between US and UK spelling, but try to find some patterns of spelling Webster changed that you were not aware of. Be careful when researching, as some of Webster's suggestions were not adopted into standard US spelling.

Further reading

For more on US/UK difference, read the blog maintained by Lynne Murphy, an American linguist who lives in the UK, called 'Separated by a Common Language'. She also posts a 'Difference of the Day' on her Twitter account.

The rise of the outer circle

In Kachru's outer circle, a standard variety of English is used for official purposes and taught as that nation's official version of English, but often there is also another, less formal and less standard version (or multiple non-standard versions). These are often described as 'hybrid' varieties and known by blended labels such as Singlish (spoken in Singapore) and Taglish (English combined with Tagalog, spoken in the Philippines).

In any multilingual or multidialectal environment, people are likely to move between varieties, often within a conversation, if they are talking to people whom they know to also be proficient in more than one language or variety. **Code-switching** is therefore common in outer circle countries in particular. It may be triggered by various factors, such as a topic being more commonly associated with one language than another. It is common to switch from the standard variety to the home language when talking about food or using family labels, for example.

Key term

code-switching: moving between language forms. This can be from one language to another, or between dialects

Case study: **Pakistani English**

Pakistan was part of the area under British rule in India, but it was annexed later than most of India, so English was less well established as part of mainstream culture. This meant that when it became an independent state in 1947, fewer people spoke English as a first language. However, it was well embedded in elite culture at that point, as the language of government, the civil service and elite schools, for example. On achieving independence, English and Urdu were both official languages, as they still are. Punjabi, Pashto and Sindhi are also commonly used, but they do not have official status. At the time of writing, it is estimated that 27 per cent of the Pakistani population speak English natively, and 58 per cent as a second or additional language.

At this time, therefore, different types of English are spoken in Pakistan. The most standard – and the form closest to British or US English – is spoken in the universities and spread through higher education. There is also a 'low' form known as Paklish. This is an 'interference language', in which words and grammatical features from other languages spoken in the region are combined with English. In common with Indian Standard English, Pakistani English has many extremely polite and somewhat archaic features in its lexis and expression. Some key features of standard Pakistani English include:

- more specific familial terms such as 'cousin-brother' and 'cousin-sister' (meaning male cousin and female cousin respectively)
- the persistence of old-fashioned terms, such as 'mugging up' to mean learning by heart, 'thrice' for three times
- polite address terms: 'sahib' (sir, master), 'uncle'/'aunty' (to refer to anyone older – not only a relative)
- verbs 'open' and 'close' used to mean turn on/off lights (due to translation from Urdu)
- pluralising some non-countable or mass nouns ('Do not throw litters'; 'There are many traffics today').
- using progressive verbs in places that British English would not:
  - For habitual action: *I am doing this weekly* (Brit: *I do this weekly*)
  - For completed action: *Where are you coming from?* (Brit: 'Where have you come from?')
  - With stative verbs: *He was having many attempts at that homework* (Brit: *He had many attempts at that homework*).

Further reading

David Crystal, *English as a Global Language*, 2nd edition (Cambridge University Press, 2012)
Peter Trudgill and Jean Hannah, *International English: A Guide to the Varieties of Standard English*, 5th edition (Hodder, 2008)
Dan Clayton and Rob Drummond, *Language Diversity and World Englishes* (Cambridge University Press, 2018)

Read Text 2, which comments on a change to BBC Worldwide's programming launched in 2017.

Text 2

BBC is right to launch Pidgin language service as part of global expansion
by Ian Burrell

[…] The tussle for viewers and listeners is particularly apparent in Africa, where the BBC is launching six of its 12 new language services: Afaan Oromo, Amharic and Tigrinya (all in the Horn of Africa), and Igbo, Yoruba and Pidgin (all broadcasting in and around Nigeria).

The unsavoury partition of the continent by European imperial powers in the late 19th and early 20th centuries is known as the "scramble for Africa". The modern media networks that will most succeed in building relations with African countries today are those that enhance the economies of their host nations and authentically represent their cultures.

Soft power does not equate to propaganda. Solomon Mugera, regional editor for BBC Africa, says the BBC's reputation is based on the independence of its editors. The new services are primarily recruiting local staff.

"It's content produced by people who live in these regions, speak the languages and know the cultural nuances," he explains.

The BBC (which aims for a global reach of 500 million by its centenary year of 2022) has shown bravery and innovation with the launch of BBC Pidgin. It will give the corporation contemporary relevance for younger audiences and underline its position as the lead player in African digital media.

This is a tongue that was recently frowned upon, even in Nigeria. Bilkisu Labaran, a BBC veteran who is the editorial lead on the new service, recalls children at her school being beaten for speaking Pidgin, an English Creole. Pupils were told by teachers: "You must not speak Pidgin because it's bad English and it's going to spoil your language." The analysis of the Angola election campaign on BBC Pidgin's new website doesn't bring to mind a Laura Kuenssberg or a John Simpson*: "Di ruling party dey set to win di election and e be like say dem already know who go be president." However, today Pidgin is spoken by 75 million people across Nigeria, with additional speakers in Cameroon, Ghana and Equiatorial Guinea.

The language crosses generations but is particularly associated with youth, in a country of 190 million with a median age of 18. Pidgin is boosted by its use in the successful "Nollywood" Nigerian film industry and on social media in a region where Facebook, Instagram and YouTube are popular. "It has a fun element, an informality," says Ms Labaran, who was the first BBC editor for Nigeria.

The launch of BBC Pidgin, in audio, video and text, represents a "360-degree turnaround", she explains, for a broadcaster that once addressed Nigerians as citizens of the British Empire.

"Many years ago the BBC was seen as a colonial service where only the Queen's English could be heard and where no variations in accent were acceptable." Nigerian media have been "amazed and impressed" by such a strategic play from the once fusty BBC. "I think this will enrich the BBC and strengthen British soft power even more," says Ms Labaran. "We are speaking in the language young people are speaking in."

From *iNews*, 29 August 2017

* Laura Kuenssberg and John Simpson are traditional BBC news journalists; at the time of writing Kuenssberg is BBC political editor and Simpson the BBC world affairs editor.

Activity 4

Discuss why the article in Text 2 presents the move to broadcast in pidgin as 'right'. What reasons for this are given or implied?

colonialisation: country is invaded by a foreign force, bringing a new culture and language

lingua franca: colonial power's language is used as a trading language between different countries occupied by that power

pidgin: words and phrases from colonial language are used with words and phrases and some grammatical patterns from local language

creole: pidgin is picked up as native language by children and filled out into a complete language, grammar is regularised

standardisation: codification occurs and rules are agreed

Possibilities for the future

Inner-circle varieties of English are stable at the moment, changing only as they always have. However, the growing number of emerging varieties around the world, and the increase in their status in a post-colonial world, shows that much change is happening within English as a whole.

English could fragment into a family of languages, like Latin did to create the modern Romance languages. In fact, this is something that Webster confidently predicted in the 19th century, stating that the British, Australians and Americans would separate linguistically and end up mutually unintelligible, just as modern Swedish, Dutch and German people speak a family of related languages, but cannot understand one another. Of course, Webster could not have predicted the many ways in which international communication and travel would bring different countries into closer contact.

Case study: **Creolisation**

Languages can be formed through contact. In some cases, the fact of speakers from different languages living alongside one another has led to the creation of new languages. If people who do not speak each other's native language want to communicate, they must find a lingua franca. However, if their contact is extended beyond single transactions, they form a pidgin, which will be made up of words and structures from both of their native tongues. When children are born hearing people communicate in a pidgin, a creole is formed. This is because children intuitively determine and apply rules to the language they hear and produce, so the creole created will eventually have patterns and rules from both (or all) of the component languages.

Some of Kachru's outer-circle countries, particularly in Africa, the Caribbean and the Pacific islands, have creole languages alongside a standard (or standardising) English. Creoles are particularly associated with the legacy of the slave trade, as slaves speaking different languages were often mixed together, sometimes as a deliberate tactic to avoid organised rebellion.

Creoles have been stigmatised as 'poor' or 'bad' language, often due to their apparent simplicity, and perceived value judgements can make it difficult to discuss them. The safest labels to use when discussing creoles are as follows:

- **Acrolect:** the most prestigious variety on the spectrum (for an English-based creole, usually the closest to Standard English).
- **Mesolect:** the medium or average variety on the spectrum (commonly, the form that most people use in everyday speech).
- **Basilect:** the lowest-status variety on the spectrum and the one furthest from the standard (this is the most stigmatised form and often not a written variety).

Final task

Select one inner- and one outer-circle variety of English not covered
in detail in this unit for this task (you may wish to look at McArthur's
circle, repeated below, for some variety names). Find out about:

- the history of each variety
- the current status of each variety (how many speak it – as first/
  other language, whether it has official status, which other languages
  (if any) also have official status in that country, whether it is used in
  education/business/government, and so on)
- key features of the variety, including lexis and grammar as a
  minimum (you may also find pronunciation and spelling).

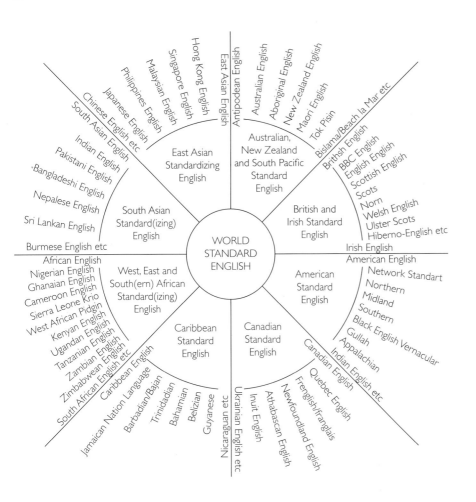

7.3 Attitudes to English issues and Englishes

What attitudes emerge in discussing global English?

Aspects of language change

Some attitudes towards global English varieties were discussed in Chapter 5, including:

- **descriptivist:** a neutral attitude, to describe how people use language
- **prescriptivist:** a critical attitude, to prescribe how people *should* use language.

Global Englishes can be seen as an aspect of language change, since they are a relatively new phenomenon and much of the discussion around them fits into that debate. People may present global Englishes in terms of:

- **progress:** a positive representation of language as moving forwards
- **decay:** a negative representation of language as being spoilt or destroyed.

For more information on this, see Unit 5.4.

Context as influence

Language is a social phenomenon. We may claim to use it to communicate, but in fact only a small part of it is really for essential communication. A huge amount of language fulfils social needs. This means that most judgments about language are ultimately social too. When people criticise a variety of language, they may really be expressing distrust or distaste for something about the people who use that variety, or the context it has come from.

Within British studies on accent and dialect, the Birmingham variety is routinely rated low. Participants in studies often place this accent at the bottom when rating speakers for attractiveness, intelligence, likelihood of having a good job, level of education and similar factors. In the British media, the Birmingham accent is rarely represented positively, and is often given to comedic and low-status characters. Conversely, when US English speakers are given UK accents to rate, they do not make the same judgments. The Birmingham accent is received more positively, due in part to its melodic qualities, but also because the people being questioned lack the contextual information and existing associations that British people have. This demonstrates that people are unable to separate social values from language, and also that there is often no linguistic reason for the judgments we make. It is only tradition and history that tells us that 'I never done nothing' is 'worse' English than 'I didn't do anything'.

Activity 1

What non-linguistic attitudes are likely to lie behind prescriptivist, negative attitudes to 'outer circle' basilect varieties such as Singlish? How are these attitudes likely to be different for people in different contexts, for example those having a different status or performing different roles?

In global English, just as in other areas of spoken language, the following tension is at the core:

```
Correctness  ⟹   On the one hand, English – and        On the other hand, home         ⟸   Heritage
and prestige     especially more standard               languages have emotional power        and identity
                 varieties – have prestige and are      and are associated with people's
                 believed to be correct. People         identity and heritage. People do
                 want their children to use it in        not want their children cut off
                 order to progress, particularly in      from their culture, which is what
                 terms of education or career.           would happen if they grew up
                                                         speaking only English.
```

Activity 2

What does 'standard' mean? What about 'standards'? Think about all the uses of these words and note down everything you can think of. When you have exhausted all your ideas, check in a dictionary and thesaurus to get all the definitions and connotations of these two words. Which of all the possible meanings are carried in the phrase 'Standard English'?

Colonial policies and lasting attitudes

During the period of colonialism, Empire countries were governed by Britain and therefore their administrations were run in English. English was often the only language spoken fluently by the ruling class in countries such as Nigeria and India. Britons had settled to work in these countries, taking on administrative government roles and imposed English as a superior or more 'civilised' language for formal state-run education, as well as managing all central administrative and legislative work in English. These policies effectively imposed English on the population at large, making essential services inaccessible to anyone unable to speak it. Education policies such as beating children who spoke local languages in class were common as recently as the late 20th century.

   Read Text 3, which is from a speech by a Scottish and Sierra Leonean writer, Aminatta Forna (pictured right). In it, she discusses the effect of colonialism on literature, and how writers can work to address the imbalance that exists in representation.

Text 3

For the first generation of African writers who came of age at the same time as their countries, this meant writing Africans into a full existence. For Chinua Achebe, writing *Things Fall Apart* meant challenging Joseph Conrad's portrayal of grunting, non-verbal Africans in *Heart of Darkness*, giving his characters the interior lives and relationships, conflicts and flaws – the very agency and subjectivity that Conrad had denied them. For Ngũgũ wa Thiong'o it meant retrieving his Kikuyu language, the language he had been beaten for speaking as a child undergoing colonial instruction. "I began to write because I did not see myself in literature, and I wanted to see myself there," said Tsitsi Dangarembga, the Zimbabwean novelist, for the western gaze had passed completely over the heads of black and African women.

   From a keynote speech given by Aminatta Forna to the African Studies Association, 17 February 2017

Activity 3

Why would literature written in global Englishes and local languages be important in post-colonial countries? What do you learn about language in Africa under colonial rule from Text 3?

Good English, bad English

Many criticisms of varieties of global English are made on the grounds that they are 'bad' English, citing grammatical irregularities or lexical usages that deviate from Standard English. However, many non-standard features of global Englishes follow more regularised patterns and structures than Standard English, making this criticism hard to justify, especially when users have no problems communicating. For example, in Singlish, yes-no questions can be made by adding 'or not' to the end of a positive sentence, or 'is it' to the end of a negative one (in place of Standard English subject-verb inversion or use of 'do'):

- *You want this one, or not?*
- *I can have this, or not?*
- *You never visit, is it?*
- *He doesn't like that, is it?*

Sometimes, however, the very simplicity of these regularised structures leads critics to present these varieties as unsophisticated or even childish.

Another strand of criticism is slightly more complex: criticism that looks like it is trying to help the speaker, such as comments like: 'You'll never get a job if you speak like that'. In this version of prescriptivism, people are still reacting negatively to the way others speak, and still trying to change it – but here it contains an element of generosity. This is more of a social argument, and it wraps the linguistic criticism up in concerns about basilect users' prospects. This could be as straightforwardly ambitious as a parent expressing 'I want you to get a job, so you need to speak well', or it could be more subtly expressed by a government or social programme intended to 'improve' or 'develop' the nation.

Key term

sociolect continuum: the arrangement of sociolects by degree, usually from the standard variety to a non-standard variety; a person will use language from different points along the continuum at different times

Case study: **Singlish and the Speak Good English Movement**

Singlish is a creole variety which draws from a wide range of local languages, including Malay, Hokkien, Cantonese and Tamil as well as English. This creates a complex hybrid, which is stigmatised in Singapore and generally viewed as a low variety, especially since the launch of the Speak Good English Movement in 2000 by then prime minister of Singapore, Goh Chok Tong to promote the use of Standard English and discourage Singlish. Since then, various workshops and programmes, as well as writing and speaking competitions, have been run to further this aim with a re-launch of the movement annually.

Singlish has been used along a **sociolect continuum** with Standard English since the introduction of English to Singapore in the early 19th century. This means that many Singaporeans will code-switch between different degrees of English and Singlish in their speech. For example, teenagers may use full formal Standard English in lessons at school or college, while speaking full Singlish in social contexts with friends and something in between with relatives, who may also encourage the use of more standard forms.

The Speak Good English Movement has been controversial since its inception and a counter-movement, Save Our Singlish, was launched in 2010. This campaign states that it is not opposed to the Speak Good English Movement, but that subtler understanding of when to use English and when to use Singlish needs to inform it, rather than simply being anti-Singlish. Save Our Singlish is opposed to the representation of Singlish as 'bad' or 'broken' English.

Activity 4

Look at the statements below, taken from people's Twitter feeds. For each statement, how would you classify the attitude to Singlish? How is Singlish being represented?

> It's kinda bad, I am too fluent in Singlish that I can't speak proper English.
>
> 👤₊ Follow

> I should stop my Singlish/ Chinglish way of speaking before its get worse.
>
> 👤₊ Follow

> So apparently, there are a total of 27 Singlish words that are officially in the Oxford English Dictionary (OED).
>
> 👤₊ Follow

> well... i don't know for certain for all singaporeans but we are able to switch off the singlish.
> i don't think the way you speak with your friends is the same way that you speak when you are having your oral exam, debate or having a presentation in school.
>
> 👤₊ Follow

> im glad i dont use singlish at home
>
> 👤₊ Follow

Heritage and identity

Nelson Mandela said: 'If you talk to a man in a language he understands, that goes to his head. If you talk to him in his language, that goes to his heart.' Language acts strongly on our emotions. It is also a core part of our identity. In many 'outer circle' countries, where English is spoken alongside other languages, it is usually the more functional and less emotional of those languages. A 'home' or 'community' language is typically the native tongue and English is learned for practical purposes. For these speakers, although English possesses a rich cultural heritage of its own, that heritage is not theirs and so they may not feel connected to it.

Activity 5

Cultural heritage includes literature written in the language, but also oral history and heritage such as nursery rhymes, myths, legends and folklore.

a) What experience of these do you have in English and/or in other languages?

b) In what ways is this heritage important in your use of the language(s)? Can you think of specific recent examples of drawing on it? How often do you think you do that?

The ideal of peace and harmony

There is an argument that if everyone spoke one language, we would all understand one another and there would be no more wars. Esperanto, a European **conlang** (constructed language) based on Romance and Slavic languages, was created between 1870 and 1887 by a Polish-Jewish ophthalmologist named L. L. Zamenhof for this reason. The idea was that sharing a single language would help everyone to share a single outlook and perspective on life, and thus reduce conflict.

Read Text 4 overleaf, a review of a book about the influence of US English on the UK variety.

Key term

conlang: a blend of 'constructed language' – a deliberately invented language, usually created either for political reasons (e.g. Esperanto) or within a novel or series (e.g. Tolkien's Elvish)

Text 4

That's the Way It Crumbles: The American Conquest of English by Matthew Engel – review

Matthew Engel urges us to hang tough against Americanisms in this entertaining history of linguistic imperialism

Toilet training: is nowhere safe from the Americanisms that have been polluting our language for years?

I worked for a few years in my 20s at the literary quarterly Granta. The magazine had been a very English institution, based in Cambridge, until it was successfully hijacked by a bullish and bearded American graduate student, Bill Buford, who had arrived at the university via Louisiana and California to help edit Shakespeare, and was looking for an excuse to stay on. I became his deputy. As a former linebacker in American college football, Buford was not always the easiest man to argue with, but when it came to questions of written style the British contingent in the office attempted to mount occasional rearguard actions.

Mostly, we followed English linguistic conventions and spelling in the magazine, but on a few issues Buford was entirely intransigent. One of these […] was the word "aeroplane". Every time it cropped up in a story – which was quite often since Granta became famous for reinventing "travel writing" – Buford would score it out fiercely, and replace it with the American "airplane" in blunt pencil. Debates over this stubborn incongruity in the mouths of English writers were long and heated, and often carried on into the pub next to the office. Buford's argument was that the ancient Greek prefix cast a typical British snobbery over what was essentially a thrusting American invention. He scoffed at our effete defences and, as editor, always prevailed.

I was reminded of those failed crusades reading Matthew Engel's typically erudite history of the battle between American English and its quaint English forebear in the ongoing war of common usage. "It's time to tell the whole story of this long campaign," Engel suggests, "from the get-go."

That story begins in 1533. The first word to enter the lexicon from the New World, was "guaiacum" which, appropriately enough, as it went viral, was the bark of a Haitian tree that was believed to be a cure for syphilis. "Tobacco" followed, literally and linguistically, along with the Spanish **bowdlerisms**, tomato, potato, chocolate, mosquito and cockroach. These imports were just the beginning, but it wasn't until independence that the real schisms began.

The prime mover of this split was the mischief-making grammarian Noah Webster, who, asked by Benjamin Franklin to prevent the spread of "Americanisms" in America, and keep close to the mother tongue, did precisely the opposite. Webster argued that if independence were to make sense politically, it should be enshrined in language. Webster believed, Engel suggests, that "American and English would drift apart to become as different as Dutch and German" and he stepped up to the plate to accelerate that process. Webster's dictionary of the "English language" in 1806 transposed the endings of "theater" and "center", insisting this was a purer form, untainted by French influence. He did a similar trick with "color", "honor", "labor" and "flavor", not to mention "defense" and "offense".

From *The Guardian*, 3 July 2017

Glossary:
bowdlerism: corrupted language forms (after Bowdler's practice of spoiling literary works by removing passages or words regarded as indecent)

Activity 6

To what extent does the argument in this text support the idea of US English infiltrating the UK variety? What are your views on this claim? Give evidence to support your ideas.

There are links here to the idea of language and identity, which is discussed in detail in Unit 8.3.

Final task

Find an article or collection of articles from local or national press that explore language issues in your country or local area. What concerns are raised? What debates exist near you? Get to know what the issues are for English (and any other languages used) in your country, so that you can confidently discuss the situation in your specific context. Make sure you consider the following:

- What attitude does the government seem to have?
- What policies (if any) exist in schools?
- How do people talk about language issues in the newspapers? What representations of language(s) are created?
- If different languages are used in your country, or clearly different varieties of English, how are users of those languages/varieties represented?
- How are debates about these issues typically framed (e.g. as concern for people's prospects, simply good/bad English or something else)?

Extension: Look at articles from another English-speaking country for comparison, researching the same issues.

7.4 Debating English in the world

**How is global English discussed in the world?
How do linguists explore the issues?**

Global English in the media

Issues surrounding English in the world are discussed in many media contexts. Specific countries' issues can be found debated in their national newspapers, such as whether there should be language policies, what the language of instruction should be in schools, colleges and universities, and even what kinds of language should be used in the media. However, all these issues are also discussed in a wider context, because issues in English — whether it is Singaporean English, Nigerian English or Texan English — are felt to affect English around the world.

Read Text 5, an opinion piece on English in South Africa.

Text 5

Country is caught up in a rip tide of English

OPPORTUNITY: There are 11 official languages in South Africa. If implemented more widely, they would open countless doors, the writers say.

February ought to be a joyful month for South African languages. It's been declared "language activism month" by the Pan South African Languages Board, a constitutionally established body tasked with the promotion and development of the 11 official languages, as well as those recognised for religious and cultural purposes. The idea is to encourage people to promote and campaign actively for the use of the country's 11 official languages in all disciplines across society.

Instead of celebrating its official languages, though, South Africa is caught in a rip current of English. This is sweeping the country further away from accepting, promoting and advancing the use of the other 10 languages.

Recently a group of parents took the Gauteng province's education department to court because of language.

They wanted their children to be accommodated in the Afrikaans-medium school and for the school to change its language of instruction to English. The parents and learners in question do not necessarily speak English as their mother tongue. But they fought for English, rather than an African language.

This is what South Africa's former Deputy Chief Justice Dikgang Moseneke, ruling in another case related to a school's language of instruction, called "collateral irony". People who speak an African language at home prefer that their children learn in English – with its long colonial history – than in their own mother tongues.

We believe there are two reasons for this. The first is political will. There's been insufficient buy-in from the government about the importance of developing, promoting and using African languages, particularly in education. Second, ordinary South Africans are ill-informed about the advantages of mother tongue being used as the medium of instruction.

Those responsible for drawing up language policies and curricula must be aware of what scholar Richard Ruí, who spearheaded a revitalisation of indigenous South American languages, calls the orientations of language planning.

There are three orientations: language as a problem, language as a right and language as a resource.

Part of South Africa's challenge is that language, and in particular multilingualism, is generally seen as a problem rather than as a rich resource. Several other African countries view their indigenous languages as resources: Kiswahili in Kenya, Tanzania and Uganda and Afan-Oromo in Ethiopia are all good examples of this. And some small corners of South Africa are getting it right; isiXhosa is used to teach maths and science in the Cofimvaba district of the Eastern Cape.

If the country's policymakers, politicians and ordinary citizens understood this it would open innumerable doors. It would create opportunities for language development and greater access to services – from government departments, courts of law, hospitals, banks and so on. This in turn would provide many new job opportunities for African language speakers.

From IOL, 22 February 2018

Studying and researching global English issues

Linguistic researchers explore variation in language by examining how people use language in as natural a setting as possible, controlling variables and exploring the features of their languages. For example, you could:

- record teachers booking in at a conference to examine pragmatics (the variables are relatively controlled by the fact that the subjects are all teachers; however there are variables in terms of age, gender, and so on, which may affect behaviour)
- interview teenagers in a multilingual setting to explore code-switching (variables are more tightly controlled here, and it would be easy to record and compare gender differences, but the situation is less natural – it would be important to ensure that conversation flows easily, by selecting topics for discussion carefully).

Linguists investigate global varieties in different places in a range of ways, but in order to explicitly compare different global varieties, you would need to either physically travel to different places to record people, or use internet data. The benefit of internet data (such as social media) is that it has been produced for a purpose and is not influenced by the researcher. If, on the other hand, you interview somebody or set up a conversational scenario to record them, however much you get the conversation flowing and natural-seeming, they are always aware of your presence and of the artificial nature of the situation.

Activity 1

Answer the following questions about Text 5.

a) According to the writer, what are the three ways language planning can be conceptualised?

b) What does the article identify as South Africa's mistake?

c) What do you understand by the other two ways of conceptualising language planning not further detailed here?

Extension: How is English represented in this article?

Activity 2

How might you try to capture and analyse the features of your local colloquial variety of English? How would you get people comfortable enough to talk casually in that variety? Would you try to use an existing context or set up a scenario?

Key term

Received Pronunciation: a specific refined accent of British English associated with the upper class and private education, sometimes colloquially known as the Queen's English or BBC English

Case study: **Giles's work on attitudes**

In 1974, Howard Giles completed a considerable amount of work on attitudes to different varieties of British English, developing a method called 'matched guise'. This involved using a speaker who was competent in two different dialects, usually **Received Pronunciation** (RP or the 'Queen's English') and another, local accent. He would record audio of this one person reading the same material in both their accents and then ask people to rate the two recordings (pretending it was two speakers) for a range of qualities such as intellect, education, friendliness, trustworthiness, and so on. The 'guise' was 'matched' because it was the same person – so he had absolute control of the variables; the subjects had no reason to judge the recordings differently except for the accent used.

In a development of this, Giles carried out an experiment known as the 'capital punishment study'. Students were asked their views on capital punishment before being given a presentation on it in one of five versions (RP, South Wales, Somerset, Birmingham, printed text only). They were asked how impressive they found the presentation and their views were sought again. Interestingly, those hearing RP and those reading the text found the presentation most impressive. Those hearing regional voices were more likely to change their views based on what they heard. This demonstrated that language variety can affect people even when they think they are not impressed by it.

Final task

What would you research in global English, given free rein? Design a project to explore any variety you like. Possible angles include:

- comparison over time
- investigating official and popular attitudes towards it
- exploring its representation and use in literature
- describing its features and comparing them to the local Standard English.

End-of-chapter task

Look back at Text 4, the review of a book called *That's the Way It Crumbles: The American Conquest of English* by Matthew Engel.

How are issues regarding English in the world presented in the article? You should:

- analyse the representation of the English language
- analyse the representation of Americanisms and the US
- discuss how these representations relate to linguistic issues.

Language and the self

This chapter follows two different strands in exploring connections between personal identity and language. Firstly, you will have the opportunity to investigate language and the self from a psycholinguistic perspective, considering how far language as a human trait is innate or learned, and exploring the relationship between language and thought. Secondly, you will look at personal identity from a sociolinguistic angle, thinking about the various aspects of identity that people can express through different forms of language. The final unit in this chapter considers the ways in which language can be, and has been, studied and discussed in terms of these topics, and asks you to look at some data and key areas of debate around language and the self.

Two key concepts are considered in this chapter. The first centres around language in the broader *context* of the sciences and human knowledge. The second is the idea of *diversity* in speech, as identity impacts upon language in a multitude of ways.

8.1 Language and learning

To what extent is language innate or learned? How would we know?

Language as human

A key part of nativist thinking is that language is essentially a trait that is specific to humans. There have been attempts to teach other species – particularly other primates – to communicate using sign language or symbols, but the results have never reached anything like the complexity of human language. Key reasons for this are:

- human anatomy can produce finer distinctions of sound than other animals, allowing for greater range in vocalisations
- humans appear to be capable of more abstract thought, which we want to share through language; animal communication is focused on the physical and the immediate.

Activity 1

What have you done with language today? Think about the conversations you have had and situations you have been in, and try to put them in the following categories (with finer details) in a list or mind map to show what you have accomplished using language in the past 24 hours:

- asked for help, advice or information
- described something that you saw or experienced but someone else did not
- explained how to do something
- explained your personal thoughts or opinions to someone else
- gave advice or recommendations
- introduced yourself or presented your skills or abilities
- narrated a story
- negotiated to make practical arrangements
- provided factual information.

Many of the ways in which we use language are abstract and complex, representing ideas and objects beyond the immediate. If you were to track the way you use language in real-time over a 24-hour period, it is likely that only a small proportion of it would deal with immediate concerns such as food and shelter. How does this relate to your thoughts on Activity 1, for example? Most of our discussions are less survival-based in intent, such as discussing hypothetical situations or popular culture. Even when they are focused on the real world, conversations are more likely to be concerned with the future or the past (or with remote locations – or even with fictional worlds) than with what is happening in the present. Thinking – and talking – about the future and the past requires a conceptual leap that many animals may not be capable of, beyond repeated searching for food in the same locations.

Ways of thinking about language and learning

Two key philosophical approaches to learning underpin the way psychologists and linguists consider language as a human trait: empiricism and innatism.

- **Empiricism** is based on the idea that a baby is born as a 'blank slate' with everything to learn; all knowledge is derived from experience, which is gained through the senses. Empiricism is associated with the theories of John Locke, David Hume and George Berkely. It became particularly prevalent in the 17th and 18th centuries.
- **Innatism** is the basic idea that humans have some key knowledge or abilities at birth.

Linked to these two broad philosophical approaches are the two schools of linguistic thought known as behaviourism and nativism, which emerged in the 20th century.

Taking things further

Innatism is linked to Plato's idea of universals and Descartes' theory of concept of thought. Find out more about these ideas and bear them in mind as you consider the discussion of innatism that follows.

Case study: **Apes and language**

The brains of apes are more similar than other animals' to human brains, so apes have been the focus of several experiments in teaching animals to use language. Apes cannot truly speak, because they are unable to produce sufficiently varied vocalisations, so researchers use sign language or symbols.

One well-known case is of Kanzi, a type of ape called a bonobo, who has been the focus of research at the Language Learning Center at Georgia State University. He has been taught to communicate using a keyboard of symbols. He has learned to combine symbols using 'proto-syntax' (his vocabulary consists of lexical words so this is a telegraphic style of syntax, omitting function words like toddlers' early sentences) and produces sentences in this way. He is able to communicate some social and more complex ideas such as 'bad' and 'now', as well as making requests relating to immediate desires such as food. However, his learning has not been the same as that of a human. A human child finds new words increasingly easy to acquire; for Kanzi, each new word is as difficult to learn as the one before.

Another famous case is that of Washoe, a chimpanzee who could use American Sign Language (ASL). She was able to label around 250 different objects and make some basic requests and comments by combining signs, such as 'please tickle' and 'me sorry'. Her adopted daughter, Loulis, who spent no time with human signers, learned around 70 signs directly from Washoe.

Activity 2

How do the cases of Washoe and Kanzi support empiricist ideas, of language as learned, or the view of innateness – that is, of language as something that is *natural* to humans? Think about:

- what in these cases supports the idea that not only humans can learn language
- what about these cases implies that there is something special about human language that cannot be transferred to animals.

What is your opinion on the 'innateness' of language at this point? Do you think we are innately equipped for language or do we start learning from the position of a 'blank slate' at birth?

Behaviourism

Building on the empiricists' idea of the 'blank slate' (or *tabula rasa*) that people are presumed to be at birth, behaviourists treat all learning as derived from the environment and reinforced through feedback. This applies to language, which is considered an aspect of behaviour rather than a unique aspect of human identity.

Behaviourists believe it is significant that other species can learn to associate particular outcomes with particular stretches of sound or even symbols or gestures – that is, they can learn the meanings of some words and phrases. This clearly demonstrates that language is a behaviour that can be learned. The fact that humans learn it in a much more complex way than apes is not surprising – this is true of many other aspects of human behaviour or understanding, such as the use of tools; other animals may use tools but they do so in a much simpler way.

Behaviourists' work is often concerned with isolating environmental stimuli and reinforcements in order to determine what associations have led to a particular behaviour. If we get social rules wrong, we do not get the response from others that we want, so we soon learn not to behave in that way again. For example, no one explicitly teaches us the rules for greetings or leave-taking, yet they clearly exist. They can be quite complex, and if you break them, people may give you negative feedback in the form of an odd look or a hesitant reply. These rules may also vary between cultures – even cultures that share a language. For example, here are some UK greeting rules:

- 'Hello' is acceptable at any time of day and in any context.
- 'Pleased to meet you' is a formal greeting for all times.
- 'Hi' is an informal greeting for all times.
- 'Good morning' is only reasonable in the morning, the first time you see someone that day; it is often abbreviated to 'morning' for informality.
- 'Good evening' is acceptable in the evening, and could be a greeting or a leave-taking.
- 'Good night' is not used as a greeting, but only as a leave-taking at the end of an evening or when going to bed.

According to the behaviourist model, people learn these complex rules by noting how others follow them, and/or by receiving feedback – perhaps by causing confusion through using the wrong register of greeting, or by using 'good night' to say hello at an evening event. This negative feedback teaches us not to do that again, so we eventually get everything right.

Activity 3

What are the rules for leaving a conversation? Pay attention to at least two conversations among different groups and notice how people leave the conversation. How many times and in how many different ways is leave-taking initiated? What role do you think context plays in this (for example, the relationship between participants, the location, the type/purpose of the conversation)? If possible, compare your findings from real conversations with representations on television. How do they differ? Why do you think that might be?

Nativism

Nativism flows from the ideas of innatism, which claims that humans are born with certain capabilities and pre-existing skills. One of these innate skills is language competence. Early innatists were mostly concerned with the idea that it was *thought* that separated humans from other creatures, but nativism began to focus specifically on language. The problem that nativists have with behaviourism is based on the sheer complexity of language – learning it from scratch seems like an impossible task without any innate competence. Chomsky believed that languages around the world have too many things in common for there not to be something innate in human consciousness that contributes to language. He spent a large part of his career exploring 'linguistic universals' – the patterns that link languages – and trying to define 'universal grammar'.

Read Text 1 below, which discusses two prominent nativists' attitudes towards the bonobo Kanzi's facility with language.

Text 1

Criticism

Although Kanzi seems to make a powerful case for the claim that some nonhuman animals are capable of learning language, Pinker and Chomsky, among others, remain unconvinced. According to Pinker, Kanzi's performance is "analogous to the bears in the Moscow circus who are trained to ride unicycles." Kanzi, he insists, does not understand the symbols he uses and is simply reacting in ways he knows will elicit food or other rewards from his trainers. Chomsky, in an interview, characterized the attempt to teach language to the great apes as a kind of "fanaticism." Apes can talk in exactly the sense in which human beings can fly. "Humans can fly about 30 feet—that's what they do in the Olympics. Is that flying? The question is totally meaningless." Although Pinker and Chomsky disagree about which of the innate cognitive systems that underlie language use are unique to humans and whether such systems could have undergone evolutionary development, they both maintain that only Homo sapiens possesses the systems and neural structures that are essential to knowing a language.

From *Advocacy for Animals*, 26 November 2007

Activity 4

What exactly does Text 1 present as nativist views on apes using language?
Why and how do Chomsky and Pinker present their ideas on apes' speech?

Case study: **The KE family**

The FOXP2 gene is a gene that has specific responsibilities for speech and language. Its discovery in the 1990s caused considerable excitement among scientists looking for a genetic reason why humans have language while other species do not.

Investigations into speech disabilities affecting three generations of a particular family (given the designation the 'KE family') determined that their difficulties with grammar were caused by a genetic mutation on the FOXP2 gene. MRI scans also showed differences in brain activity when compared to the brains of other members of the family with 'normal' speech. Interestingly, one of these differences was increased activity in Broca's area – a part of the brain associated with speech production, and one which, if damaged by stroke, for example, causes speech and language problems.

Final task

Using the information in this unit, present the central ideas of behaviourism and nativism in a mind map or similar diagram. What supporting evidence or ideas can you add to each school of thought from your own knowledge of language? Which ideas make sense to you? You may wish to refer back to child language acquisition theories, or conduct wider research on how language seems to be innate or learned.

8.2 Language and thought

What is the relationship between language and thought? To what extent is each dependent on the other?

How do we think?

A considerable amount of psycholinguistic study and effort has gone into the question of the relationship between language and thought. We still know relatively little about the workings of the human brain, although we can now identify some specific areas that are associated with language: Broca's area and Wernicke's area. These are broadly associated with speech production and reception respectively, but it is more complex than this. People with injuries to these areas may still have some speech, and individuals with injuries to other parts of the brain have been known to lose aspects of speech. There is still a lot we do not know about the physical connections between language and the brain.

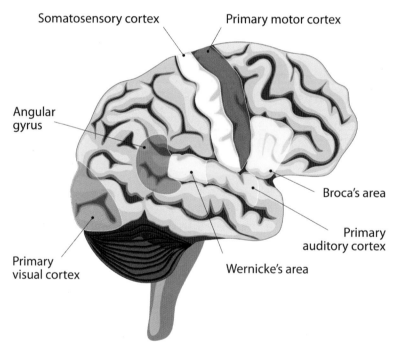

However, more abstract ideas about the link between language and thought have been discussed by philosophers for many years – since long before psycholinguistics was recognised as a discipline. It can be dated to the 17th century, and Descartes' famous declaration of thought as central to human identity: 'I think, therefore I am.' Key questions to consider here include the following:

- Can you/do you ever think without or outside of language?
  - o Do you ever find it hard to put your thoughts into words to explain them to others?
  - o Are your thoughts ever visual? Do you ever hear your thoughts?

- Does (or can) language exist separately from human thought?
  - o What would that mean?
  - o Can a language exist without anyone thinking it?
  - o Do we speak without thinking first?
  - o To what extent can language be outside of us?
- Does the language available to us affect the way we are able to think?
  - o If we had a different vocabulary, might we be able to think differently?
  - o If you speak more than one language, are you aware of which language you think in, or does it change depending on circumstances?

Activity 1

Note down answers to the questions above. Do not simply answer yes or no; try to think of examples or scenarios that might support your ideas. These are questions that have been discussed by philosophers for centuries, so do not think that you should have an answer immediately. A 'maybe' or 'it depends' with specific context may be more appropriate!

Linguistic universalism

There are two main theories to consider in this topic, which take broadly opposing views on the relationship between language and reality: linguistic universalism and linguistic relativity.

Linguistic universalism is the concept that ideas are shared between languages, because reality is constant. As well as linguistic universals (such as most languages having something like nouns, something like verbs, and so on), there are other points of comparison. This is because around the globe, people try to express similar ideas – we all live in the same world and experience it in similar ways. This theory is associated mostly with the ideas of Noam Chomsky, under the heading of 'universal grammar'.

Linguistic relativity

Linguistic relativity is the idea that the specific language people speak affects their experience of the world, because everything is relative. For example, if two languages do not express time in the same way, people who speak those languages will not experience time in the same way.

This theory is particularly associated with Benjamin Whorf, a student of Edward Sapir, who formed the Sapir-Whorf Hypothesis in 1956. Also known as 'linguistic determinism', this is the idea that language determines reality. The 'strong' version of the hypothesis (which few experts now agree with) claims that the language someone speaks *absolutely controls* the way they experience the world. The 'weak' version maintains that the language someone speaks, and the resulting vocabulary and structures they have access to, *influences their understanding* of the world. For the relativist or determinist, therefore, language affects reality.

Various studies in comparative linguistics have been carried out to test linguistic relativity. Results include the following:

- People tend to experience colour in the same way (controlling for colour blindness), even though languages have different systems for labelling colours, varying on a scale from two main descriptors (light/dark) up to 11, as in English. People all use longer descriptions to go beyond the basic

Taking things further

Find out more about the connection between language and the experience of time. For example, most people who speak Proto-Indo-European-derived languages experience time in a linear way, while it is experienced in more of a cyclical mode for Uto-Aztecan-derived languages such as Hopi.

labels, and there is less agreement between individuals once you move away from the standard/basic/central labels in any language, as descriptions become more individualised.

- Depending on the gender of nouns in languages that use grammatical gender (such as French, German and Russian), people tend to choose different adjectives to describe the physical objects. For example, in a language that designates 'bridge' as a masculine word, words used to describe bridges tended to be more masculine adjectives such as 'strong' or 'sturdy'. Speakers of a language in which 'bridge' is a feminine noun, however, tended to describe bridges using adjectives such as 'elegant' or 'slender'.

Activity 2

a) How would you label these 11 colours? If you are bilingual, what are they called in your other language?

Colours

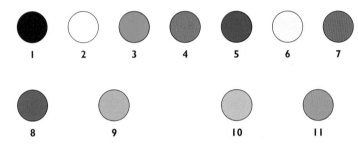

b) What about these 11 colours?

Colours

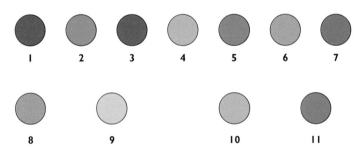

c) Now ask at least five other people to label these colours. Do you get the same results from everyone? Do you notice any patterns in your data?

d) Find out about colour terms in other languages. You could start by looking at Russian and Welsh, then look for some minority languages such as a Native American, Aboriginal Australian or Pacific Island language to see how they describe colours.

Read Text 2 opposite, an extract from an article by cognitive scientist Lera Boroditsky, in which she introduces her work on linguistic relativity.

Text 2

How Does Our Language Shape the Way We Think?

Follow me to Pormpuraaw, a small Aboriginal community on the western edge of Cape York, in northern Australia. I came here because of the way the locals, the Kuuk Thaayorre, talk about space. Instead of words like "right," "left," "forward," and "back," which, as commonly used in English, define space relative to an observer, the Kuuk Thaayorre, like many other Aboriginal groups, use cardinal-direction terms – north, south, east, and west – to define space. This is done at all scales, which means you have to say things like "There's an ant on your southeast leg" or "Move the cup to the north northwest a little bit." One obvious consequence of speaking such a language is that you have to stay oriented at all times, or else you cannot speak properly. The normal greeting in Kuuk Thaayorre is "Where are you going?" and the answer should be something like "Southsoutheast, in the middle distance." If you don't know which way you're facing, you can't even get past "Hello."

The result is a profound difference in navigational ability and spatial knowledge between speakers of languages that rely primarily on absolute reference frames (like Kuuk Thaayorre) and languages that rely on relative reference frames (like English). Simply put, speakers of languages like Kuuk Thaayorre are much better than English speakers at staying oriented and keeping track of where they are, even in unfamiliar landscapes or inside unfamiliar buildings. What enables them – in fact, forces them – to do this is their language. Having their attention trained in this way equips them to perform navigational feats once thought beyond human capabilities. Because space is such a fundamental domain of thought, differences in how people think about space don't end there. People rely on their spatial knowledge to build other, more complex, more abstract representations. Representations of such things as time, number, musical pitch, kinship relations, morality and emotions have been shown to depend on how we think about space. So if the Kuuk Thaayorre think differently about space, do they also think differently about other things, like time? This is what my collaborator Alice Gaby and I came to Pormpuraaw to find out.

To test this idea, we gave people sets of pictures that showed some kind of temporal progression (for example, pictures of a man aging, or a crocodile growing, or a banana being eaten). Their job was to arrange the shuffled photos on the ground to show the correct temporal order. We tested each person in two separate sittings, each time facing in a different cardinal direction. If you ask English speakers to do this, they'll arrange the cards so that time proceeds from left to right. Hebrew speakers will tend to lay out the cards from right to left, showing that writing direction in a language plays a role. So what about folks like the Kuuk Thaayorre, who don't use words like "left" and "right"? What will they do?

The Kuuk Thaayorre did not arrange the cards more often from left to right than from right to left, nor more toward or away from the body. But their arrangements were not random: there was a pattern, just a different one from that of English speakers. Instead of arranging time from left to right, they arranged it from east to west. That is, when they were seated facing south, the cards went left to right. When they faced north, the cards went from right to left. When they faced east, the cards came toward the body and so on. This was true even though we never told any of our subjects which direction they faced. The Kuuk Thaayorre not only knew that already (usually much better than I did), but they also spontaneously used this spatial orientation to construct their representations of time.

From Edge.org, 6 November 2009

Activity 3

a) How does Boroditsky's account of Kuuk Thaayorre show a relationship between language and thought?

b) How is time represented in the language(s) you know? Think of the metaphors people use (for example, 'the past is behind us' – is the past ever represented as anywhere but behind in English?).

c) Why do you think linguistic determinism – the idea that our language governs or determines our thoughts absolutely – is now viewed mostly negatively? If language controls how we think, what limits does that create? How might linguistic relativity as an idea offer more flexibility?

Key term

political correctness: the idea that language and actions that might be considered offensive to others should be avoided, particularly with regard to race or gender

Activity 4

The Sapir-Whorf Hypothesis can be said to underlie the concept of **political correctness**, or the project of replacing language that is outdated and offensive in its representation with new, more neutral labels.

Explain the conceptual relationship between the Sapir-Whorf Hypothesis and the aim of political correctness. You may find it useful to include examples of politically correct terms.

A middle ground?

Although the theories of universalism and relativity oppose each other, it is possible to argue that both views offer truth.

It is clear that there are universal elements of human experience, such as sensory information and the act of thought itself. It is also clear that we all process many of our thoughts using language, although there are times when it can be difficult to explain our thoughts to another person, which implies that thought comes before language. At the same time, language can and frequently does influence people's perception of reality, as the existence of persuasive language and rhetorical technique attests.

Case study: **Eyewitness testimony research**

Further evidence can be found in psychological research into eyewitness testimony. An example of this is research carried out by Elizabeth Loftus, who found that people's perception of a car's speed appeared to be influenced by the choice of verb in a question. Test subjects were shown a video of a car accident and were then asked a series of questions. Different people received different versions of questions to test the idea that language could influence the result.

		Average speed response	Percentage saying they saw glass on the road* (not all participants were asked this)
Approximately how fast were the cars going when they…	contacted?	31.8 mph	
	hit?	34.0 mph	14%
	bumped?	38.1 mph	
	collided?	39.3 mph	
	smashed?	40.8 mph	32%
(no speed question asked)			12%

*There was no glass on the road

Loftus's research shows a clearly demonstrable effect on people's perceptions with only the wording of the questions they were asked being changed.

The language of thought hypothesis

Conceived in the late 1970s by US philosopher Jerry Fodor, the language of thought hypothesis suggests that thinking has its own language, known as 'mentalese'. The hypothesis has been tested in various empirical studies, with mixed results. Some linguists believe that our private language – the language we think in – is the same as our public language – the one we speak. Others are interested in the idea that thought is possible in those without a public language, such as pre-verbal babies. One group of particular interest in terms of mentalese is in Deaf people who have not learned an official sign language – known as homesigners. Some adults in this group were able to communicate with other homesigners and hearing people, and to do so to express abstract concepts as well as to discuss immediate needs. This demonstrated clear cognitive activity despite having learned no language.

Final task

Imagine there is going to be a debate in your school or college on the topic of language and thought, with both universalist and relativist speakers. Write the text of a flyer (approximately 350 words) to advertise this debate to students and the local community. You will need to:

- introduce the key ideas
- use the structure and form of a flyer/leaflet
- use persuasive techniques
- be impartial.

8.3 Language and personal identity

How do different aspects of people's identity affect their language?

Social groups and language

We all have our own individual way of speaking, known as our **idiolect**. This is influenced by a range of factors, including the social groups we belong to, each of which may collectively be described as having a **sociolect**. People can be grouped according to different classification systems, several of which will be explored in this unit, and all of which, arguably, have some impact on people's use of language.

Key terms

idiolect: an individual's personal style of speech

sociolect: a non-standard variety of language spoken by a particular social group

Activity 1

Which aspects of your identity affect your language? For example, you may be aware of using particular words and phrases that are influenced by your friendship group, or a particular pronunciation that is specific to your area.

Two key theories surrounding how groups influence and affect an individual's language are explored below.

Social network theory

According to social network theory, some types of network are particularly efficient at reinforcing non-standard uses of language. These networks need to be 'dense' in order to achieve this. Density is described in terms of the following:

- **multiplexity:** people within the network have many things in common (for example, they work together, live near each other, are related, spend social time together); a multiplex (as opposed to uniplex) network is dense
- **connections between participants:** people within the network all know each other in a dense network (that is, person A is linked to person B and C; person B is linked to person A and C).

Loose, open networks (where person A knows person B and C, but person B knows person A and person D, and person C knows person A and person E) are less likely to maintain non-standard language. This may be because a dense network (where everybody knows everybody else and they share multiple connections) has less need to communicate with the 'outside world'. This means it is easier to maintain inside jokes and for features such as accent to get stronger.

Activity 2

Map out a social network of your closest 10–15 connections. First, list the people you spend most time with. Then, make a mind map of those people around your name, connecting any names who also know each other. Draw additional lines to show where you have more than one link to a person, and write the connection along the line (for example, they are in your class and you play on a sports team with them). Do the same for links between others. If you can, add more connections, working in order of the people you spend most time with (whether that's virtual time or real time).

How dense does your network appear to be? Are there areas where you can already identify shared language links (for example, in-jokes/references, common lexis, **accent**/**dialect**/sociolect)?

Community of practice

Another useful concept is that of a 'community of practice'. This is a group of people joined by something they do – a practice. That may be a hobby, a sport, an occupation, a religion or a craft, but it requires the members of the community to carry out some kind of activity – the practice at the core. According to Lave and Wenger, the theorists who created the term, a community of practice requires three things:

- **a domain:** a field of knowledge that participants acquire and operate within (the rules of a sport, for example)
- **a community:** recognition that there are others (you do not have to belong to a 'club' in order to know you are part of the community); for a fandom, this would be awareness of 'the fandom' as a whole, and participation might include online activities or real-life events
- **a practice:** there needs to be a thing, or a set of activities that people do, which forms the core – for a religion, this would include regular worship and following daily rules.

Within communities of practice, additions to participants' language are most likely to be lexical and/or semantic, as people learn a specialist vocabulary or jargon – and occasionally develop special slang – relating to the practice. This specialist lexis will probably not be understood by those outside the community, but it will either support the practice itself or affirm the identity of members of the community as belonging to the group. For example, within a sport, there may be technical terms relating to rules and techniques (for example, 'offside rule' in soccer), but there are often also slang terms used by fans of the sport which emphasise the bonds between them and facilitate conversation about the sport (for example, 'group of death' to describe a group with all the good teams in it in the soccer World Cup).

Activity 3

Choose a community of practice that you have personal experience of, or are otherwise familiar with. Explain what the domain is, where the community might be found and what the practice entails. List some examples of language that participants in the community use that are non-standard or would not be understood by others and explain their usage.

Social networks and communities of practice are two communities that you might belong to by choice. However, there are other aspects of social identity over which you have less control, but which might still have an impact on your idiolect.

Regional diversity

Regional variation is what gives us dialect. In the UK in particular, regional variation is particularly pronounced due a number of historical factors, including different invading forces going back centuries, and the spread and separation of rural communities (until relatively recently). In the USA, this variation is less pronounced due to factors including colonisation, less time for different dialects to evolve and a different attitude towards social class than in the UK.

Key terms

accent: pronouncing the words of a language in a distinctive way that shows which country, region, or social class someone is from

dialect: a regionally specific non-standard variety of language, including accent, grammar and word variations from the standard variety

Case study: **Milroy's Belfast study**

The social networks study conducted in Belfast by Leslie Milroy in the 1980s identified that dense multiplex networks – which were typical in working-class culture at the time – were reinforcing local dialect over Standard English. In one community taking part in the study, high male unemployment forced a change in women's behaviour, causing them to operate in denser networks than previously. This was because women now had full-time factory jobs and were spending more time together than before. When they did not work, or worked part time, they had been more mobile, operating in far looser networks.

Before Milroy's study, it was widely believed that women used more standard forms of language and men more non-standard language for gender-based reasons (such as needing to be 'ladylike' or a role model for children). This study demonstrated that the difference was, in fact, associated with people's networks. It seems that previously, when women had been mixing with a wider range of people, for example by travelling outside the area more frequently, they had used more standard forms – probably to aid mutual comprehension. When they started spending almost all their time with the same kind of people, they were more comfortable using a stronger version of local dialect.

Milroy's findings – that network strength enables non-standard usage – also apply to other types of social group. For example, if the network in question is a fandom community, such as a Taylor Swift fan group online, features of regional speech would not increase, but lexical examples specific to that fandom would, such as references to Swift's songs.

The opposite is happening in many regions of the UK. Linguists describe a phenomenon known as '**dialect levelling**', in which people's dialects are becoming less distinct and more neutral. There are various reasons for this:

> **Key term**
>
> **dialect levelling:** the decrease in differences of people's dialects

- reduced geographical isolation for many rural areas
- greater physical and social mobility
- exposure to a wider range of voices via the media.

Activity 4

Find out about a particular variety of English. This might be in your local area, or you could research one of the three below. Try to find out about/describe lexical, grammatical and phonological differences from the national Standard English:

- Newcastle English (Geordie)
- Chicago English
- Southland (New Zealand) English.

Different kinds of prestige

People may unconsciously and gradually shift their dialect to fit in with others and to gain status and prestige. Many different linguistic studies have shown that there are two key types of prestige, and that they are opposites – people seek and acquire one or the other.

Overt prestige:

- comes from using the socially approved forms of language such as Received Pronunciation (RP), Standard English or General American (the standard or neutral form of US pronunciation)
- is equivalent to high status.

Covert prestige:

> **Key term**
>
> **anti-language:** a form of language designed to exclude outsiders, like a code (for example, Cockney rhyming slang or leet)

- comes from using forms of language approved by a group rather than by wider society (for example, a local dialect, slang, youth dialect or **anti-language**)
- is equivalent to 'cool factor'.

There have been many studies of social class and attitudes to language, especially in the UK. Howard Giles's work on attitudes is seminal, and Ellen Ryan's 'solidarity vs status' study is very useful in demonstrating how people respond to accents. Ryan compiled a meta-study (a large-scale project taking many studies together) on attitude, and concluded that all accents were rated by participants highly either for solidarity – that is, traits such as likability and trustworthiness – or for status – that is, traits such as intelligence and presumed income. Ryan's work combined many different attitude studies in which participants were asked to rate or respond to accents in various ways. She concluded that participants were highly unlikely to believe that the owner of one accent could hold traits in both these areas.

For more detail on Howard Giles's studies on attitudes, see Unit 7.4.

This finding supports the reduction in RP speakers in recent years, and the related increase in speakers of Estuary English.

Case study: **RP and Estuary English**

Received Pronunciation is not simply the absence of an accent. It is a particular accent in its own right, with distinct vowel shapes. To hear it, simply play a broadcast of the Queen's Christmas speech, or a 1950s BBC television or radio programme. In 1974, sociolinguist Peter Trudgill said that only 3 per cent of the UK population spoke RP. That figure is even lower today, and many in the public eye choose instead to speak Estuary English. Estuary appeals to upper working-class and lower middle-class speakers who want to 'speak up' from London or Essex varieties and sound 'better'; it also appeals to upper-class speakers who want to avoid the more negative connotations of RP and be seen more positively. For that reason, you will hear many politicians use it, despite their private educations.

Estuary English was first defined in the 1980s by David Rosewarne as a 'variety of modified regional speech' and has since been much debated. It is now best seen as an umbrella term for a group of accents used around the Thames estuary in Kent, Essex and London, which includes such features as glottal-stopping (for example, missed 't's in 'butter'), l-vocalisaton (pronouncing 'l' like 'w', for example in 'football') and yod **coalescence** (a process where 'y' sounds, or yods, traditionally inserted between plosives and certain vowels, are combined with the plosive to produce a 'ch' or 'j' sound instead, as in 'duty' or 'Tuesday'). It is sometimes described as sitting between Cockney and RP, but this is a broad area to inhabit; Estuary English is not as 'posh' as RP (there are no elevated vowels) and not as 'common' as Cockney (no dropped 'h's or rhyming slang).

Activity 5

Explain, in terms of type of prestige, why people are shifting to Estuary English. Refer to any other concepts you feel are relevant.

Key term

coalescence: the combining of phonemic elements to produce a new phoneme (e.g. 'duty' pronounced as 'juty' instead of 'dyuty')

Final task

Choose a community you are part of or know very well.

- Identify and explain at least three examples of language use specific to that group, ideally using more than one approach (that is, not just lexical variation).
- Apply at least two different theories or concepts to explain how and/or why language is used in a particular way within the group.

Write in paragraphs to produce a short, coherent essay.

8.4 Language and social identity

To what extent do broad social categories such as age and gender affect people's use of language?

Age as a variable – youth dialect

As well as dialect – where the region in which a person lives determines their language – someone might also speak using a sociolect. This is determined by a social factor such as age, race or gender (this last is also known as **genderlect**).

Many teenagers use a youth sociolect or youth dialect, which some experts consider to be an aspect of language change. Youth sociolects often attract considerable covert prestige from the target group, but they can be heavily stigmatised in institutions such as schools, where they are seen as low-status and judged as potentially affecting future employment opportunities. However, as users of youth dialect can often code-switch into a more standard variety when necessary, a lot of the panic around youth dialect is unnecessary and based on imaginary situations rather than real ones.

Key term

genderlect: a style of speech affected by gender

Activity 1

Copy and complete the table to show which words you would use in the following situations.

	Informal/social situation (for example, with friends)	Mid-register situation (for example, with family)	Formal situation (for example, at work/ school)
You're really pleased about something: that's ____!			
Something is annoying or rubbish: that's ___!			
You're annoyed: ___!			
Someone is attractive: s/he is ___			

Collect between two and five other people's words for the same situations, gathering ideas from people of different ages if possible. What do you notice?

Attitudes to youth sociolects show a clear link to prescriptivism, particularly 'golden age thinking'. These attitudes have persisted for centuries. In 1274, Peter the Hermit observed:

> The world is passing through troublous times. The young people of today think of nothing but themselves. They have no reverence for parents or old age. They are impatient of all restraint. They talk as if they knew everything, and what passes for wisdom with us is foolishness with them. As for the girls, they are forward, immodest and unladylike in speech, behaviour and dress.

Multiculturalism is a relatively new aspect of youth sociolect. In the late 20th and early 21st centuries, studies carried out in London by Sue Fox and Elvind Torgersen identified a variety of English that they named 'Multi-Ethnic Youth Dialect' (MEYD). Key to this variety is the mixing of words and phrases from a range of nationalities and ethnicities, including Australian (for example, 'nang' to mean 'good' or 'cool') and Jamaican (for example, 'bare' to mean 'a lot'. According to Fox and Torgersen's study, the key to whether a young person speaks this variety is their network: the more mixed this is, the more likely they are to speak it. A young person with a very 'anglo' network would be unlikely to use MEYD.

Originally called 'Multicultural London English' (MLE), the label MEYD was preferred as it made clear that the variety was not only found in London, but in other cities with mixed ethnic populations such as Birmingham and Manchester as well. More recently, however, there has been a move to rename it Multicultural Urban British English (MUBE), as it is losing its association with youth culture, at least partially through urban music culture in the UK, such as the grime scene.

Does gender make a difference?

People have been considering the ways in which gender affects language since the 1970s, when Robin Lakoff first gave her ten-point description of 'women's language'.

Feature	Example
hedges	It's kind of difficult
tag questions	He's a good man, isn't he?
rising intonation on declaratives	I really don't want to?
empty adjectives	sweet, divine, cute
precise colour terms	aquamarine, fuchsia
intensifiers	He's such a great guy
superpolite forms	Could you possibly pass the salt please?
hypercorrect grammar	Between you and I
avoidance of swearing	Oh sugar!
emphatic stress	She's SOOO late!

This was relabelled as 'powerless language' following William O'Barr and Bowman Atkins' more in-depth study. They examined 150 hours of courtroom interactions and gave all speakers, male and female, a 'women's language score' based on how many of Lakoff's features they used per utterance. O'Barr and Atkins found that gender had far less effect on the likelihood of these features appearing than a person's previous courtroom experience and their status in that context (for example, the judge has most status in the courtroom context and the defendant has the least).

Activity 2

Lakoff felt that the women's language features made them look weak, and believed that they reflected a kind of internalised patriarchy or learned submission to the social order of the 1970s. Look at the features listed in the table above. For which of them does that argument work most effectively? For which might it not be so useful? Can you suggest an alternative argument for those features, bearing in mind the 1970s patriarchal social order?

In the 1990s, Deborah Tannen put forward her theory of gender – that men and women often struggle to understand one another because they basically want different things out of conversations. She explained that male/female communication is essentially cross-cultural communication – like trying to speak to someone out of their native language.

The core of Tannen's argument is a set of six pairs of desires that men and women are socialised into holding when they communicate and which are at odds with one another:

- Men seek STATUS, Women seek SUPPORT: According to Tannen, men essentially see conversation in battle-like terms and want to come out on top, whereas women see it as a quest to earn friendship and gain backing for their ideas.
- Men seek ADVICE, Women seek UNDERSTANDING: This particular misunderstanding causes the most difficulties when people share problems. Women, according to Tannen, share problems in order to gain sympathy and share their experience, but men's instinct is to offer solutions, which women experience as telling them what to do and fobbing them off with practicalities.
- Men give ORDERS, Women offer PROPOSALS: The idea of directness comes up again and again in gender debates and here is Tannen's version of it: men tell others what to do in a direct (and clear, or perhaps aggressive) way, while women make suggestions, which men might interpret as weak.
- Men seek CONFLICT, Women seek COMPROMISE: In disagreeing with others, men's aim is to highlight disagreement and win, whereas women want to find common ground and work together to find a solution. Women are more likely to negotiate, men more likely to argue.
- Men seek INDEPENDENCE, Women seek INTIMACY: This is about people's goals for conversations overall: men want ultimately to be seen as separate, individual entities with their own ideas and achievements recognised, whereas women seek to be part of something and aim to join with others.
- Men share INFORMATION, Women share FEELINGS: This pairing is about how people make connections and create friendships within their same-sex communities, which they then try to take out into the wider world. Little boys (in this narrative) trade facts in order to bond, while little girls will tell each other what they think and feel about things to make a connection.

Activity 3

How convincing do you find Tannen's theories? What evidence and/or arguments might there be both for and against them?

Types of gender theory

More recently, people have clustered the various strands of genderlect theory and characterised them all according to their approach to gender.

Approach	Explanation
deficit approach	This basically measures women against men and finds them wanting. It was common before the theories and research on gender and language described above. For a deficit theorist, women are not capable of using 'strong' or 'powerful' language in the same way as men are, so they speak indirectly, and so on.
dominance approach	This takes language as an expression of the social relations between men and women, seeing language differences as caused by patriarchy. For dominance theorists, women's language may appear weaker than men's language because women do not have 'permission' to use stronger language. Equally, men may use more powerful constructions because they assume they have the right to more space and power.
difference approach	This suggests that language differences between men and women are due to cultural differences and differences in emphasis in their interests and desires. This approach is keen to present neither as 'stronger' or 'better', but to highlight the ways that the differences may lead to difficulties, in order to foster better understanding between the sexes.

The diversity approach

A post-2000 theory, the diversity approach, has been led by Deborah Cameron. This approach emphasises that gender is just one facet of identity, and highlights how other genderlect theories have worked to generalise and summarise 'men' and 'women' as categories. For Cameron, any individual man may have more in common with a woman than with another man linguistically, just as not all men are tall and not all women are short, even though it may be true that generally, women are shorter than men.

Cameron also points to meta-research carried out by Janet Hyde, who drew together the results of hundreds of gender studies and found no significant differences in the language used by men and women. This huge study looked at a wide range of areas of psychological research and found only two differences in the language area, both of them small: in smiling and spelling.

Cameron believes that despite this lack of empirical evidence, genderlect theories are so compelling because people have expectations of behaviour – including linguistic behaviour – based on gender. This fits into the larger concept of performative identity, especially performative gender identity, as proposed by Judith Butler in her 1990 book *Gender Trouble*. To some extent, we all choose how to perform our gender identity, including whether and how to conform to expected gender norms of linguistic behaviour. We also notice behaviour that fits these expectations rather than behaviour that does not. This is called 'confirmation bias' – we are biased towards noticing things that confirm our expectations rather than question them.

Read Text 3 overleaf, which is an extract from Deborah Cameron's blog.

Text 3

It ain't what you say…

February 22, 2018

If you look at the way the act of speaking is described in everything from news reports to Great Literature, you'll soon discover that it's persistently represented in stereotypically gendered and sexist ways.

The most neutral way to describe the act of speaking is by using the generic verb 'say'. 'X said' is the reported speech equivalent of Lochhead's 'men talk': it conveys no more than 'this person uttered these words'. But writers often add colour by choosing something a bit less basic. Here's an example, from a political sketch that appeared in the Telegraph after the second TV debate of the 2015 General Election campaign.

"Ed Miliband is scared to be bold," **scowled** Ms Sturgeon. "We don't want a pretend alternative to austerity." "Exactly right!" **squeaked** Ms Bennett.
   "Labour are letting the Tories off the hook!" **snapped** Ms Wood. The audience applauded.
   Desperately Mr Miliband tried to steer the debate back to his absent foe. "Let's not pretend there's no difference between me and David Cameron," he **said**, rather pleadingly. "There's not a big enough difference!" **barked** Ms Sturgeon.

Notice that it's the only male participant in this exchange, Ed Miliband, whose contribution is reported using the basic 'said' (though the writer does add some extra information with the adverbial 'rather pleadingly'). The three women, by contrast, don't just 'say' things, they 'scowl', 'squeak', 'snap' and 'bark'.

These verbs aren't literally describing how the women sounded. They've been chosen to help the writer tell a story, in which a hapless male is ganged up on and berated by three angry and aggressive females. If we only had the speakers' own words to go on, we might not make that interpretation: we're directed to it mainly by the writer's choice of verbs ('scowl', 'snap', 'bark') and adverbs ('desperately', 'pleadingly'). The verbs also say something about the power dynamic among the women. Whereas 'squeaked' casts Natalie Bennett as a small animal, 'snapped' and 'barked' suggest bigger beasts.

From debuk.wordpress.com, 25 June 2018

Activity 4

Discuss Deborah Cameron's arguments in Text 3. How do you respond to them? To what extent do you think society and the media make us expect gender to be significant in the way people speak?

Final task

Consider the features of your own linguistic identity. Try to explain the key features of your own idiolect. Think about:

- the range of languages or dialects you speak – do you code-switch on a regular basis?
- the extent to which you 'perform' the norms of your gender
- any regional variations which appear in your speech
- any communities of practice you belong to – how have they influenced your speech?
- your age and other social group markers – can you identify any features relating to these in the language you commonly use?

Further reading

Dan Clayton, *Attitudes to Language* (CUP, 2018)

Peter Trudgill and Arthur Hughes, *English Accents and Dialects: An Introduction to Social and Regional Varieties of English in the British Isles* 5th Edition (Routledge, 2012)

Dan Clayton, *Language Diversity* (CUP, 2018)

Deborah Cameron, *The Myth of Mars and Venus: Do Men and Women Really Speak Different Languages?* (OUP, 2008)

8.5 Debating language and the self

How do people research social variation in language? How are philosophical concepts about language discussed?

Sociolinguistic research

There are several key considerations when planning research on how people's identity is reflected in the language they use:

- how to get people to speak naturally
- how to isolate the social variables you want
- how to obtain data in an ethical way.

You can obtain more natural data if you do not tell participants what you want the data for. For example, you might ask participants their views on the local area or last night's football match or whether teenagers should be allowed to drive – leading them to believe that these topics are the focus of your research, when really the subject of the conversation is less important than the speech. Conducting research this way raises ethical issues, though, as you are deceiving people. Permission would need to be sought afterwards, and you would need to explain that, in fact, you wanted to record people speaking in order to analyse their dialect.

Key term

diphthong: a sound formed by the combination of two vowels in a single syllable, where the sound begins as one and then moves towards the other (for example, 'coin', 'side')

Case study: **William Labov's pilot study**

In 1966, Labov's Department Store Study in New York was ground-breaking for sociolinguistic method. To examine the variable of social class, he looked at the speech of staff in three different stores in New York, whose language he believed would need to suit the class of their customers. The linguistic variable he focused on was the post-vocalic 'r' (the phoneme 'r' following a vowel, as in the word 'car'), which is a prestige pronunciation in US English.

Labov tested his theory by finding out ahead of time what was on the fourth floor of each store, then going in and asking an assistant where that item could be found. He would then pretend not to have heard them, to get them to repeat their reply, making sure everyone he spoke to would say 'fourth floor' twice, the second time potentially more carefully. He did this many times, speaking to multiple members of staff, recording his findings each time.

In the 'lower class' store (S. Klein), the post-vocalic 'r's were not usually pronounced either time of speaking. In the 'upper class' store (Saks Fifth Avenue), the 'r's were pronounced each time and in the 'middle class' store (Macy's), the 'r's were often not pronounced the first time but were almost always pronounced on repeating. This, he concluded, suggested that lower-middle class speakers were less confident in their social position and more likely to adjust their speech to try to please others.

In the 1970s, Peter Trudgill developed further detailed methods for studying accent and dialect in a range of registers. He wanted to test whether and to what extent people's accent varied when speaking in different contexts, so he had them read individual words in a list, read a passage, answer structured questions in an interview and narrate an experience in order to try to replicate the most natural speech possible. His findings on social position, confidence and identity relating to speech were similar to Labov's.

Trudgill's word list contained 52 words, chosen to exemplify groups of sounds which show differences from RP in a range of accents. It opens with short vowel sounds such as 'pit' and 'pat', moving into **diphthongs** such as 'buy' and 'boy', a group of words to test the shift from short 'a' to long 'a' (hat, dance, daft, half, father, farther) and then including selections of words which are homophones (or near-homophones) in some accents but not others such as 'poor', 'pour', 'pore' and 'paw'.

Activity 1

a) Trudgill's word list was designed for UK accents. A similar list to test US accents might include words such as 'Mary', 'merry' and 'marry'. From your knowledge of accents local to you, or from international English, what additional groups of words might you suggest to add to an international English word list?

b) What benefit do you think including reading a list and a passage has, alongside interview questions and more spontaneous speech for collecting accent data?

What research shows

As the genderlect studies in particular have shown, there can be problems even with empirical evidence. Studies may show only what we expect because we only look for what we expect. In addition, we may interpret results in a biased way. For example, in comparing data showing that women used less direct means to make requests of others, people who subscribed to the different approaches would make different inferences.

- A deficit theorist would say that women are indirect because they lack the clarity to be direct.
- A dominance theorist would come to the conclusion that women's indirectness is due to their relative lack of power in society generally, and because women are used to not having power, they feel uncomfortable in making direct requests of others.
- A difference theorist would claim that women's indirectness is about how they would want to be approached themselves – women appreciate cooperation rather than power plays, so they prefer to be asked rather than told to do things and therefore extend the same courtesy to others.
- A diversity theorist might question the size of the study and ask whether it really, definitively showed women being less direct, or they might ask what other contextual factors played out to make the women in this study feel that indirectness was more appropriate.

Activity 2

How might the four genderlect approaches interpret women's use of tag questions? You can draw examples from the dataset below.

We liked that, didn't we?	She's really sweet, isn't she?	I'm coming to that one, aren't I?
You won't go yet, will you?	He didn't eat it all, did he?	That's a bit silly, isn't it?

Text 4

Men 'much more likely to ask questions in seminars' than women

Male academics two and a half times more likely to speak up, as women cite lack of confidence and 'intimidating' speakers.

Men are two and a half times more likely to ask a question in an academic seminar than women, according to a major study that offers further explanation of female under-representation in science.

Researchers who collected observational data from 247 departmental seminars from 35 institutions in 10 countries found that the two and a half times difference significantly misrepresented the gender ratio of the audience, which was, on average, equal.

In a paper published on the ArXiv preprint server, the authors argue that the lack of female visibility in seminars may be both a symptom and a cause of the "leaky pipeline", which describes the high attrition rate of women in science fields, with a lack of female role models leading junior researchers to believe that the academy is not a place where women succeed and subsequently to choose a different career.

The observational data were backed up by an online survey completed by 638 academics in 20 countries, which found that 60 per cent of women and 47 per cent of men believed that there was bias towards men asking questions.

While the vast majority of both male and female survey respondents (92 per cent) admitted that they did not always ask a question when they had one, women were much more likely to report that they "couldn't work up the nerve", that they found the speaker too "intimidating" or that they did not "feel clever enough".

Alecia Carter, Alyssa Croft, Dieter Lukas and Gillian Sandstrom write that most men are simply "not aware of the bias" and most women "identify internal factors as holding them back from asking questions".

Interestingly, the observational data indicated that if a woman asked the first question, the people who asked subsequent questions were generally representative of the audience. If a man asked the first question, however, men were disproportionately more likely to ask questions.

The length of time allowed for questions also had a significant effect, with the imbalance shrinking over time and typically disappearing at about 50 minutes of questions.

The paper suggests that moderators could play an important role in stopping questioners "showing off", taking too much time or digressing.

From *Times Higher Education*, 12 December 2017

Activity 3

Which of the four genderlect approaches does the research cited in Text 4 appear to be taking? Choose examples to back up your ideas. How important do you think the four approaches are in gender studies? How might other approaches have studied or interpreted the same phenomenon?

Discussions about language and the self

The media has long been fascinated with language, and regularly includes articles about research into child language, findings in neuroscience and, of course, opinion pieces on sociolinguistic issues such as new words and varieties. More philosophical areas of psycholinguistics are also often discussed in the media and online. They are as likely now to be concerned with replicating human language in Artificial Intelligence as animals.

Read Text 5, which is an article about speech recognition technology.

Text 5

Language Pragmatics: Why We Can't Talk to Computers
by Cody Adams

Speech recognition technology continues to fascinate language and cognitive science researchers, and Apple's introduction of the Siri voice assistant program in its recent iPhone 4S was heralded by many as a great leap toward realizing the dream of a computer you can talk to. Fast-forward half a year later and, while Siri has proved to be practically useful and sometimes impressively accurate for dictation, the world has not been turned upside down. A quick Google search for "Siri fail" will provide you with the often unintentionally funny attempts by Apple's voice recognition service to answer abstract questions or transcribe uncommon phrases.

But in a day and age when computers can win at Jeopardy and chess programs can consistently defeat the best human players, why hasn't voice technology reached a similar plateau of mastery? [...]

In short, it's all about context, and the kinds of leaps easily achieved by humans in casual conversation have thus far remained outside the reach of dynamic language processing programs. One need only watch the infamous 2008 Microsoft demonstration of its Windows Vista voice recognition software to be reminded how nascent this technology remains for the most part.

But Siri works *pretty* well *much* of the time, right? Interestingly, Apple approached the voice recognition game using a framework that is about as far from how humans understand speech as you can get. Every time you speak to Siri, your iPhone connects to a cloud service, according to a Smart Planet article by Andrew Nusca, and the following takes place:

The server compares your speech against a statistical model to estimate, based on the sounds you spoke and the order in which you spoke them, what letters might constitute it. (At the same time, the local recognizer compares your speech to an abridged version of that statistical model.) For both, the highest-probability estimates get the go-ahead.

Based on these opinions, your speech – now understood as a series of vowels and consonants – is then run through a language model, which estimates the words that your speech is comprised of. Given a sufficient level of confidence, the computer then creates a candidate list of interpretations for what the sequence of words in your speech might mean.

In this sense, Siri doesn't really "understand" anything said to it, it simply uses a constantly expanding probability model to attach combinations of letters to the sounds you're saying. And once it has computed the most likely identity of your words, it cross checks them against the server database of successful answers to similar combinations of words and provides you with a probable answer. This is a system of speech recognition that sidesteps pragmatics by employing a huge vocabulary and a real-time cloud-based feedback database. And Siri's trademark cheekiness? Apple has thousands of writers employed inputting phrases and responses manually into the Siri cloud, continually building out its "vocabulary" while relying on statistics for the context.

Does this constitute true speech recognition, or is this just a more robust version of old-time AOL chat bots? If this is the way that speech recognition technology will evolve in the future, do you think that it will cross a database threshold so as to be indistinguishable from true speech recognition, even if there's no pragmatic "ghost in the machine," as it were? Or will computers never be able to truly "learn" language?

From *Big Think*, 17 Feb 2012

Activity 4

Discuss the ideas presented in the article. How does it relate to the ideas of universalism and nativism? Write a short essay explaining your ideas.

Final task

Write an article for your school or college magazine, in which you explore some key ideas about language and the mind. You might include some or all of the following, or ideas of your own/from your own research:

* the extent to which language is learned or innate
* the extent to which we can think without/outside of language
* the language of thought hypothesis
* evidence from studies with animals
* work with computers to replicate human language.

End-of-chapter task

Reread Text 2 in Unit 8.2. Discuss what you feel are the most important issues raised in the text in regard to the ways in which language can reflect social identity. You should refer to specific details from the passage as well as to ideas and examples from your wider study.
Do this by:

* commenting on the ideas raised in the text by relating them to your knowledge of language concepts, theories and research
* expressing your opinions on the ideas raised.

Applying key skills

This chapter provides a selection of tasks that will allow you to practise your skills. It also offers suggestions for how to revise and put together your own practice tasks to test yourself. There are models and worked examples here, with some demonstrations of strong practice to help you prepare. You will also find some examples of more average performance as the basis for development tasks.

When looking at models of analytical and writing tasks, remember that there is never just one correct way of addressing a task. Although these are offered as examples of good practice, they are not the only possible way to success. If you have attempted the task and have an answer that is very different to a model here, do not assume it is wrong. There are many possible valid responses, so check with a mark scheme or ask your teacher for their comments on your work.

9.1 Text analysis

What makes a successful text analysis?

Key requirements of a text analysis task

When analysing a text, you need to demonstrate that you can:

- understand the context of the text – its audience, form and purpose(s)
- use the context to explain and interpret meanings and effects intended and constructed by the writer/speaker of the text
- select and label the most appropriate features of language and structure to demonstrate the above.

Even if a task does not explicitly mention a key contextual factor such as audience, you should always include all three central ideas – audience, form and purpose – in an analysis. These are key to creating meaning, and how the writer approaches and positions the audience is crucial to how meaning is constructed.

Developing an analysis of a text

Look again at this text from Unit 3.1 – an extract from a tourist brochure about the Canada Goose Arctic Gallery.

ARCTIC

What happens here, doesn't stay here

CANADA GOOSE ARCTIC GALLERY

The new Canada Goose Arctic Gallery is a window on the intimate connection between people and nature in Canada's North. Discover this region through authentic specimens and artefacts. Walk through real ice as part of a National Film Board of Canada multimedia experience. #ArcticAtTheMuseum

Activity 1

Your task is as follows:

> Analyse the text, focusing on form, structure and language.

Make notes on the following questions to help you start planning an answer.

- How does the brochure form affect the text's language and structure?
- How is the text structured? How does this help it to communicate to its target audience?
- What is interesting or effective about its language? How does this relate to its purpose, its audience and/or its form?

Copy and complete the table below to help you get started.

	Features	Example	Comment
Form			
Structure	subtitles	'Canada Goose Arctic Gallery'	organises the text, coheres to form as short brochure text
Language	pun	'What happens here, doesn't stay here'	shared resources – reference and implies visitors will talk about experience

Now read the example of an analysis below.

The Canada Goose Arctic Gallery text is a clear example of a commercial brochure, with a clearly defined audience of potential tourists who might be interested in visiting the museum. The brochure form requires a concise text and this example aims to appeal to young families with references to 'real ice' and 'a National Film Board of Canada multimedia experience', to make it sound appealing and modern.

reasonable identification of audience, if a little broad/obvious

better point on audience, once linked to some language, although this could be more specific

The structure of the text is also straightforward, due to its short length. It uses titles and subtitles and closes with a hashtag, again in an attempt to appeal to a modern audience.

bit vague/undeveloped

sound explanation

The language of the text includes an appeal to shared resources with the gentle pun in the title, playing on the well-known phrase of 'what happens in Vegas, stays in Vegas', the pragmatic implication being that visitors will want to talk to others about their visit. The imperatives 'discover' and 'walk' are also used to direct the audience and make them feel as though they are visiting the museum already, as these verbs direct them on what to do once they are there.

this is the best point – a fully developed explanation and with linguistic terminology

clearly labelled language feature

interesting interpretation, but could be more clearly explained and developed

Comment

The analysis is a reasonable attempt which covers the key ideas, although it could be more detailed. The main issue here is the way the response is structured, considering language separately. It would be better to weave in language comments, linking them to other points. It is acceptable to consider language, form and structure separately in the planning stage, but treating them discretely in writing can result in a disjointed and undeveloped analysis.

Activity 2

Write an improved version of the analysis. You may use and develop the ideas within it, restructuring it and expressing it more precisely, or you may choose to add your own ideas from Activity 1 if you noted different features.

Activity 3

Find a text of your own that would be appropriate for analysis (for example, in a magazine, something delivered to your home). Copy and complete the table below by writing the contextual factors in the left-hand column and selecting textual evidence that supports each one. If you identify more than one audience/purpose, select language or structural features for each one.

	Language/structural feature used to suit identified contextual factor	Quotation as evidence
Form		
Purpose(s)		
Audience		
Two most interesting aspects of mode		

Activity 4

Read through your text and decide on its most important language feature. Then challenge yourself to produce a paragraph which:

- makes a comment about how that feature relates to the text's audience (for example, the pronouns in an advert make the audience feel personally involved)
- explains how the feature helps the text in relation to its form – for example, direct address using second person pronouns are a common feature of advertising (synthetic personalisation)
- discusses how that feature supports the text's purpose – for example, if an advert can make the audience feel that the product/service provider understands them, the audience is more likely to respond positively.

Tackling a new question

Read Text 1 below, which is a piece of autobiographical writing from a newspaper series. Consider the same task:

Analyse the text, focusing on form, structure and language.

Text 1

Derek Redmond: The Day That Changed My Life

27 July 2012

The former British 400 m record-holder, now 46, was at his peak when he lined up for the 400 m semi-final in Barcelona in 1992. Here he relives the day that ended his career but made him an inspiration to millions.

'When I took my place on the starting blocks I felt good.

'For once I had no injuries, despite eight operations in four years, and I'd won the first two rounds without breaking sweat – including posting the fastest time in the first round heats. I was confident and when the gun went off I got off to a good start.

'I got into my stride running round the first turn and I was feeling comfortable. Then I heard a popping sound. I kept on running for another two or three strides then I felt the pain. I thought I'd been shot, but then I recognised the agony.

'I'd pulled my hamstring before and the pain is excruciating: like someone shoving a hot knife into the back of your knee and twisting it. I grabbed the back of my leg, uttered a few expletives and hit the deck.

I couldn't believe this was happening after all the training I'd put in. I looked around to see where the rest of the field were, and they had only 100 m to go. I remember thinking if I got up I could still catch them and qualify.

'The pain was intense. I hobbled about 50 m until I was at the 200 m mark. Then I realised it was all over. I looked round and saw that everyone else had crossed the finishing line. But I don't like to give up at anything – not even an argument, as my wife will tell you – and I decided I was going to finish that race if it was the last race I ever did.

'All these doctors and officials were coming onto the track, trying to get me to stop but I was having none of it. Then, with about 100 m to go, I became aware of someone else on the track. I didn't realise it was my dad, Jim, at first. He said, "Derek, it's me, you don't need to do this."

'I just said, "Dad, I want to finish, get me back in the semi-final." He said, "OK. We started this thing together and now we'll finish it together." He managed to get me to stop trying to run and just walk and he kept repeating, "You're a champion, you've got nothing to prove."

'We hobbled over the finishing line with our arms round each other, just me and my dad, the man I'm really close to, who's supported my athletics career since I was seven years old. I've since been told there was a standing ovation by the 65,000 crowd, but nothing registered at the time. I was in tears and went off to the medical room to be looked at, then I took the bus back to the Olympic village.

My dream was over. In Seoul four years earlier I didn't even get to the start line because of an Achilles injury and had "DNS" – Did Not Start – next to my name. I didn't want them to write "DNF" – Did Not Finish – in Barcelona.

'When I saw my doctor he told me I'd never represent my country again. I felt like there'd been a death. I never raced again and I was angry for two years. Then one day I just thought: there are worse things than pulling a muscle in a race, and I just decided to get on with my life.

Today I don't feel anger, just frustration. The footage has since been used in adverts by Visa, Nike and the International Olympic Committee – I don't go out of my way to watch it, but it isn't painful any more and I have the Visa ad on my iPad.

'If I hadn't pulled a hamstring that day I could have been an Olympic medallist, but I love the life I have now. I might not have been a motivational speaker or competed for my country at basketball, as I went on to do. And my dad wouldn't have been asked to carry the Olympic torch this year, which was a huge honour for him.

From *Daily Mail*, 27 July 2012

Now read this opening section of a sample response.

In this text, Derek Redmond uses many features from narrative writing, as he is retelling an event that happened to him in order to explain about 'the day that changed my life'. The form is autobiography and he is writing for readers of the newspaper, but also probably for his fans who might find the article online.

The article's structure sets up that the day was tragic at the time with the verb phrase 'ended his career' in the opening statement, but it also had a positive aspect as shown by the abstract noun phrase 'an inspiration to millions'. This opening part is not written by Redmond himself, but introduces his words. Once he is writing, the text has a more chronological structure and goes through the day, explaining what led to it, what happened and how he was feeling.

Activity 5

What strengths and weaknesses can you identify in the opening to the analysis? How do you think this answer or its approach might be improved? What features of this answer would be worth keeping and perhaps trying to use in responses to other analysis tasks?

Now look at this annotated sample answer to the same task.

As is typical for autobiographical writing, Redmond's article shares some features with narrative writing, mostly in its structure, but also in its use of tense, pronouns and dialogue. All of these features help Redmond re-create the day he is describing for his readers, but also put it into context in order to fit into the newspaper's series 'the day that changed my life'.

> clear understanding of form

> strong and concise overview helps set up effective structure

> precise explanation of purpose

> sophisticated understanding of precise form

The inclusion of this episode in the series enables Redmond to use some key structural features of narrative, such as clear evaluation at the end, which explains the value of the event and its ongoing meaning in his life. Redmond marks the shift from describing immediate events to evaluating them with the conjunction 'then' and time adverbial 'one day', also a common narrative-style phrase, to highlight his change of attitude.

> effective comments on combining of forms

> precise analysis of features leads to sophisticated comment on meaning as well as structure

The paragraph following this shift is the evaluation part of the narrative, where he considers the whole episode, and this part of the text is presented in the present tense 'I don't feel anger', as it relates to his feelings now and the impact of this event on his life in the present day. The final paragraph is more complex in its tense usage including a past perfect in the opening subordinate clause, which leads to a past conditional in the main clause and is then followed by a simple present: 'If I hadn't pulled a hamstring that day I could have been an Olympic medallist, but I love the life I have now.' This section enables Redmond to leave the audience in no doubt that he is grateful for what he has in his life despite the tragedy, closing the text with a positive and inspirational message, which is likely to be what regular readers of this series are seeking.

> coherent writing makes points fully clear

> fully explains how language features link to structure and meaning

> description of features here is less purposeful

> focus on audience and meaning at end of paragraph is effective and cohesive

A key feature of autobiographical writing – which is also common in narrative – is the use of a first-person perspective. Redmond narrates his experience using the first-person pronoun 'I' throughout, with an occasional second person 'you' used in the universal sense 'like someone shoving a hot knife into the back of your knee'. This use of perspective is essential in autobiographical or memoir writing, as the audience wants to be able to understand the writer's

> clear identification and overview

> sophisticated understanding of pronoun use

helpful return to focus on audience as link between form and meaning

experience as closely as possible, so they need to be able inhabit the narrative space with the writer/speaker.

less useful link between paragraphs here

helpful to comment on tone as a way to relate to audience

Another way that Redmond helps the reader feel present with him is the spoken tone of the piece. This is achieved largely through the use of colloquial language, including idioms such as 'hit the deck' and some phrasing typical of speech such as the noun phrase 'All these doctors and officials'.

effective linking of different features

continued focus on audience engagement is cohesive and coherent

Including dialogue is a further way in which Redmond engages the audience by obeying narrative rules and making it entertaining. It is also far more powerful to read his father's words directly, than to have them reported at a distance. The length of time this exchange took is also emphasised through the effort implied by the verb phrase 'managed to get me to stop trying', which conveys the difficulty of that task through its length as well as its three verbs, all of which can imply a hard task, and through use of the progressive verb phrase: 'kept repeating'.

sophisticated and precise analysis of meaning of detailed language feature

Overall, Redmond's piece is designed to appeal to a broad newspaper audience who are looking for an uplifting story in the series 'the day that changed my life'. It may also be found and read by those who are already fans of his or are familiar with his story, as it is likely to be available online. His usage of features of narrative structure, particularly using the section at the end which puts the event into the broader context of his life, makes it highly effective as an entertaining and engaging read.

effective closing comment on audience – and a good choice for conclusion of this answer as it has been the main focus

useful to select one feature of this aspect as an evaluative comment

concluding evaluation to end on

Activity 6

a) How has this response addressed or avoided the weaknesses you identified in the mid-level response you looked at in Activity 5?

b) What lessons can you learn from this response? Does it help you with issues you have either seen in feedback on your own work or not fully understood how to do? Make a note of these issues to refer back to when writing your own responses.

Revising for analysis work

It can be difficult to revise for analytical tasks, as they are skills-based rather than fact-based. However, there are some things you can do to build your skills.

- Make sure your knowledge of terminology is as good as it can be – use glossaries, index cards, mind maps and posters to revise this core knowledge.
- Practise applying analytical skills to random texts from food packaging to flyers, official letters (for example, from school/college) to online articles.
- Also practise analysing language that you hear, including 'live' (for example, on the bus, walking down the street, sitting in a café) as well as on the radio/television/online. Think about how the speakers select language appropriate for the audience (and try to be precise about those audiences).

Creating exam practice for yourself

You may want to produce practice tasks for yourself that are more in line with what you will be asked to do in an assessment. Here are some tips:

1. Follow the format of the questions here and in the samples in Chapter 10.
2. Choose texts of approximately 550–750 words. Possible sources for texts include:
   - newspapers and magazines – for all kinds of articles
   - the internet – for podcasts, blogs, articles and videos of all kinds
   - your mailbox – for flyers/leaflets and brochures.

You could include writing to review, narrate and describe, as well as travel writing, (auto)biographical work, diaries, essays, advertisements and scripted speech.

Final task

Reread Text 4 in Unit 4.2, the opening of the story 'A Temporary Matter'. Analyse this text, focusing on form, structure and language.

9.2 Writing creatively

How should you approach narrative and descriptive writing tasks?

Addressing the brief

You may be asked to write:

- a short piece based on a prompt, followed by a reflection on the writing (reflective writing is discussed in Unit 9.5)
- an extended piece, from a list of options
- a directed response based on a text (this will be explored specifically in Unit 9.4).

If you are given specific guidance in the task, make sure you consider it in your response. For example, an extended descriptive task might be:

> Write a descriptive piece entitled 'Entering the Cave'. In your writing, focus on smell and sensation, and on creating a sense of atmosphere to help your reader imagine the scene. Write between 600 and 900 words.

Activity 1

Which of the two openings below do you think shows a better understanding of the task above? Give evidence for your response.

Student A

> The cave was eerily cold and damp. There was an unmistakable odour of mould, creating an atmosphere of decay.

Student B

> I stepped into the cave unsteadily, slippery rocks underfoot. The temperature dropped as I went inside, leaving the comforting rays of the sun behind.

As the examples above show, you do not need to try to address everything in the brief in the first paragraph. However, you should make sure that you do not miss something vital such as the exact title or the main purpose of the task.

Now look at this sample brief for a short narrative writing task.

> Your class has been asked to contribute stories for a writing competition run by your town/city. The theme is *Be the Change*. Write the opening for the story. Write around 400 words and concentrate on creating a realistic setting and an optimistic tone.

When responding to short creative tasks like this, you are likely to be writing only part of a longer text. It is therefore important to zoom in on relevant details. Do not write a long introduction that tries to explain a character and setting in broad terms; start the narrative at an important point for the story. This is where planning is essential – a good plan will help you avoid including unnecessary information.

Activity 2

Plan your approach for the task above, bearing in mind the following.

- You are only required to write the *opening* of the story, not the whole thing.
- You need to set up a scene and make sure the tone is clear.
- You should limit the number of characters, perhaps even focusing on just one character.
- It may help to plan the whole story in broad terms, with more detail for the first part.

The table below shows two possible approaches to planning narrative tasks that you could use. Both include a combination of ideas and would work well (other approaches are also possible). In narrative writing, personal preference can be crucial to success.

Plan 1	Plan 2
Key idea:	Key idea/situation:
Setting:	Opening:
Key character(s):	Development:
Tone:	Climax/high point:

Producing effective narrative responses

Remember, the key skills for effective narrative writing include:

- creating and sustaining a strong voice
- choosing devices such as vocabulary, description and imagery carefully to contribute to mood/tone and atmosphere
- structuring your story effectively, to control pace and the reader's discovery of events and information
- creating characters that feel real to the reader by making them behave and speak in realistic and believable ways.

Read this section from a sample response for the *Be the Change* task above.

rather a literal interpretation of the theme

opening with an alarm going off is a narrative cliché and not relevant to the story

very sudden mention of litter not very realistic

rather clumsy attempt to introduce the theme

dialogue is not very natural

speech tags not needed for every turn

I Am the Change

I reach for my phone to shut off the alarm. Another school day. After a healthy-ish breakfast of wholemeal toast and a green juice concoction, I'm out of the door and on my way. As usual, I'm swinging by Sami's house on my way but before I get there, my mood is seriously brought down by all the litter cluttering up the streets. Why haven't I noticed it before? OK, so slipping on a can just a few steps from my door may have brought it to my attention a little, but really, has it been this bad for long?

So, soon I get to Sami's. 'Hey, man,' I say. 'Have you noticed all the stuff on the street here?'

'Yeah, dude,' he replies. 'Bad, isn't it.'

'Someone should do something about it, you know,' I responded.

Activity 3

How might a story about an environmental problem be created? How could you create a plot around someone 'being the change' where green issues are concerned?

Plan a sensible plot. Try to give your character a reason to notice the problem, or a reason that a new problem might emerge, then draft the first two or three paragraphs of a story, building up the atmosphere/tone to make the narrative both realistic and optimistic.

Now read the first part of a sample response to the following extended narrative task:

Write the opening section of a story called 'Viral'. In your writing, aim to build tension and to create a threatening atmosphere. Write between 600 and 900 words.

effective variety in sentence length and type

hint that something happens to Marco – withheld information builds tension

I should have known it would be a terrible idea, but I was only thinking about the potential for fame and glory. A viral video. What could be hard about that? Idiots manage it all the time, don't they? Marco and me, we were going to be made. Now I can hardly bear to think about Marco.

We had everything lined up, perfect. All it needed was that little burst of action – that extra injection of je ne sais quoi and we'd be off, riding the wave of YouTube hits and associated ad revenue.

> metaphor works well in context, if somewhat clichéd

I just hadn't figured on Hector coming along and destroying it all. But no one ever does figure on Hector Martinez – that's the problem with him. Well, part of the problem with him, anyway. The main problem, of course, is the gang of nodding knuckleheads he's surrounded himself with.

> sentence structure effectively creates voice, mimicking spoken register

> alliteration adds to threatening tone

It all started in Maths last Monday. Mrs Whitmore had set us a tonne of formulae to deal with, so Marco and I were taking the opportunity to plan our production.

'Wednesday should be good, there's supposed to be a storm,' Marco had said, chewing his pen like he always did.

> more hints of terrible changes with Marco

'Ooh, that could be good – dramatic backdrop.' I sketched out some storyboard ideas in my smuggled notebook.

> effective use of an action instead of repeated speech tags to show who is speaking

'Yeah, that's what I was thinking,' Marco agreed. He pointed to one of the panels I'd drafted. 'Nice idea. Think we can pull it off?'

'What are you two losers whispering about?' Hector leaned back from his position at the front of the class.

My notebook was whipped into my bag in an instant. 'Nothing,' I said. 'Well, just these formulae, of course. Having trouble with them, Hector?'

'Sure,' he replied. 'Sure, that's what you were talking about. You two are up to something, and I'm making it my business to find out what.'

> explicit threat to contribute to the atmosphere

Activity 4

Although this response is quite effective as a story opening, it could be improved. What kinds of choices would be likely to be more successful in this context? Think about organisation and language as well as ideas for content.

Now look at this extended narrative writing task and the start of a response overleaf.

> Write the opening of a story called 'The Gift'. You are free to interpret the title however you like, but should write 600 to 900 words and ensure your writing explores a relationship between characters.

unusual structure as diary entry	
use of pronoun initially obscures recipient of gift to increase tension	
again, use of pronoun is realistic for a diary but increases tension and engages reader	
mystery recipient revealed along with some interest	
effective characterisation, and a link between mother and daughter created	
sentence variation, and further details of mother's unusual character	
less positive side of mother expressed using passive – avoids direct criticism here	
use of euphemism again avoids direct criticism of mother – hint at difficulties but reader can infer complexity in relationship	
detail offered on the sister, beginning to see relationship between narrator and Chloe	
direct criticism of mother for first time here – sense of anger from narrator	
strong vocabulary skills, and sense of events as important	
effective description of mother and sense of foreboding through the image	
engaging and effective characterisation of Chloe	
clear sense of narrator as caring for mother	

Sunday 3rd March

So, tomorrow's the day.

I really hope she'll like it, or at least acknowledge our efforts. Surely she'll see we tried? Chloe and I have planned for weeks, scouring eBay and Etsy until up popped the perfect thing.

Sometimes, I just wish she was more like a regular mother, although I suppose flowers and hand-cream wouldn't really do it for me either. Is it really appropriate to buy rock concert tickets, obscure fandom merch and stuff from random corners of the internet for your mother's birthday, though? Although, to be fair, most of those have not exactly been deemed acceptable offerings.

Better try and get some sleep – tomorrow could be quite the ride. Hope Chloe's OK. She still kind of expects normality around here…

Monday

Every year it's the same – we agonise over the perfect way to commemorate the birth of the woman who bore us, while simultaneously knowing it doesn't really matter. She can't be satisfied; it's an impossibility. Why on earth do we put ourselves through this?

Allow me to record this evening's debacle for posterity:

Chloe and I got home from school to find Mum wrapped around a cup of coffee, crow-like in her huge black sweater.

'Happy birthday!' Chloe obviously couldn't read the look I was desperately shooting her way.

'Hngh!'

Mum's grunt was pretty clear, but still the cheer machine that is my sister kept on going. 'I hope you'll like your present, we – ow!' Finally she stopped, rubbed her ankle and looked my way.

'Tough day, Mum?' I asked.

'Aren't they always?'

'Need another cup?' I gently lifted the mug from her curled fingers.

244

Comment

Overall, this succeeds in beginning to build up a clear sense of the
relationship between the narrator and her mother (and sister) in a short
space. We can clearly see some of the difficulties that exist between the
mother and the girls, and the different ways they respond to their mother.
The difference in the girls' ages is also apparent, without being stated. The
response also uses structure thoughtfully, applying a less common form
which is appropriate to the personal nature of the story.

Activity 5

Look at the following three narrative writing tasks.

- Write a story in which a character has a decision to make.
- Write a story entitled 'The Leader'.
- Write a story that takes place on water.

Write paragraph plans for all three of these titles. Remember that the final
response should be between 600 and 900 words.

Creating effective descriptive pieces

There are various ways of approaching descriptive writing, but it is important
to remember not to include narrative features when responding to
descriptive tasks. This means:

- no plot (nothing should particularly 'happen')
- no character development (you might describe people as part of the
  scene, but they should not be experiencing conflict and growing and
  changing, as they would need to in a story).

However, there are some key skills that narrative and descriptive writing share:

- aim to show rather than tell – in description, you need to create an
  atmosphere gradually through lots of small details, rather than just stating
  'it was miserable' or 'it was calm'
- use imagery
- any dialogue must be realistic
- follow a clear structure – in description, this means leading the reader
  around the scene with a mixture of 'big picture' and small details
- show off your language skills, using varied vocabulary and sentence structures.

Look at this extended descriptive writing task:

> Write a descriptive piece called 'Centre of the City'. In your writing,
> create a sense of atmosphere and focus on colours, sounds and
> movement to help your reader imagine the scene. Write 600–900 words.

Here is a plan for this task, which clearly shows how to structure a description
effectively by creating contrast and movement through changes in focus and
the passage of time.

Overview: wall of shops, crowds, majestic clock tower surrounded by unworthy stalls

Para 1: shouting from one of stalls, shift focus to stall, colours, trying to attract attention

Para 2: mother and child walking away from stall – snippet of dialogue, lead towards shops, lose in crowd

Para 3: crowd itself – movement, noise, riotous colours, clash of different speeds of movement

Para 4: focus on shop doorway – crowd movement becomes coordinating (nature simile: like fish swimming in harmony? Birds flying in formation?)

Para 5: zoom back out to bigger picture – attention to skyline, clock tower and pigeons (colours)

Para 6: pigeon swoops down to ground, crumbs from a stallholder, movement of pigeons on ground

Closing: by the end of the day, stalls closing up, people leaving, pigeons taking over

Activity 6

What kind of atmosphere do you think would result in writing from this plan? Create an alternative plan for the task to create a different kind of atmosphere.

Now read the following opening paragraph for the task above.

useful to give a time reference at or near the start

helpful to anchor this as a description (for yourself as much as your reader)

clearly atmospheric through strongly evaluative vocabulary

slightly weaker choices here

more strongly evaluative use of figurative language – may be a little overdone here

use of personification

more evaluation; needs more description to show why stalls are 'unworthy' (although that might come next)

Noon in the centre of the city. The backdrop to the scene is a wall of shops, assaulting the senses with an array of clashing colours, as the army surplus shop's olive green stands against the neon blue and hot pink of the cheap fashion boutique. Flowing in and out of these brightly lit temples to capitalism is a never-ending stream of people, while the ancient clock tower stands majestically in the centre, surrounded by various stalls, each more unworthy to stand in its shadow than the last.

Activity 7

The introduction above is a mid-level opening to a piece, which has some good points that could be developed. Using the original plan, write the description. Write 600–900 words, using the comments on the introduction to ensure that you create an atmosphere through your use of descriptive detail and techniques.

Final task

Choose and complete one of these tasks.

a) Write a descriptive piece called 'Rainfall'. In your writing, create a sense of atmosphere and focus on sounds and movement to help your reader imagine the scene. Write 600–900 words.

b) Write the opening for a story called 'The Race', producing 600–900 words and concentrating on creating a sense of conflict and tension.

9.3 Writing for an audience

What makes effective writing for an audience?

What is writing for an audience?

In the context of your assessment, writing for an audience usually means non-fiction or transactional texts, rather than narrative or descriptive writing. It is writing where the audience, form and purpose is more tightly defined than with a story or descriptive piece. It includes forms such as essays, leaflets, articles and reviews. You may be required to create this type of writing in response to:

- longer, extended writing tasks of between 600 and 900 words
- short writing tasks of around 400 words
- writing tasks based on a text, which would require 150–200 words (this is known as a 'directed response', and is covered in more detail in Unit 9.4).

Activity 1

Look at the three different short (400-word) writing tasks listed in the table. They all share a topic focus. Identify the contextual factors for each one, then note three key features that your writing would need in order to be successful in each task. For example, if one of these tasks were a formal letter (form) making an argument (purpose) to a government representative (audience), your writing should include formal address, detailed reasons/ evidence and counter-arguments. Planning consciously in this way will make your writing more effective and may help you when you come to writing reflectively.

Task	Form	Purpose	Audience	Features of writing to use
Write the text for a leaflet advising students on their educational choices at 16. You should outline the range of possibilities to them in an unbiased way.				
Write the opening of a speech to 16-year-old students explaining why your school/college is the best choice for A Level studies. The speech would be given as part of a visit to the institution.				
Write the opening of an opinion article for your local newspaper in which you outline how the post-16 education system should be changed. Aim to express views clearly and with passion.				

Now read this sample response to the speech task in the table on the previous page.

Good afternoon everyone. Thank you for visiting Town Green School at this critical time in your educational career, when you are considering the move to A Level study. We at Town Green School are delighted that you are considering us as a possible home for that study and we want you to know how proud we are as a school community of all that we have achieved so far, and we look forward to celebrating your successes with you in the future.

Town Green is a success largely because of the culture that thrives here. You will see it and probably feel it as you walk around this evening. There's a happy buzz. Students are definitely happy here; they enjoy their studies, they enjoy their enrichment activities, they enjoy being a part of this school community. If you are willing to put in, this school will undoubtedly pay you back with interest.

Obviously, you will be aware of our great academic record, but do just indulge me for a second. If you can't bring it out and show it off on occasions like this, when can you? Town Green is the highest-performing A Level provider in the region on every measure. That means that not only do more students pass, but also that more students go on to further study than anywhere else in the area. It is likely that you will do better here than anywhere else – as simple as that. This is because we specialise in A Levels. We offer a lot of different subjects, which means that you can do the subjects you want to, which also helps you be more likely to succeed.

As a staff, we are also A Level specialists. Teachers are all well-qualified experts in their subjects, with experience teaching A Level, or if they are new and enthusiastic young teachers, we nurture that while supporting them with good subject- and A-level-focused training, so that they can be up to speed quickly. Support staff are also expert in the needs of A Level students in particular. One of the ways we support student achievement is by looking after wellbeing by having qualified youth workers to help in those difficult times that are somewhat inevitable within a large community of teenagers. So if you encounter problems while you are here, there are places you can go where someone who understands will listen and be able to offer support and real help.

Activity 2

Find appropriate points in the speech above to place these feedback annotations:

- clear use of address showing understanding of audience
- euphemistic reference to emotional and social problems implies tact and discretion responses to such problems, encouraging trust
- repetition of quantifier emphasises number effectively
- request and rhetorical question effectively soften tone before 'hard sell'
- sets up representation of the school using triple patterning/listing.

Activity 3

Now choose one of the other tasks from the table in Activity 1 and write up a full response of around 400 words. Remember to keep your writing focused and aim to use language that will suit the context identified in the brief.

Practising structured writing

Writing 'skeleton essays' can be a good way of revising writing tasks that require a structured argument or have a clear direction, such as critical writing. They allow you to consider a complete argument without writing the whole text. A skeleton text consists of the following:

- a full introduction
- bullet-pointed body paragraphs to summarise the main points
- a full conclusion.

Skeleton texts can also be used to practise analysis and discussion tasks, such as those explored in Units 9.1, 9.6 and 9.7.

Look at this example essay-writing task and the skeleton essay below.

In class, you have debated whether animals' rights should be more protected. Write an essay that discusses both sides of the argument and presents your views. Write between 600 and 900 words.

Animals' rights are currently protected under law to an extent. However, these laws are not simple to enforce and the issues surrounding them are complex. Different categories of animal, such as pets, livestock and wildlife, have different welfare legislation attached to them, and therefore different rights are enforceable. These differences stem from human perceptions of these animals being separate, but the basic moral belief that a good person would not kill or cause harm without good reason underwrites all the policies and rules regarding animals and their rights.

- Animals should have more rights – people are not punished sufficiently for animal cruelty.
- Animals should have more rights – livestock/lab animals can be very poorly treated.
- Animals should have more rights – native species under threat from farming, building, etc. (need to already be 'threatened' to stop habitat being removed, but this is happening at high speed and will lead to more threatened species).
- Animals should not have more rights – humans more important, e.g. medical testing.
- Animals should not have more rights – rights/laws already exist but need stronger enforcement.
- My views – more rights are needed, animals feel, our greater intellectual capacity requires greater moral responsibility.

In conclusion, I would argue that animals' rights should be increased, as they need our protection and do not get it even to the extent that the law allows at present. Our intellectual superiority to animals is sometimes used as an argument for our mastery over them, but to me it is obvious that this puts a moral imperative on us to protect them and act as their custodians, not take advantage of them or use them as a resource in a callous and inhumane way.

Activity 4

Draw up a skeleton essay for the following practice task:

In class, you have been discussing the pros and cons of parental controls on computers for younger teenagers. Write an essay that discusses both sides of the argument and presents your views. Write between 600 and 900 words.

Activity 5

Create skeleton versions of each of the following 600–900-word tasks:

- Write a review of a film or television series that you have seen recently. This can be either positive or negative but should share a definite opinion.
- Write the text of a leaflet for a fundraising event aimed at families.

Final task

Choose and complete one of the following tasks.

a) Write the text of a speech outlining a social problem to be given in a school assembly. You should introduce two different views of the problem, along with any possible solutions. Write between 600 and 900 words.

b) Imagine that a new restaurant has opened in your town. Write a review of that restaurant for your local newspaper/news website. Write between 600 and 900 words.

c) Write the script for a radio advert for a charity of your choice. Use your writing to convince people to support the charity. Write around 400 words.

9.4 Directed response

How can you produce a successful, directed response?

What is a directed response?

In a directed response task, you will be given a text to read and then you will be asked to use this as the basis for writing a new text. That new text may:

- have a different context, but use the information from the original text *or*
- be in the same style as the original text but take a different topic.

The key skills you need to demonstrate here are:
- selecting the most appropriate content from the source text
- writing accurately to a brief
- changing the content to make it appropriate for a different context.

In both cases, you may be asked to follow this with a comparative analysis, where you compare your writing to the original text, demonstrating your understanding of audience, form and purpose more explicitly. This is covered in detail in Unit 9.5.

Mimicking a text's style

For a directed response, you need to swiftly analyse the text provided in order to borrow its features in your own writing. The trick is to do so in a creative way, to best show off your writing skills. The new piece must follow the conventions of the same form and appeal to the same audience, but it should not feel like a line-by-line translation into new subject matter.

Reread Text 6 in Unit 4.4 – the review of *Thor: Ragnarok* – then look at the task related to it:

> Write a review of a different film, basing your text closely on the language and style of the original. Write 150–200 words.

To do this, you need to:

- understand how the text works linguistically
- make decisions about what related topic to write about
- select features to include in your text
- write the piece using those features.

Look at the initial notes for the task below.

> Typical features of reviews: comparatives and superlatives, proper nouns to situate this film in relation to others/discuss the actors and director; middle register, mix of polysyllabic, complex lexis, film-related jargon, some colloquialism.

Content: feelings and opinions

Clear structure: overview at beginning/clear recommendations at end.

Activity 1

The notes above cover the first bullet point: 'understand how the text works linguistically'. Now choose a film and work through the other three bullet points to create a review as outlined in the task. Remember to select what you feel are the most important features to help you base your text 'closely on the language and style of the original'.

Using information from one text to produce a new text

Look at this task:

Read the following text, which is a letter to parents explaining a change to school policy. Imagine that this letter has been issued from your school/college, and you have been asked to present the student-body perspective on the matter at a meeting. Write the opening text of the speech you would deliver, expressing opinions on behalf of all students. Write 150–200 words, using the information in the text.

Dear parent/guardian,

I am writing to introduce a new policy which will take force with immediate effect. As of this term, Town Green School will no longer run trips during term time. There are various reasons for this change to procedure, both educational and logistical.

As I am sure you will appreciate, having students out of lessons in term time is less than ideal. Trips can, of course, have educational benefits of their own, but these are often offset by the fact that it is rarely the whole class that is able to participate, making the learning gained unequal. Furthermore, teachers running trips are, obviously, out of school and unable to take their usual lessons, leading to further disruption to learning in other classes who are not benefitting from the trip. We therefore expect this change of procedure to lead to an improvement in our already excellent examination results.

Additionally, the disruption alluded to above can be unhelpful to behaviour and discipline within the school environment in general. We expect that having all teachers present in a more predictable manner will therefore have a positive effect on the overall culture and behaviour in the school.

We will continue to offer a selected few trips, but these will be outside lesson times, and will necessarily be fewer in number, allowing us to be more selective. This will also enable you as parents to experience less financial pressure in the form of trip requests from your child(ren).

Thank you for your support in this, as with all, matters.

Yours faithfully,

Mrs G. Tomasz
Headteacher

Activity 2

Copy and complete the table below to help you plan an answer to the directed response task opposite.

Form	
Audience	
Key information from the text, with counter-arguments	
Structural features	
Language features	

Activity 3

Read the following two sample responses carefully. One is a mid-level response and one a higher-level. Which aspects of the responses explain the difference in their levels of success?

Thank you for inviting me to speak on behalf of the student body at this meeting. We welcome this opportunity to express our views on this change to policy regarding trips, as we are very concerned at the likely outcomes of this short-sighted and sudden change.

Firstly, in academic terms, we are not convinced by the argument that ceasing to run trips will have an appreciable and positive impact on results. Trips add a wealth of knowledge and understanding to the syllabus of many courses, particularly those which benefit from a practical appreciation of the subject, such as geography and languages. These benefits cannot be replicated in the classroom, or using virtual tools, as many of these benefits are unpredictable and are gained from additional or emotional experiences on trips, not just the core academic material. We are not convinced that regaining the handful of lessons missed in other subjects to gain this wealth of other material is a valuable trade.

Further, we reject the behaviour argument, as Town Green does not have behaviour problems, having reported no permanent exclusions in the past three years and having fewer temporary exclusions than the other high schools in the region.

I am here today to provide the student body view on the new trip policy. I am here to tell you: we are outraged. As students we feel that trips have been a valuable addition to our learning here at Town Green School, and something that puts this school above other schools. We feel that it is a great shame to take that away, to the extent that it feels like a punishment, although we have done nothing wrong. Our results are strong, and behaviour is good, so we do not understand why the school board wants to take trips away from us like this.

If behaviour had been slipping lately, or if results had been falling, then this decision would make more sense, but as it stands it feels like a pointless punishment. Do you want us to do less well? Or do you want rebellion? Students feel that you are taking something away from them without a good reason.

Activity 4

Reread the article about sleep in Text 2 in Unit 3.1. Write the text of a leaflet aimed at teenaged students on how they can improve the quality of their sleep. Write 150–200 words.

Revising for directed response

Directed responses are brief writing tasks based on a longer reading text. To practise your skills at writing such pieces, try reusing texts that you have previously used for analysis as directed response prompts. Some ideas for building transformative tasks of your own are provided in the table below, but you can go beyond these ideas. Remember to practise writing texts of the same type on a different topic, too.

Base text	Try writing...
a review (of a restaurant, tourist attraction, hotel, film, game, book, and so on)	a response in letter form, disagreeing with the writer's point of view on a particular issue
an advert for a tourist attraction or event	a review as if you have been there
a news article	a diary entry as though you were a witness to the event being described in the article a letter/email to a friend as though you were a witness
an opinion/feature article or blog on a particular issue	an advice leaflet
a recipe	an opinion piece/blog article on the style of cooking

Final task

Reread the letter to parents on page 252. Using the language and style of this text as a model, create a letter to your government representative, explaining your views on an important issue so that they would be able to represent your views. Use 150–200 words.

9.5 Reflective writing

What makes strong reflective writing? How should you approach comparing your writing to a base text?

When and how to write about your own writing

You may be asked to write analytically about your own writing in two different contexts:

* reflective commentary
* comparative analysis.

In both reflective and comparative writing, you should explain your choices by reference to the contexts and intended meanings of the text. Focus on the techniques you have used, rather than the content you have included.

Reflective commentary

In a reflective commentary, you need to explain the choices you made in order to meet the brief in a short writing task. Focus on form, structure and language, and explain how your choices are connected to audience and create meaning in the text.

A reflection should be written in the first person, showing how you took these decisions as a writer. For example, if the task had been to write a leaflet for children persuading them to eat healthily, your reflection might point out the structure you used for the leaflet, breaking the information up with headings and subheadings, and using imperatives to direct the reader. You might also explain your decision to avoid jargon and instead use simple lexis to explain the effect food has on children's bodies, using semantic fields of body parts and health, or of illnesses that they would want to avoid.

Comparative analysis

A comparative analysis follows a directed response task. In it, you should compare your new text with the original, demonstrating understanding of how language works by making links between the two texts and identifying similarities and differences. A comparative analysis shows either how you have adopted and adapted features of the original text to write about a new topic or explains how your text differs from the original because it is written in a different form with a different form, purpose or context.

Writing a reflective commentary

Look again at the task linked to Activity 1 in Unit 9.3:

Write the opening of a speech for 16-year-old students explaining why your school/college is the best choice for A Level studies. The speech would be given as part of a visit to the institution.

Section D: Applying key skills

The second part of this task might be:

Write a reflective commentary on this text, explaining how your linguistic choices contributed to fulfilling your brief.

Reread the sample response to the task itself, then look at the opening to a reflective commentary below.

> I wrote this speech using a plural first-person perspective, 'we at Town Green School', because I felt that was cohesive with the form of a speech, particularly in a formal context like this one, but where the speaker is trying to be friendly and persuasive. I used a lot of synthetic personalisation by including second person direct address, such as 'we look forward to celebrating your successes with you in the future' to imply that the listeners would have already chosen to go to that school. This directs the audience quite strongly but in a subtle way, which is a technique used in advertising and I felt it was appropriate for a speech like this.
>
> Rhetorical techniques were also important, as the form of this text is a speech and the audience would be listening to it rather than reading it. For example, the triple repetition of 'they enjoy' reinforces the positive atmosphere claimed in the sentence before. This emphasis on student satisfaction would definitely appeal to the audience, helping me to meet the brief.

Activity 1

Annotate a copy of the sample response above to indicate what makes it a successful reflection. Consider how the student identifies features of language they have used and explained their purpose.

Now look back at the short narrative writing task in Activity 2 in Unit 9.2 and the sample response. The task was:

Your class has been asked to contribute stories for a writing competition run by your town/city. The theme is *Be the Change*. Write the opening for the story. Write around 400 words and concentrate on creating a realistic setting and an optimistic tone.

Now look at the reflective commentary below.

identifies perspective but does not explain *why* this would make it more engaging

states that the story is meeting the brief but does not clearly explain how

makes an assertion – stories do not have to be informal

gives a reason for using a rhetorical question, although a bit broad

> I wrote using the first person to make my story more engaging for my audience and to link with my title 'I am the Change'. This links with the theme and shows how I am meeting the brief. I also used casual language because it is informal writing, being a story and I brought the theme of litter in quickly as I wanted to make it clear that this was going to be the problem to be dealt with. My story had a rhetorical question in it as well because that would help to make the audience think, which is important for an issue-based story.

Activity 2

How might this student have explained their choices more effectively? Choose two or three of their choices in writing *I am the Change* and write explanatory statements as though you are the writer of the story.

Revising reflection

Here are some ideas for practising reflective writing:

* After any writing practice, challenge yourself to identify the three most effective features of it and write a quick paragraph explaining each, preferably with reference to context.

Writing a comparative analysis

Structure is key in comparative analysis. You cannot compare effectively if you write two mini essays – one about your text and one about the source text. It is essential to keep making links between the two texts, identifying how they relate to one another. Approach the structure in the same way as you would for any other analysis task: select the most important points for a particular text, rather than trying to work through a text or through an arbitrary list of features. The most important points are the features you can comment on in context, relating them to audience, purpose or form.

In a comparison, you need to identify both similarities and differences, but you should not try to create an artificial balance between these. If it is a 'same form, different topic' task, there are likely to be more similarities than differences; if it is a 'same information, different context' task, there are likely to be more differences than similarities.

Activity 3

Reread the higher-level answer to the directed response task in Activity 3, Unit 9.4 (the speech to the school board about its decision to offer no more trips in school hours). The second part of this task might be:

> Compare your speech with the letter, analysing form, structure and language.

Complete a copy of the table below to create a plan for a comparative analysis of this response.

	Source text	New text
Form		
Feature(s) that suit the form		
Audience		
Feature(s) that suit the audience		
Purpose		
Feature(s) that suit the purpose		

Read the annotated opening of a sample comparative analysis, overleaf.

opening offers a straightforward comparison immediately

audience identified clearly and linked to language, if rather straightforwardly

this point is better than the above, as it is a little more precise

useful topic sentence showing focus on a similarity and a shift to looking at structure

link to a language feature

a difference noted within this similarity – subtlety of comparison

precise language labelling – there could be a little more on how these are used to create meaning

My speech differs from the letter in a range of ways, most of which are due to the different modes. As the letter is written and sent to a wide audience of parents, it uses formal language such as 'with immediate effect'. Although the speech is also formal, being delivered in a formal meeting context, as it is written to be heard rather than read, the lexis is slightly lower in register and less complex: 'thank you for inviting me'.

One aspect that is similar in both texts, however, is their structure. As both are argumentative texts, they have a clear structure, setting out an overall idea at the start and then providing reasons for that view in the paragraphs that follow. This is also highlighted with fronted adverbials in both texts, although again these tend to be longer constructions in the letter, due to the different needs of listeners and reader. For example, where I have used the simple adverb 'firstly', the letter uses the subordinate clause 'as I am sure you will appreciate'.

Activity 4

Continue writing this comparison, using the table you produced in Activity 3 to help you. Produce two more paragraphs, each discussing a different aspect of the texts, and then write a conclusion to draw together the arguments.

Revising comparative analysis

The easiest way to revise comparative analysis is to add this step when practising directed response tasks, and analyse the form, structure and language of the two pieces. You could also challenge yourself to produce short writing tasks based on existing texts, then to identify:

- ways in which your use of language is different from the original text (and reasons for this, linked to the contexts)
- ways in which you have used similar features to the original text – again, with a reason linked to both texts' context(s).

Final task

Your local newspaper news website has been featuring stories about unruly teenagers all month and you have had enough. You have decided to write a letter explaining to them the positive aspects of teenagers. In your writing, provide clear arguments about the positives teenagers have to offer.

a) Write the letter, using no more than 400 words.

b) Write a reflective commentary for this text, explaining how your linguistic choices contributed to fulfilling your brief.

9.6 Analysing for language change

What makes successful analysis of language change texts and data?

Integrating data into analysis

Tasks relating to language change may include data in the form of an *n*-gram graph and a brief corpus table, to be discussed alongside a piece of text. This may seem daunting, but in fact such data can be very helpful in indicating some of the features which should be explored in the text.
Look at this sample question.

> Read Texts A, B and C.
>
> Analyse how **Text A** exemplifies the various ways in which the English language has changed over time. In your answer, you should refer to specific details from **Texts A**, **B** and **C**, as well as to ideas and examples from your wider study of language change.

Text A

Extract from the introduction to a book written in 1653, in which the author, Izaak Walton, contextualises the book.

Next let me tell the Reader, that in that which is the more useful part of this Discourse, that is to say, the observations of the nature and breeding, and seasons, and catching of fish, I am not so simple as not to know, that a captious Reader may find exceptions against something said of some of these; and therefore I must intreat him to consider, that experience teaches us to know, that several Countries alter the time, and I think almost the manner of fishes breeding, but doubtless of their being in season; as may appear by three Rivers in Monmouthshire, namely Severn, Wie, and Usk, where Cambden (Brit. f. 633) observes, that in the river Wie, Salmon are in season from Sept. to April, and we are certain, that in Thames and Trent, and in most other Rivers they be in season the six hotter months.

Now for the Art of catching fish, that is to say, how to make a man that was none, to be an Angler by a book; he that undertakes it shall undertake a harder task than Mr. Hales (a most valiant and excellent Fencer) who in a printed book called, A private School of Defence, undertook by it to teach that art or science, and was laugh'd at for his labour. Not but that many useful things might be learnt by that book, but he was laugh'd at, because that art was not to be taught by words, but practice: and so must Angling. And in this Discourse I do not undertake to say all that is known, or may be said of it, but I undertake to acquaint the Reader with many things that are not usually known to every Angler; and I shall leave gleanings and observations enough to be made out of the experience of all that love and practise this recreation, to which I shall

encourage them. For Angling may be said to be so like the Mathematicks, that it can ne'r be fully learnt; at least not so fully, but that there will still be more new experiments left for the trial of other men that succeed us.

But I think all that love this game may here learn something that may be worth their money, if they be not poor and needy men; and in case they be, I then wish them to forbear to buy it; for I write not to get money, but for pleasure, and this Discourse boasts of no more; for I hate to promise much, and deceive the Reader.

Izaak Walton, from *The Compleat Angler*

Text B

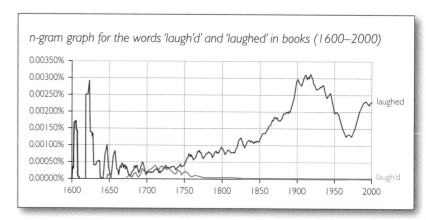

n-gram graph for the words 'laugh'd' and 'laughed' in books (1600–2000)

Text C

The top five collocates for 'art' and 'science' from the British National Corpus (1980–93).

art	science
contemporary	political
gallery	social
historian	fiction
form	natural
history	medical

Activity 1

In Text A, what is Walton saying about his book? How would you characterise his attitude and/or the text's tone?

The data presented in Texts B and C suggests two different areas that must be looked at in relation to Text A. Note that the question will require you to consider more than this, but Texts B and C will always point to something significant in the main text, which is therefore a good place to start your planning.

Activity 2

What is significant about Text B and C? What information do they point you to in Text A? Are there any links you can make to other knowledge about language change that you have? How might you begin to comment on these aspects (e.g. using particular approaches to English that you have studied)?

Writing successfully about language change

Look at this opening to a sample response to the task above.

Text A shows how grammar has progressed over time as it uses lots of commas instead of breaking the text into sentences in the first paragraph. It also uses capital letters for some common nouns, like 'Mathematicks' and 'Discourse', which does not happen in Contemporary English. As Text B also shows, Text A includes the Early Modern feature of using an apostrophe in the past tense, such as 'laugh'd'. In Text B, it is clear that this stops being common around 1800. Today we only see it in older texts and poetry.

Activity 3

How might the opening above be improved? What weaknesses does it show?

Now read this second opening to a sample response. Does it show improvements in the areas you noted in Activity 3 above?

Text A demonstrates many aspects of how language has changed since its publication in 1653, notably in syntax and orthography, as the sentence structures are very long and convoluted and there are a few orthographical differences to Contemporary English.

clear introduction with an overview

good focus on particular frameworks

In Text A, Walton seems almost apologetic for the book and explains humbly how it may not be able to teach people to fish, and may not be accurate for everyone, due to differences in seasons. In doing this, he shows good knowledge of rivers across the country, which is likely to have been unusual in the 17th century, as travel was far more difficult and less common than today.

interesting attention to meaning

clear awareness of period and relevance of context

detail of syntax is appropriately described

The sentence structures of the first paragraph of Text A defy contemporary labelling, consisting of many clauses linked simply with commas and semicolons. This was acceptable in Early Modern English, but is more challenging for a modern reader, used to more regimented syntax and shorter sentences. The second paragraph includes full stops, so they had been introduced, but the idea of shortening sentences came considerably later.

data is linked in well to sound linguistic detail

As is also clear in Text B, apostrophes were used in past tense verbs, especially those with a short plosive sound, such as 'laughed' (and 'walked' etc). This tapers off around the turn of the 19th century, as the n-gram graph of book publications shows.

Activity 4

The opening above is a good start. Now continue this response, writing at least another paragraph. You could try bringing in the second dataset, Text C, in order to do this.

Revising language change

It can be challenging to find appropriate texts and data for revising and practising language change. Start by searching online for examples of Early Modern English or 19th-century English, or look for particular text types, such as letters, travel writing and diaries. The Google Ngram Viewer and British National Corpus are both freely available.

Once you have your text, you simply need to identify the words you want to use. For *n*-grams, it is a good idea to look for a word that exists in alternative spellings or forms, or a word that may have been replaced over time, in order to compare them. For collocates in the corpus, identify a word or two in the text that has a different usage to its use in Contemporary English, or that you feel might be used more frequently in different senses today.

When revising language change, it is also important to have a strong overall sense of how language has changed. Building yourself a good chronology can be extremely helpful, so creating a timeline is a good revision task. Index cards of influences and effects of different factors over time are also useful (and can be added to a timeline).

Final task

Analyse how Text A exemplifies the various ways in which the English language has changed over time. In your answer, you should refer to specific details from Texts A, B and C, as well as to ideas and examples from your wider study of language change.

Text A

Extract from Chapter 1 of a novel originally published in 1847 and written by Charlotte Brontë.

John Reed was a schoolboy of fourteen years old; four years older than I, for I was but ten: large and stout for his age, with a dingy and unwholesome skin; thick lineaments in a spacious visage, heavy limbs and large extremities. He gorged himself habitually at table, which made him bilious, and gave him a dim and bleared eye and flabby cheeks. He ought now to have been at school; but his mama had taken him home for a month or two, "on account of his delicate health." Mr. Miles, the master, affirmed that he would do very well if he had fewer cakes and sweetmeats sent him from home; but the mother's heart turned from an opinion so harsh, and inclined rather to the more refined idea that John's sallowness was owing to over-application and, perhaps, to pining after home.

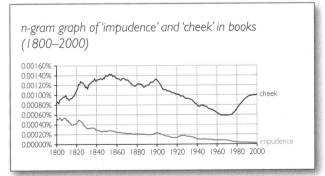

John had not much affection for his mother and sisters, and an antipathy to me. He bullied and punished me; not two or three times in the week, nor once or twice in the day, but continually: every nerve I had feared him, and every morsel of flesh in my bones shrank when he came near. There were moments when I was bewildered by the terror he inspired, because I had no appeal whatever against either his menaces or his inflictions; the servants did not like to offend their young master by taking my part against him, and Mrs. Reed was blind and deaf on the subject: she never saw him strike or heard him abuse me, though he did both now and then in her very presence, more frequently, however, behind her back.

Habitually obedient to John, I came up to his chair: he spent some three minutes in thrusting out his tongue at me as far as he could without damaging the roots: I knew he would soon strike, and while dreading the blow, I mused on the disgusting and ugly appearance of him who would presently deal it. I wonder if he read that notion in my face; for, all at once, without speaking, he struck suddenly and strongly. I tottered, and on regaining my equilibrium retired back a step or two from his chair.

"That is for your impudence in answering mama awhile since," said he, "and for your sneaking way of getting behind curtains, and for the look you had in your eyes two minutes since, you rat!"

Accustomed to John Reed's abuse, I never had an idea of replying to it; my care was how to endure the blow which would certainly follow the insult.

Charlotte Brontë, from *Jane Eyre*

Text B

n-gram graph of 'impudence' and 'cheek' in books (1800–2000)

cheek

impudence

Text C

The top five collocates for 'sallow' and 'pale' from the British National Corpus (1980–95).

sallow	pale
face	blue
skin	face
complexion	green
man	very
droopy-leaved	grey

9.7 Analysing child language acquisition

How can child language data be effectively analysed?

Analysing a transcription

When asked to analyse features of child language acquisition in a single data source (for example, a transcription), it is important to be clear on factors such as children's ages, who is speaking when, and understanding what is meant by utterances. You also need to be clear on reasons for things like repetitions and questions, whether from adults or children, in order to interpret and comment appropriately.

As with other analysis tasks, organisation is important when responding to child language questions. Do not simply work through the transcription from top to bottom; instead pick out and cluster features, to enable you to talk about patterns and to make points efficiently. Use the data in front of you to show that you understand how children learn to speak. Ask yourself: what does this data let me show that I know? Do not focus on one idea, but try to demonstrate a range of knowledge.

Look at this question.

Read the following text, which is a transcription of conversation during play between six-year-old Adam, three-year-old Zoe, their cousin, Freya (aged 14) and Adam and Zoe's mother. Adam and Zoe are visiting Freya and her family. They have just finished playing a game called 'Mousie Mousie'.

Analyse ways in which the participants are using language in the conversation. In your answer, you should refer to specific details from the transcription and also to ideas and examples from your wider study of language acquisition.

Freya:	you alright ↗ (.) are you bored ↗ (.)
Adam:	lets play another ↘ game
Freya:	yeah (.) this games confusing (.) isnt it ↗
	//
Adam:	i want to play mousie mousie
Freya:	you just said you wanted to play
	//
Mum:	yeah (.) play another game now
Adam:	but (2) zoe cant play that other game
Mum:	well therell be something ↘ that you can play
Freya:	yeah (.) we dont have to play THAT
Mum:	you havent even looked ↘ at your comic yet (.) have you ↗
Adam:	comic (1) [*runs away from table and grabs comic*]
Mum:	you need to help Freya tidy up first (.) darling
Zoe:	i play other game

Freya:	yeah (.) shall we put (.) will you help me pack this one away ↗ (3) thank you zoe (.) very helpful (2) theres all the counters (.) thats it (.) good ↗ girl
Zoe:	how i do the mouses ↗
Freya:	adam ↗ (1) dont worry (.) we can definitely play cluedo tomorrow if we dont get to today ↘ ok (.) can you get them all off the floor for me ↗ (.) ok (1) youre a bit tired anyway so im not sure how cluedo will go (4)
Zoe:	mousie mousie
Freya:	mousie mousie (.) very good (.) what do you want to do next ↗ (.) zoe (1) do you want to do some colouring at the table ↗
Zoe:	i want do some and sit here
Freya:	zoe (1) will you come round here ↗ (.) you can sit here if you want (.) let adam sit there ↗
Zoe:	i done it
Freya:	what you doing ↗ (2) get down (2) come on (2) zoe (2) thats ↘ it (1) sit on that seat (2) good ↘ girl (1) you just have to ask her nicely ↘ adam (1) it's okay (.) you don't have to get upset ↘ (7) [*zoe tips pens everywhere*] no no no zoe (.) whatve you done ↗ (.) put them in here (.) put them in the box ↘ (1) just put them in the box

Transcription key

(1) = pause in seconds
(.) = micro-pause
<u>underlined</u> = stressed sound/syllable(s)
// = speech overlap
[*italics*] = paralinguistic features
[UPPER CASE] = words spoken with increased volume
↗ = upward intonation
↘ = downward intonation

Activity 1

Copy and complete the table to identify the key features of the interaction above.

Lexical features of children's speech	
Grammatical features of children's speech	
Pragmatic features of children's speech	
Features of caregivers' speech	
Relevant theories and links to the data	

Look at this sample skeleton answer:

In this conversation, there is evidence of both Chomsky's LAD at play, mostly in Zoe's speech, and also Bruner's LASS in the way that Freya and the children's Mum speak to the children. Although Zoe's speech is not yet fully realised and is still telegraphic at times, the syntax follows a standard order

useful overview statements for introduction, linking theory to the data

clearly connecting Zoe's speech to LAD – needs development through examples

linking caregiver speech to LASS – will need development with concrete examples

and she follows morphological rules. Also, the teenager and adult address the children using many questions and lots of praise and encouragement.

Para 1: Zoe syntax/word order

Para 2: Zoe pluralisation

Para 3: Freya questions and modal verbs

Para 4: Freya and Mum praise/encouragement/address terms

In conclusion, this interaction clearly shows how innate ability to develop language, together with the right kind of input, enables children to learn to speak. Adam has obviously already been benefitting from this environment as the sentences he produces are complete and adult-equivalent.

appropriate conclusion connecting these two linked theories

broad statement to end on, and it is inappropriate to comment on Adam's speech in the conclusion when it has not been discussed earlier

Activity 2

Choose paragraph 1 or 3 to write up fully. Make sure you include an example from the data, precise linguistic labelling and an explanation of what this shows about child language development, using theories. For more support, see paragraph 2 below.

Extension: Add in one or more paragraphs to include further points from the table you created in Activity 1.

Paragraph 2:

accurate term

clear labelling

accurate explanation

subtle contextual reading

detailed and sophisticated explanation of link to Chomsky

Zoe's use of non-standard pluralisation, rendering mice as 'mouses' can be seen as a virtuous error as it shows knowledge of how regular plurals are formed, applying an 's' ending to the noun. In the case of 'mouse', however, a vowel change is applied instead. In this particular case, it is unclear whether Zoe may have been confused by the name of the game 'Mousie Mousie', so we do not have enough information as to whether she usually uses this plural form or whether a kind of assimilation has occurred on this occasion. Assuming, however, that it is a virtuous error (which is, after all, age-appropriate), this is support for Chomsky's LAD theory, which posits that children absorb and apply grammatical rules and thus may appear to learn non-standard forms first correctly, since they are copied, then to get them wrong, as they overgeneralise the rule, then to learn the exceptions and finally fit with adult patterns.

Final task

Read the following text, which is a transcription of a conversation during a bedtime routine between mother and daughter (aged 29 months).

Analyse ways in which the participants are using language in the conversation. In your answer, you should refer to specific details from the transcription and also to ideas and examples from your wider study of language acquisition.

When you have finished, compare your work with your earlier comments on this transcription in Unit 6.2.

Mother:	you ready for stories now
Freya:	yep
Mother:	what are ya doing
Freya:	its trousers
Mother:	yep (.) which book are you having first ↗
Freya:	that one
Mother:	this one (.) ok (.) come here to mummy then ↘ (2) right this is called scratch and sniff food (.) which smell do you prefer ↘ whats this ↗
Freya:	its nana
Mother:	its a banana yes (.) can you smell it ↗ (4) nice fruity smell ↘ (1) whats that ↗
Freya:	its pizza
Mother:	dyou like pizza ↗
Freya:	i did eat it
Mother:	did ↗ you
Freya:	mm
Mother:	whats this ↗
Freya:	onange
Mother:	oranges (.) thats right (.) can you smell them ↗ (1) dyou like oranges ↗
Freya:	yeah
Mother:	yeah (3) ah (1) whats that ↗
Freya:	cocklut
Mother:	what is it ↗
Freya:	its cocklut
Mother:	chocolate (.) thats right (.) what kind of chocolate do you like ↗
Freya:	mm I like them
Mother:	you like them do you
Freya:	yeah {unintelligible – tries to say 'chocolate} is down there
Mother:	downstairs (.) its downstairs (1) yeah (.) we havent got any chocolate upstairs ↘ have ↗ we (6) sthat a nice smell
	//
Freya:	yeah
Mother:	good (.) what about this one ↗
Freya:	this one nice dawbries
Mother:	strawberries (.) thats right (1) and wha whats this ↗ (3) theres some strawberries (1) theres a strawberry (.) tart (1.5) and whats this ↗ (2)
Freya:	sambuh
Mother:	what is it ↗
Freya:	samp
Mother:	isnt it ice cream ↗
Freya:	its amb (1) not samidge (.) peam
Mother:	its ice cream (.) thats right (2) allgone {closing book}

9.8 Writing in response to language topics

How can you respond effectively to questions on English in the world or language and the self?

What is the task?

In a language topic task, you may be asked to respond to either one or two texts. You need to identify the points the text is raising and how they relate to what you have been studying. You then need to write those thoughts up into a coherent essay, using your argument writing skills. Remember that you need to focus on ideas contained within the text — you can add to them if relevant, but every point you make should link clearly and explicitly to the text.

Read the following example task on the topic of English in the world, and the text below, which is an article from an Indian current affairs website.

> Discuss what you feel are the most important issues raised in the text relating to the changing use of English in the world.

Text 1

Thirteen Ways of Looking at English: This Language Gets Work Done in India
SREETILAK SAMBHANDA, 21 March 2018

Love-hate
The debate whether we should love or hate English has now been concluded heavily in favour of the lovers. The main ideas of the anti-English argument, keeping mother tongues alive, preserving traditions, cultural protectionism, fighting the linguistic class system, etc. have been trumped by one simple idea: *Erst kommt das Fressen, dann kommt die Moral.* First comes food, then come ideals. In the knowledge economy, English is a breadwinning skill. Culture can barely put up a fight against economic whirlwinds, let alone resist them. In other words, turning against English is costly.

India's first minister of education Maulana Azad wrote: "One thing is quite clear and definite, and I have no doubt that any Indian will disagree with me. The position English occupies [...] in our educational and official life cannot be sustained in future." He couldn't foresee that in future Indians would, in fact, quite disagree with him. In reality, has English displaced our languages any more than computers have taken away our jobs? Even if it has, India has beaten English by learning it.

The unstoppable pro-English cult today has such swashbuckling poster boys as Shashi Tharoor, who would address questions as national and existential as "Why I am a Hindu" in English.

The talisman

Like it [or] not our educational and economic system favours people skilled in English. This is very similar to the good fortune enjoyed by Sanskrit and Persian at different points of our history. English has come to be a passport to personal progress and a talisman to ward off socioeconomic backwardness. What is the most visible thing about those whose success is powered by their education? In most cases, it is the fact that they speak English.

Get things done

Even though the quality of English hasn't improved much, its spread has. This is understandable as people's interest is primarily in the things available through English – education, technology, the Internet, products and services – and not in English itself. From the smartphone keyboard to social media apps, from bank statements to medical prescriptions, the average Indian faces more screens, signboards and printed pages in English than in any other language. English is, overwhelmingly, the language that gets things done.

Winners and winners

Why does English always win? Because no one loses when it wins. Numerous historical, political and economic factors massively favour English. Among them are globalisation and the information revolution. The displacement of local knowledge and languages from the education system has been blamed, unfairly, on English instead of on misguided policy and muddle-headed implementation. English is a valuable skill, and having one skill will not need you to lose another.

At the bottom of the webpage where the particularly censorious 2014 article that calls English an oppressor were four advertisements, placed presumably by text-analysing algorithms: "Learn English Fast", "English as a Second Language Courses", "Learn English with audio", "English Learning Course"! Poetic justice.

From dailyo, 21 March 2018

Activity 1

Gather your ideas in a copy of the table below. (Note that you can use a similar table to gather your ideas when preparing an answer on the topic language and the self.)

Key ideas in the text	Links between the text and your own study	Key ideas from studying English in the world

Organising the information you have for a discursive essay on language topics may seem daunting, but the key is to let the ideas lead you. Once you have gathered the main ideas, you will have a summary of the most important information in front of you and can more easily identify what to prioritise in your response. Like an analytical answer, you need to choose the most important/interesting ideas, rather than working through the text from start to finish. Remember, you are being assessed on your understanding of the language issues and the subtleties of the text. Some of these will be implied within the text, while you will need to introduce others yourself.

Activity 2

Using the information in the table you completed in Activity 1, create a plan for the task relating to Text 1. You could extend this into a skeleton essay for further practice.

Now read this opening section of a sample answer.

English in India is presented as the most important language, even though it acknowledges that only a few years ago, many were arguing against its importance. This shows how contested it has been, as the status of English has been in many of the countries described as 'outer circle' by Braj Kachru, who identified English as being no longer under the control of Britain.

According to Kachru, English has been controlled by mainly Britain, but also the other 'inner circle' countries of the US, Canada, Australia etc for a long time, as these were the norm-establishing countries. However, due to population change, the internet and international power shifts, this is no longer the case. The 'outer circle' countries, almost entirely former colonies of the UK and Commonwealth countries, have more power and freedom than they used to and in many cases this includes linguistic choice.

However, the issues are not simple. While many might feel that English represents the old order, this language also represents the possibilities of trading with global powers and accessing all that the internet has to offer. This means that avoiding it entirely becomes inadvisable.

Activity 3

Assess the strengths and weaknesses of this answer. To what extent does it:

- show knowledge of linguistic issues?
- show knowledge of language theories and concepts?
- engage with the text?

How could you rework it to bring it back in line with what the task requires? Which parts of the answer are worth retaining and adding to? Where do you need to add material?

Now, look at this task related to the topic language and the self, and read Text 2.

Discuss what you feel are the most important issues raised in the text relating to the ways in which language can shape and reflect social identity. You should refer to specific details from the text, as well as to ideas and examples from your wider study of English and the self.

Text 2

The Grand Divisiveness of Political Correctness
Reflections on Orwell, Sapir, and those damn liberal kids.

When the topic of political correctness comes up in casual conversation, one of two things tends to happen. One, your conversation partner takes another sip of their artisanal[1] tea as they complacently nod and murmur, "Yes, yes, that is good." Or two, they bare their sharpened teeth at you, hissing like a feral cat and growling incoherently, "You – goddamn – hippietrash[2] – scum – !"

Yes, lately it seems as though language has become one of the most divisive political issues to date. Everywhere we turn there appears a fresh new article (or collegehumor video) about taking political correctness too far – an occurrence recorded almost exclusively on college campuses. In fact, "language policing" is quite an old phenomenon, constantly rebirthing and presenting itself anew with each generation. I believe that political correctness takes as an assumption the idea that, in changing our words, we can change the way we think, and thus influence the world around us for the better.

On the other hand, besides the fact that trying to casually say the phrase "houseless persons" in any conversation makes you sound like the linguistic equivalent of a vegan, the backlash against politically correct language is either based on legitimate Orwellian concerns about individual freedoms or the fatigue of having to constantly filter your words and […] think before you speak. Let's explore these things for a minute.

In the world of George Orwell's popular dystopian novel, *1984*, a new kind of language has developed called "Newspeak". It was created by the novel's totalitarian government in order to further their "Ingsoc" political agenda by limiting the English vocabulary, stripping speakers of words formerly used to express concepts of political equality and freedom, thus eliminating these concepts altogether.

"Don't you see that the whole aim of Newspeak is to narrow the range of thought? In the end, we shall make thoughtcrime literally impossible, because there will be no words in which to express it." – George Orwell, *1984*

The functionality of Orwell's Newspeak, then, is solely dependent upon the idea that language – its very grammatical structure and vocabulary — determines the way we think. The birth of this idea can be traced back to the 1930s and the studies conducted by linguist Benjamin Lee Whorf (encouraged by his mentor, Edward Sapir) on the Hopi peoples; Whorf arrived at the conclusion that the Hopi have a different concept of time because of the way the Hopi language expresses time, which became the basis for Whorf's theory of linguistic relativity; or, as it is more commonly known, the Sapir-Whorf Hypothesis.

Alluring conclusion, yes? Whorf's theory gained much popularity in the decade following its publication (*1984* was published in 1949)... only to be violently criticized, upon further inspection, by linguists in the '50s. And I mean, come on. The realities we can perceive are limited by the language(s) we speak? If you think about it hard enough (that's what scientists do, crazy enough), it's a bit of a reach.

Let me provide an example from home to illustrate. In Tagalog, an official language of the Philippines, speakers do not make the distinction between gender in pronoun use. There is simply one word for "he" or "she": siya. And so on: The gendered spousal terms "husband" and "wife" are encompassed under a single word, asawa; "son" or "daughter" becomes simply anak, "brother" or "sister", kapatid. Following the logic of the Sapir-Whorf Hypothesis, should we then conclude that the entire Tagalog-speaking community – the population of an archipelago larger than Great Britain, plus millions of souls dispersed around the world besides – has no concept of gender difference, and is thus more progressive in terms of gender equality?

Absurd.

From *theodyssewyonline*, 16 April 2016

Glossary:
[1]*artisanal*: crafted in a small company (here, used with a slightly mocking tone)
[2]*hippietrash*: pejorative term for a liberal-minded individual

Read this clear introduction and first paragraph to a response to the task.

identifies key idea straight away

links to another important idea

explains text's views

This article takes the Sapir-Whorf hypothesis as its central linguistic idea, explaining it in context and relating it to the concept of political correctness in order to support a discussion of the concept. The central thesis is generally in support of PC language, whilst acknowledging its limitations due to difficulties with linguistic determinism more generally.

shows wider knowledge of language ideas

The text discusses the extent to which it is reasonable to assume that language controls or affects thought, by making a series of comparisons, in order to help readers who may not be familiar with the concept of determinism or relativity. George Orwell's 1984 as a reference point is likely to be familiar to far more people, and is often referenced in articles on political correctness, particularly when the writer wishes to imply that having to avoid racist and sexist language is akin to living in a dystopian society. Orwell's 'Newspeak' was designed explicitly to change how people thought: by removing the language associated with thought the government deemed unacceptable, they intended to remove those thoughts themselves. Perhaps for some, the aim of political correctness is similar – if we can't express racism, we will no longer experience it. This has, however, not proved to be the case.

explains the link between PC and Orwell succinctly

concludes this point and enables further discussion of PC as an idea

Activity 4

Gather your ideas in a copy of the table below.

Key ideas in the text	Links between the text and study	Key ideas from studying Language and the self

Having collected your ideas, organise them into a plan by selecting the two or three most important ideas to cover in your essay.

Revising language topics

Many websites discuss language topics and these are suitable places to find material to serve as prompt pieces for revision, or to get you thinking and familiarise yourself with the way language is often discussed. Many university linguists have social media accounts where they share links to useful pieces in the press, and there are also linguistics podcasts and blogs which do the same.

Further reading

Some useful web resources:
Lingthusiasm is a linguistics podcast with a twitter account that shares lots of linguistics news and content from which it is easy to find other sources of language content.
The Language Logs is a very prolific linguistics blog.
EngLangBlog is a blog aimed at A Level English Language students, also with a busy Twitter account linking to lots of useful media stories about language.

Final task

Choose one of the tasks in this unit and write a full answer for it.

End-of-chapter task

Plan your revision. Work out how much time you have, what your commitments are (be realistic) and start sorting out what you need to cover and when you need to cover it. Think about the following:

- revision of knowledge
- practise of skills
- allowing time for last-minute changes.

Remember that you might find it helpful to overlap topics, rather than completely revise one topic at the start and then leave it alone until the exam. It is usually better to do rounds of revision, rather than one big shot at each topic.

Strategic revision planning

Make sure that you factor yourself into your revision planning!

- What are you best at? (Don't only work on that topic/skill because it is easiest.)
- What do you find hardest? (Make sure that aspect gets enough time.)
- Some skills are harder to revise for (analysis, for instance – factual-based topics lend themselves to revision much more easily). Don't neglect skills-based revision, that is, practice.
- What are your habits when it comes to study? (Are you best in the morning? In big chunks? Little and often?) Figure out what works and stick to it.

This chapter contains sample exam-style papers, to give you an opportunity to consolidate and apply your learning.

10.1 Practice Paper 1: Reading

Section A – Directed response

Question 1

Read the following text, which is a book review of travel writer Alexander Frater's memoir entitled *Tales from the Torrid Zone: Travels in the Deep Tropics*.

(a) The publishers of the book are holding a book-signing event at a major bookstore near where you live. You have been asked to write the text for a flyer which will advertise the event. Use 150–200 words.

[10]

(b) Compare your flyer with the book review, analysing form, structure and language.

[15]

For those of us who live in the temperate zones, the tropics tend to be perceived in one of two very different ways. There are the tropical paradises – islands graced with palms, white-sand beaches and luxury hotels, and inhabited by laid-back, happy people, or virgin[1] rainforests peopled by indigenous tribes who value earth's abundant treasures. And then there are the tropical hells, home to half the world's illnesses – […] former colonies torn apart by tribal fighting, or climatically challenged countries lashed by hurricanes of skin-shredding violence. One of the fascinations of Alexander Frater's mix of memoir and travelogue is the way that he acknowledges these extremes yet locates his tropics somewhere between the two.

Whereas most of us are obliged to buy our way into the torrid zone, Frater was born into it, the son of a doctor on a South Sea island. He has emerged as a self-confessed 'tropophiliac', a man with a chronic case of le coup de bambou (a blow of bamboo), which he describes as 'a mild form of tropical madness for which, luckily, there is no cure.' The only relief for this condition is regular sojourns in that third of the world where the sun rises at the same time each day and where, at midday, people cast no shadows, 'their heads swallowed by their feet.'

Frater was brought up on Iririki, a tiny island in the Vanuatu archipelago of the New Hebrides, little dots in the Pacific 1,200 miles east of Australia. While his father was a tropic-loving, religious man, his mother feared the mind-fuddling[2], piano-rotting weight of the heat and humidity. Their son shared something of both of their reactions. When his father's church refused to pay for life-saving surgery for his mother, Frater left Iririki for an opening in journalism in Europe, but has spent much of his adult life coming to terms with his legacy.

As a journalist, Frater is best known as the former chief travel correspondent of a broadsheet newspaper; his editor's aunt just happened to have been brought up near the author's island. The obvious satisfaction that Frater drew from his job is apparent on every page of *Tales from the Torrid Zone*, as are the skills he has honed over the years, particularly his energetic use of language and his eye for telling detail. A foreign correspondent or war reporter would have had a tougher tale to relate: Frater's interest, however, has not been conflict or politics, but the tropical life itself. Into this long and entertaining narrative, which has the tone and texture of the stories one hears at sundown on a tropical veranda while nursing a tumbler of whisky, he has distilled a lifetime of experiences.

By the end of the book it is clear that, above all, these travels describe the effect that the tropics can have on a person who, most of a lifetime after leaving the area, still regards himself as a tropicano. *Tales from the Torrid Zone* is Frater's love letter to the region.

Notes:
[1] *virgin:* unspoilt
[2] *mind-fuddling:* very confusing

Section B – Text analysis

Question 2

Read the following text, which is an extract from the opening chapter of Eowyn Ivey's novel, *The Snow Child*.

Analyse the text, focusing on form, structure and language.

[25]

Wolverine River, Alaska, 1920

Mabel had known there would be silence. That was the point, after all. No infants cooing or wailing. No neighbor children playfully hollering down the lane. No pad of small feet on wooden stairs worn smooth by generations, or clackety-clack of toys along the kitchen floor. All those sounds of her failure and regret would be left behind, and in their place there would be silence.

She had imagined that in the Alaska wilderness silence would be peaceful, like snow falling at night, air filled with promise but no sound, but that was not what she found. Instead, when she swept the plank floor, the broom bristles scritched like some sharp-toothed shrew nibbling at her heart. When she washed the dishes, plates and bowls clattered as if they were breaking to pieces. The only sound not of her making was a sudden "caw, cawww" from outside. Mabel wrung dishwater from a rag and looked out the kitchen window in time to see a raven flapping its way from one leafless birch tree to another. No children chasing each other through autumn leaves, calling each other's names. Not even a solitary child on a swing.

***

There had been the one. A tiny thing, born still and silent. She should have cupped the baby's head in the palm of her hand and snipped a few of its tiny hairs to keep in a locket at her throat. She should have looked into its small face and known if it was a boy or a girl, and then stood beside Jack as he buried it in the Pennsylvania winter ground. She should have marked its grave. She should have allowed herself that grief.

It was a child, after all, although it looked more like a fairy changeling. Pinched face, tiny jaw, ears that came to narrow points; that much she had seen and wept over because she knew she could have loved it.

***

Mabel was too long at the window. The raven had since flown away above the treetops. The sun had slipped behind a mountain, and the light had fallen flat. The branches were bare, the grass yellowed gray. Not a single snowflake. It was as if every-thing fine and glittering had been ground from the world and swept away as dust.

November was here, and it frightened her because she knew what it brought – cold upon the valley like a coming death, glacial wind through the cracks between the cabin logs. But most of all, darkness. Darkness so complete even the pale-lit hours would be choked.

She entered last winter blind, not knowing what to expect in this new, hard land. Now she knew. By December, the sun would rise just before noon and skirt the mountaintops for a few hours of twilight before sinking again. Mabel would move in and out of sleep as she sat in a chair beside the woodstove. She would not pick up any of her favorite books; the pages would be lifeless. She would not draw; what would there be to capture in her sketchbook? Dull skies, shadowy corners. It would become harder and harder to leave the warm bed each morning. She would stumble about in a walking sleep, scrape together meals and drape wet laundry around the cabin. Jack would struggle to keep the animals alive. The days would run together, winter's stranglehold tightening.

All her life she had believed in something more, in the mystery that shape-shifted at the edge of her senses. It was the flutter of moth wings on glass and the promise of river nymphs in the dappled creek beds. It was the smell of oak trees on the summer evening she fell in love, and the way dawn threw itself across the cow pond and turned the water to light.

Mabel could not remember the last time she caught such a flicker.

She gathered Jack's work shirts and sat down to mend. She tried not to look out the window. If only it would snow. Maybe that white would soften the bleak lines. Perhaps it could catch some bit of light and mirror it back into her eyes.

10.2 Practice Paper 2: Writing

Section A: Shorter writing and reflective commentary

Question 1

Your school principal has asked you to give a short speech to students in the year group below you about coping with the stress of exams. In your speech, offer advice and guidance on how to cope with this stress.

(a)   Write the text of the speech, using no more than 400 words.

[15]

(b)   Write a reflective commentary on this text, explaining how your linguistic choices contributed to fulfilling the task.

[10]

Section B: Extended writing

Answer **one** question

EITHER

Question 2

You have decided to enter a short story competition. Write a story called *Never Again*, in which someone regrets a decision they made. In your writing, create a sense of the person's mood and how it changes. Write between 600 and 900 words.

[25]

OR

Question 3

There have been several letters in your local newspaper about the bad behaviour of teenagers in your country and about whether their behaviour is better or worse than it was 20 years ago. Write a letter to the newspaper, giving your views on the issue. Write between 600 and 900 words.

[25]

OR

Question 4

A website aimed at young people wants to publish an article called *Time to get a Job?* The article offers guidance and advice to students thinking about getting a part-time job. Write the text for the article. In your writing, discuss both the pros and cons of working while studying. Write between 600 and 900 words.

[25]

10.3 Practice Paper 3: Language analysis

Answer **both** questions.

Section A – Language change

Question 1

Read **Texts A**, **B**, and **C**.

Analyse how **Text A** exemplifies the various ways in which the English language has changed over time, and discuss which factors you consider to be most significant with respect to these changes. In your answer, you should refer to specific details from Texts A, B and C, as well as to ideas and examples from your wider study of language change.

[25]

Text A

Excerpt from *The Grasmere Journals* by Dorothy Wordsworth, written in 1802. Dorothy Wordsworth was the sister of the poet William Wordsworth.

Tuesday 15th. A sweet grey mild morning. The birds sing soft and low. William has not slept all night. It wants only 10 minutes of 10, and he is in bed yet. After William rose we went and sate in the orchard till dinner time. We walked a long time in the evening upon our favourite path; the owls hooted, the night hawk sang to itself incessantly, but there were no little birds, no thrushes. I left William writing a few lines about the night-hawk and other images of the evening, and went to seek for letters --- none were come.---We walked backwards & forwards a little, after I returned to William, & then up as far as Mr King's. Came in. There was a Basket of Lettuces, a letter from MH about the delay of mine & telling of one she had sent by the other post, one from Wade & one from Sara to C---William did not read them---MH growing fat.

Wednesday 16th. We walked towards Rydale for letters ---met Frank Baty with the expected one from Mary. We went up into Rydale woods & read it there, we sate near an old wall which fenced a Hazel grove, which Wm said was exactly like the filbert[1] grove at Middleham. It is a beautiful spot, a sloping or rather steep piece of ground, with hazels growing 'tall and erect' in clumps at distances almost seeming regular as if they had been planted. We returned to Dinner. I wrote to Mary after dinner while Wm sate in the orchard. Old Mr Simpson drank tea with us. When Mr S was gone I read my letter to William, speaking to Mary about having a cat. I spoke of the little Birds keeping us company---& William told me that very morning a Bird had perched upon his leg---he had been lying very still & had watched this little creature, it had come under the Bench where he was sitting & then flew up to his leg, he thoughtlessly stirred himself to look further at it & it flew into the apple tree above him. It was a little young creature, that had just left its nest, equally unacquainted with man & unaccustomed to struggle against Storms & winds. While it was upon the apple tree the wind blew about the stiff boughs & the Bird seemed bemazed & not strong enough to strive with it.

Notes:
[1]*filbert:* a hazel tree

Text B

n-gram graph for the words *sat* and *sate* (1650–2000)

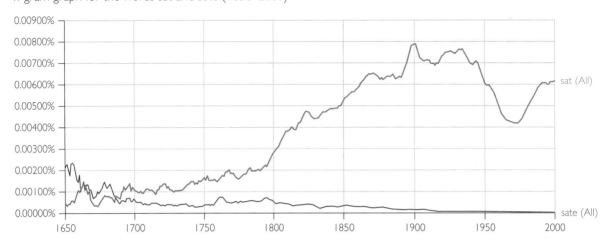

Text C

a word table of concordances of the word *hooted*, generated from the British National Corpus (1980s–1994)

Centre for Translation Studies   **IntelliText 2.6**

| Home Page | Choose Language | Choose Corpora | Choose Type of Search | View Results | Build Your Own |

Frequency Comparison Table | Empty | Affix Main Table | Affix Forms Table | Empty | Frequency Comparison Chart | KeywordsConc Table | KeywordsTable | KeywordsFreq

Concordances for [word="hooted"]

titleid	left	match	right
A15	Permission to come ashore? " The others	hooted	with laughter. Evening drew in while we
A3U	city 's overhead railway, two trains	hooted	in solidarity, to the crowd 's delight
A73	she was then about six — he almost	hooted	aloud, so grotesque was the likeness between
A7A	flat settled down to slumber. As the owl	hooted	and the night train called, Erika was already
A7A	sounding a friendly, human signal. The owl	hooted	in the beech tree and, to Erika 's
ABF	in Rennes on March 15th-18th. Delegates	hooted	in disgust or yanked up their ties to imitate
AC6	your German friends saw us doing this, they	hooted	with derision. Fortunately, the church was
ALS	Gingarden to the Baddie 's Tower. Owls	hooted	and bats fluttered, and the pirates were
ASE	miles away, at Lulling Station, a train	hooted	, and from Lulling Woods, in the valley on
B1N	seats), to convey them to Glasgow; they	hooted	, yelled, swore, crushed, and fought like
BMS	again (nothing in it …) and she	hooted	and said, " I 'll bet. Thought you
BMX	started if a mouse stirred, and when an owl	hooted	they seized their swords. " His chuckle
CAB	shop dreamily as he crossed the road. A car	hooted	at him. " Mind where you'se goin'

Section B – Child language acquisition

Question 2

Read the following text, which is a transcription of an extract from a conversation between Poppy (age 3 years 6 months) and her mother. Poppy is pretending that it is her sixth birthday.

Analyse the ways in which Poppy and her mother are using language in this conversation. In your answer, you should refer to specific details from the transcription, relating your observations to ideas and examples from your wider study of language acquisition.

[25]

Poppy:	hooray (2) oh <u>jos</u> here (1) my friend
Mother:	has she come to your party ↗
Poppy:	yes (.) and lots of people are (.) to our party (1) YEAH
Mother:	hooray
Poppy:	YEAH (1) im six (.) and im going to make (.) a cake (1) and a ballerina on the top
Mother:	wow
Poppy:	(7) happy (.) you have to say (.) you have to sing happy birthday first
	//
Mother:	alright
	//
Poppy:	when i sit down (.) here [*sits on the floor*] (1) sing happy (.) birthday
Mother:	happy birthday to you (.) happy birthday to you
Poppy:	[*pretends to blow out the candle on the cake*]
Mother:	what are you doing ↗
Poppy:	i bow the candles out
Mother:	ahh
Poppy:	one each (.) theres one for [*pretends to give her mother a piece of cake*]
Mother:	thank you
Poppy:	and a plate (1) and now (.) i put lots on yours (.) i di (.) i did a big (.) big cake on yours (.) cos (.) youre (.) youre four (.) cause its (.) its your birthday too
Mother:	oh right

Poppy:	and one for me (.) im six (1) so i put six (.) and now (1) one for you (.) one for you (.) one for you [*pretends to give her friends a piece of cake each*] (1) there (4) now (.) theres some music going to come on now [*plays some notes on her toy keyboard*]
Mother:	thats nice
Poppy:	cause its my happ (.) birth (1) its my (.) birthday music (2) happy birthday happy birthday [*sings while she plays some notes on her toy keyboard*] happy birthday to you (.) mummy
Mother:	hooray
Poppy:	was that nice ↗ (.) song
Mother:	yes lovely
Poppy:	now we going to eat the (.) ballerina cause the ballerina isnt real cause its made from icing
Mother:	is it ↗
Poppy:	so (.) im going to eat the ballerina (.) cause that is the ballerina six (.) cause it got a baller (.) it got six on her (1) umm on her skirt (.) so im going to eat it (2) you can (.) you can eat the (.) head (.) you can eat the head
Mother:	oh lovely (.) delicious
Poppy:	its all gone now (4) now its (.) whose birthday is it now ↗
Mother:	i dont know
Poppy:	its your (.) your own birthday
Mother:	is it ↗
Poppy:	your only birthday (1) i'll ring (.) lots of people (.) lots of people
Mother:	ok
Poppy:	im ringing myself (.) im ringing some people (.) lots of people (.) up
Mother:	ok

TRANSCRIPTION KEY
(1) = pause in seconds
(.) = micro-pause
underlined = stressed sound/syllable(s)
// = speech overlap
[*italics*] = paralinguistic features
[UPPER CASE] = words spoken with increased volume
↗ = upward intonation

10.4 Practice Paper 4: Language topics

Answer **both** questions.

Section A – English in the world

Question 1

Read the following text, which was published on *The Guardian* website in 2017.

Discuss what you feel are the most important issues raised in the text relating to the changing use of English in the world. You should refer to specific details from the text as well as to ideas and examples from your wider study of English in the world.

From Seaspeak to Singlish: celebrating other kinds of English

Dialects that blend, bend and offend the rigid rules of traditional grammar can be a delight

A poster in Singapore advertising a comedy album in Singlish says: "Eh, buy leh! Got 33 tracks, one! Very the wurf! You sure chio kao peng! It roughly translates as "Buy our CD, it's very worthwhile and will make you laugh till you fall over".

It was recently reported that the British government is being urged to create opportunities for Britons to learn languages like Polish, Urdu and Punjabi, in order to effect more social cohesion. According to Cambridge professor Wendy Ayres-Bennett, language learning, and indeed social integration, should not be a one-way street; rather, the onus should also fall on British people to learn community languages.

Part of that process is ceding British English to the prospect of change, noting the ways in which ethnically marked forms of English, such as Bangladeshi and African-Caribbean varieties, have played their part in shaping how new generations across the country will speak: take Multi-Cultural London English, the dialect that has almost completely replaced Cockney on the streets of the capital.

Outside the UK too, creoles and dialects have bent, broken and downright flipped the bird at the rules, offering not only musicality and freshness, but new ways of conceiving of language that staunch protectionism doesn't allow for.

Grammar rules have their place, of course. But rules can be learned to be broken, leading to the formation of identities, cultural protests and unique means of expression.

Not persuaded? Then consider these examples of syntactic rule-bending and linguistic intermarriage that have taken English into intriguing and delightful new directions.

Section E: Help to prepare for examination

Irish English

This refers to dialects spoken across Ireland. Frank McCourt immortalised West and South-West Irish English in his memoir *Angela's Ashes*, with its liberal use of the definite article ("Do you like the Shakespeare, Frankie?"), and the unbidden musicality that comes with inverted word order ("Is it a millionaire you think I am?").

Singlish

Short for Colloquial Singaporean English, this creole language produces some extremely interesting grammatical structures. Take Singlish's being topic-prominent, for example: like in Mandarin, this means that Singlish sentences will sometimes start with a topic (or a known reference of the conversation), followed by a comment (or some new information). For example, "I go restaurant wait for you." Grammatically, it's worlds apart from "I'll be waiting for you at the restaurant," but it's evolved in a region where that kind of sentence structure is the order of the day.

Seaspeak

A controlled natural language (CNL) based on English that provides a lingua franca for sea captains to communicate. First conceived in 1985, the premise is simple, grammar-free phrases that facilitate comprehension in often fraught and dangerous situations. It has now been codified as Standard Marine Communication Phrases.

Ultimately, English grammar has always been in flux: both in its native land and abroad. When it comes to 'offshoots' of the language, whatever label we apply – be it dialect, patois, creole or CNL – each exists as a yardstick for linguistic evolution, and ought to be celebrated as such.

Section B – Language and the self

Question 2

Read the following text, which was published on *The Guardian* website in 2016.

Discuss what you feel are the most important issues raised in the text relating to the ways in which language can shape and reflect social identity. You should refer to specific details from the text as well as to ideas and examples from your wider study of Language and the self.

There's nowt wrong with dialects, nothing broke ass about slang

Policing children's language encourages them to think nonstandard English is substandard. Linguistic diversity should be celebrated, not banned.

Language use is one of the last places where prejudice remains socially acceptable. It can even have official approval, as we see in attempts to suppress slang and dialects at school. Most recently, Ongar Academy in Essex launched a project to discourage students from using words like 'ain't', 'geezer', 'whatever', 'like', and 'literally'.

Banning words is not a sound educational strategy. Research shows that gradual transition towards standard English works better. But because dialect prejudice is so prevalent, this must be done in such a way that children understand there's nothing inherently wrong with their natural expression.

Ongar Academy says it's not banning words, but "evolving" its pupils' speech. The head teacher, David Grant, says that students' dialect "may not favourably reflect on them when they attend college and job interviews". This may seem a reasonable position, when even those who work in education are subject to linguistic intolerance. But to assume that students who use slang – i.e., most of them – will do so in interviews does them a disservice. Native speakers of English are generally at least bidialectal. We have the dialect we grew up using, with its idiosyncrasies of vocabulary, grammar and pronunciation, and we learn standard English at school and through media like books and radio. As with any social behaviour, we pick up linguistic norms and learn to code-switch according to context. Just as we may wear a T-shirt and slippers at home, but a suit and shoes at work, so we adjust our language to fit the situation.

Standard English is a prestige dialect of huge social value. It's important that students learn it. But the common belief that nonstandard means substandard is not just false but damaging, because it fosters prejudice and hostility. Young people can be taught formal English, and understand its great cultural utility, without being led to believe there's something inferior or shameful about other varieties.

Grant says that in Shakespeare's anniversary year, we should "ensure the way the pupils talk gives a positive impression". But Shakespeare's plays abound in slang and informal language. "Geezer" appears in books by HG Wells, Graham Greene, and Anthony Burgess. Charlotte Brontë, Charles Dickens and Vladimir Nabokov used non-literal 'literally'. Rather than spurning such words, we can teach students when and why they are used. Learning different Englishes gives us command of different domains, a skill we can then put to creative and appropriate use. Facility with slang is a real advantage in some jobs.

James Sledd once wrote: "To use slang is to deny allegiance to the existing order ... by refusing even the words which represent convention and signal status." That is, slang lends covert prestige – however anathema to those in authority who prefer teenagers not to be teenagers. There's nowt wrong with regional dialects, nothing broke ass about slang. They're part of our identities, connecting us to time, place, community, and self-image. They needn't be displaced by formal English – we can have both. As David Almond wrote, in a wonderful response to one school's linguistic crackdown: "Ye hav to knaa the words the world thinks is rite and ye have to knaa how to spel them rite an speek them rite ... But ye neva hav to put the otha words away."

Glossary

A

accent: non-standard and regionally-specific pronunciation features of language

acquisition: A native language is described as acquired rather than learned to highlight the naturalness of this process, and its apparent effortlessness.

acrolect: When discussing Creole language; the most prestigious variety on the spectrum (for an English-based creole, usually the closest to Standard English)

adjective: words that add information and detail. Common types include evaluative, emotive and descriptive

adverb or adverbial: a word or group of words that modifies a verb by saying when, how or where the action was performed. Types include manner, place, degree and frequency.

affixation: the creation of a new word by adding a suffix or prefix to an existing one

amelioration: when a word takes on a more positive connotation over a period of time

anti-language: a form of language designed to exclude outsiders, like a code (e.g. Cockney rhyming slang or leet)

archaism: a word that has fallen out of use entirely

aspect: the form of a verb that indicates duration or completion

auxiliary verb: a verb that supports the main verb in constructing the tense or voice (in English, this can only be either 'to be', 'to do', 'to have' or a modal)

B

basilect: when discussing Creole language; the lowest-status variety on the spectrum and the one furthest from the standard (this is the most stigmatised form and often not a written variety)

borrowing: the adoption of a new word directly from another language

C

characterisation: the creation of a fictional character in a narrative text, establishing their distinctive features

cliché: an overused idea, phrase or image

coalescence: the combining of phonemic elements to produce a new phoneme

code-switching: moving between language forms. This can be from one language to another, or between dialects.

collocate search: a search conducted in a corpus of language to find the words that occur most commonly on either side of a search term (e.g. for 'majority', 'vast' would be a left-hand collocate and 'rule' a right-hand collocate)

collocation: words commonly found near or next to one another

colloquialisms: language used commonly in conversation and informal contexts

conlang: a blend of 'constructed language' – a deliberately invented language, usually created either for political reasons (e.g. Esperanto) or within a novel or series (e.g. Tolkien's Elvish)

connective: a word or phrase that joins ideas together

connotation: the cultural, social or personal associations surrounding a word

connotations: the emotional or sensory associations that a word has

coordinating conjunction: a word or phrase that links main clauses or other sentence elements (e.g. 'and', 'or', 'but')

corpus: (plural corpora) a large and structured set of texts, usually stored electronically

D

demonstrative: a pronoun or adjective that indicates which one of various possibilities is being discussed (e.g. 'his', 'these', 'that', 'those')

denotation: the dictionary definition of a word

derivation: the act of creating new words from existing words; the origin of a word

descriptive: an approach to language that seeks to describe how people actually use it

determiner: a modifying word that limits the field of reference of a noun – article (e.g. 'a', 'an', 'the'), possessive (e.g. 'my', 'his'), numeral (e.g. 'three'), quantifier (e.g. 'many', 'few') or distributive adjective (e.g. 'each', 'any')

dialect: a regionally specific non-standard variety of language, including accent, grammar and word variations from the standard variety (e.g. 'I done it')

dialect levelling: the decrease in differences of people's dialects

diphthong: a sound formed by the combination of two vowels in a single syllable, where the sound begins as one and then moves towards the other (for example, 'coin', 'side')

discourse marker: a word or phrase that signals a change of topic and may provide a link between parts of a conversation or text

E

ellipsis: the omission of words or phrases

elision: the omission of sounds or syllables

emphasis: giving a little more volume or time to a word to show its importance in an utterance

etymology: the origin and formation of a word or phrase

euphemism: a phrase used to avoid saying something thought to be unpleasant

F

figurative meaning: the metaphorical meanings of words/phrases

filler: a word used to avoid pausing too long or frequently

flashback: a literary device in which the narrative of a story jumps back in time to tell about an earlier event

frequency: a measure of how often a word/phrase is used in everyday language/ by the average speaker

fricative: a set of consonant sounds produced using friction

G

genderlect: a style of speech affected by gender

grapheme: the smallest written representation of meaning (that is, a single letter or symbol)

H

holophrase: a single word carrying the meaning of an entire utterance or sentence (e.g. 'juice' to mean 'I want juice' or 'give me juice')

homograph: a word that is written in the same way as another, but which has a different meaning

homophone: a word that sounds the same as another word, although it may be spelled differently

hyperbole: exaggeration for effect

hypercorrection: using a non-standard form of language (usually phonetic or grammar) that the speaker mistakenly believes to be the prestige form (e.g. 'between you and I')

I

idiolect: an individual's personal style of speech

idiom: a typical phrase common to a language (e.g. 'dead funny' meaning 'really funny'; 'a right laugh' meaning 'a lot of fun')

implicature: the meanings intended in what someone says or writes which are not stated explicitly

in medias res: 'in the middle of things' – structural term used for a narrative opening in the middle of the story

in ultimas res: 'at the end of things' – structural term for a narrative which opens with the ending or the outcome of the story and then goes back to explain how it all happened

infer: to work out what a writer means by using evidence from a text

inference: the meanings drawn out of a text by a listener or reader

inflection: a form or change of form that distinguishes different grammatical forms of the same lexical unit (e.g. the ending '-s' to distinguish certain plural forms from their singular forms)

informalisation: the idea that language, in line with society, has become more informal over time

interactional: describing a conversation whose purpose is entirely social

intertextuality: the ways in which texts are interrelated and meanings that arise out of this

intonation: the pattern of pitch within speech, which varies according to meaning; the rise and fall of the voice while speaking

J

jargon: technical terminology used within a specific field of study or work

L

lexical field: the topic of the text

lexical gap: space in the language for a new word to come in

lingua franca: a language used to communicate that is not the native language of either speaker in the interaction

literal meaning: the exact, dictionary meanings of words/phrases

M

melodic utterance: the use of realistic-sounding intonation without speaking in actual sentences

mesolect: when discussing Creole language, the medium or average variety on the spectrum (commonly, the form that most people use in everyday speech)

metaphor: a figure of speech comparing two unlike things to highlight the qualities of one

micropause: a pause of less than half a second

mismatch: when people or things are put together that would not normally be associated

monolingual: describing someone who only speaks one language

monologue: a long speech given by a character in a film or play

more knowledgeable other: (MKO) an individual who models and guides language for a child

morpheme: the smallest unit of grammatical meaning (e.g. 's' – a marker of plurality, 'dis' – a negative prefix)

morphology: the study of how words are built from morphemes, for example, 'runs' = 'run' + 's' (verb + present tense marker)

N

negative reinforcement: A response is strengthened by stopping or avoiding a negative outcome such as correction or disapproval.

neologism: a new word or expression in a language

non-finite verb: a verb that is not conjugated to agree in person and number – either an infinitive ('to eat', 'to laugh', 'to go'), a progressive ('eating', 'laughing', 'singing') or a perfective ('eaten', 'laughed', 'sung')

non-verbal filler: a non-verbal sound like 'um' used to avoid pausing too long or frequently

noun: words that provide labels for things, people and places. Common types include proper/common, concrete/abstract and (non-)countable.

O

object permanence: the understanding that objects exist always, even when not in view

over-extension: taking something too far

P

perfective: a non-finite verb form used to create a perfect tense; in regular verbs the form is the same as the simple past ('I walked', 'I have walked') but in irregular verbs it is usually different ('I was', 'I have been'); the aspect form that suggests an event is complete at the time of speaking

personification: attributing human qualities to an inanimate object or an animal

phoneme: the smallest spoken representation of meaning (that is, a single sound)

pitch: the measure of whether a voice is high or low

plosive: a set of consonant sounds produced by expelling all the air at once

political correctness: the idea that language and actions that might be considered offensive to others should be avoided, particularly with regard to race or gender

positioning: a description of where, symbolically, the writer, audience and subject of the text are located in relation to one another

positive reinforcement: A response is strengthened when a favorable outcome occurs, such as praise.

prescriptive: an approach to language that seeks to prescribe how it should be used

progressive: the aspect form that suggests an event is in progress at the time of speaking

pidgin: a form of speech created when people who do not share a language communicate

Pidgin: a language spoken across West and Central Africa, e.g. in Nigeria, Ghana and Equatorial Guinea

pronoun: words that replace nouns and noun phrases. Types include subject/object, possesive and reflexive.

prosodic features: category of terms which includes phonological features applying to speech and affecting more than a word, e.g. rhythm, intonation, pitch

proto-word: an early form of a word, not pronounced as an adult would, but recognisable by the child's caregivers to have a specific meaning due to its consistent use

Q

qualitative analysis: (in language) methods of analysis primarily concerned with the qualities of language used

quantitative analysis: methods of analysis concerned with statistics and numerical assessments of data

R

Received Pronunciation: a specific refined accent of British English associated with the upper class and private education, sometimes colloquially known as the Queen's English or BBC English

reduplication: repetition of a sound or syllable in a word

referent: the item or concept that a word refers to

register: a description of the level of formality or specialism of the lexis of a text

rhetorical devices: language techniques used for effect, such as questions that make a point rather than seeking an answer

S

semantic field: a group of words that belong to the same category of meaning (e.g. 'bicycle', 'car' and 'truck' all belong to the semantic field of vehicles)

shared resources: the sum of knowledge and references that it is reasonable to expect members of a culture to have access to

simile: a figure of speech that compares two things using the word 'like' or 'as'

slang: highly informal language used in speech by a particular social group or used for a short time

sociolect continuum: the arrangement of sociolects by degree, usually from the standard variety to a non-standard variety; a person will use language from different points along the continuum at different times

sociolect: a non-standard variety of language spoken by a particular social group

Standard English: the most widely used form of English that is not specific to a particular location or region

stative verb: a verb that expresses a state, such as a feeling or emotions, rather than an action

stress: the pattern of emphasis within a spoken word, usually common within a language or dialect

subordinating conjunction: a word or phrase that opens a subordinate clause (e.g. 'because', 'although')

synonym: a word with the same or similar meaning as another

syntax: the arrangement of words into well-formed sentences

synthetic personalisation: the use of inclusive language when addressing a mass audience to make them feel like they are being addressed individually

T

telegraphic: describing an utterance typified by the missing out of function words such as auxiliary verbs, determiners, conjunctions and prepositions

tense: the way a verb phrase indicates time

tone: the attitude of a writer towards a subject (similar to the tone of voice that a speaker uses)

topic sentence: the sentence in a paragraph that states the main topic of that paragraph; the topic sentence is often (but not always) the first in the paragraph

transactional: describing a conversation with a clearly defined purpose or function

V

variegated babbling: early speech consisting of different consonant-vowel combinations

velar: a sound produced using the back of the tongue against the velum, or soft palate (e.g. g/k)

verb: a word that shows actions, processes and states. Types include dynamic/stative and modal auxiliary

verb phrase: a verb with other words that are attendant to it, which function together as a verb

voiced pause: a non-verbal sound like 'um' used to avoid pausing too long or too frequently

Z

zone of proximal development: the space in which the MKO (more knowledgeable other) instinctively works, just ahead of where the child is currently capable.

Index

Text acknowledgements

We are grateful to the following for permission to reproduce copyright material:

Recipe on page p.10, 'Lemon Poppy Seed Cake Recipe' from *Cake: 200 Fabulous Foolproof Baking Recipes* by Rachel Allen, p.10, copyright © Rachel Allen, 2012. Reproduced with permission from HarperCollins*Publishers*; The article on p.40, 'Taking Sleep Seriously' by Mark Parkinson, *New Delhi Times*, 03/02/2018, http://www.newdelhitimes.com/taking-sleep-seriously/. Reproduced with permission; Extracts on pp.44, 232 from 'Arctic: Arctique' from the Canadian Museum of Nature leaflet, September 2017, copyright © Canadian Museum of Nature, https://nature.ca/. Reproduced with permission; An extract on p.57 from 'Dark Is the Hour' by Jacob Ross from *Tell No-One About This: Collected Short Stories 1975–2017* by Jacob Ross, 2017, Peepal Tree Press. Reproduced with permission of Peepal Tree Press; An extract on p.61 from 'Great Gold v Great White: Olympic legend Michael Phelps on what it's like to take on the ocean's most fearsome predator' by Rachel Corcoran and Emily Retter, *The Mirror*, 18/07/2017, copyright © Mirrorpix 2017; An extract on p.62 from 'A Walk with the Valiant' by Bruce Holmes, *Traveller*, 06/11/2011, http://www.traveller.com.au/a-walk-with-the-valiant-1mx8j. Reproduced with permission of the author; An extract on p.74 from *Playing It My Way* by Sachin Tendulkar, Hodder & Stoughton, copyright © Sachin Tendulkar, 2014. Reproduced by permission of Hodder and Stoughton Limited; An extract on p.77 adapted from 'Hockey in Canada: More than just a game!', leaflet by the Canadian Museum of History, https://www.historymuseum.ca/hockey. Reproduced with permission; An extract on p.80 from ''Will coffee in California come with a cancer warning?' by Alexander Nazaryan, *Los Angeles Times*, 18/02/2018, http://www.latimes.com/opinion/op-ed/la-oe-nazaryan-acrylamide-20180218-story.html. Reproduced with permission of the author; An extract on p.85 from the podcast 'Writing Excuses 13.2: Writing Active Characters' by Brandon Sanderson, Maurice, Amal, Mary Robinette Kowal, 14/01/2018, https://www.writingexcuses.com/2018/01/14/. Reproduced by permission of Writing Excuses LLC; An extract on p.93 from *Interpreter of Maladies* by Jhumpa Lahiri, copyright © Jhumpa Lahiri 1999. Reprinted by permission of HarperCollins*Publishers* and Houghton Mifflin Harcourt Publishing Company. All rights reserved; An extract on pp.101–102 adapted from 'Mark & Vinny's' review by Terry Durack, *Good Food*, 11/05/2018, https://www.goodfood.com.au. Reproduced with permission of the author; An extract on p.108 from *Fast Food Nation* by Eric Schlosser, Penguin Books Ltd, copyright © Eric Schlosser, 2001. Reprinted by permission of Penguin Books Ltd and Houghton Mifflin Harcourt Publishing Company. All rights reserved; Screenshots and collocates on pp.124, 125, 260, 263, 280 generated from the British National Corpus, (1980s–1994), IntelliText 2.6 by James Wilson, Anthony Hartley, Serge Sharoff and Paul Stephenson. Advanced corpus solutions for humanities researchers, in *Proc Advanced Corpus Solutions*, PACLIC 24, pp.36–43, Tohoku University, November 2010, http://www.aclweb.org/anthology/Y10-1089. Reproduced with permission; Screenshots on pp.126, 154, 156, 260, 263, 280 from Ngram Viewer graphs, Source: Google Books Ngram Viewer, http://books.google.com/ngrams; The article on pp.142–143, "From Silver Surfers to Social Seniors - half of older people now have a Smartphone and are on social media" by Jonathan Owen, *PR Week*, 28/06/2017. Reproduced with permission of Haymarket Media; Concordance entry on pp.152–153 for 'sea', from *CLiC Dickens: Novel uses of concordances for the integration of corpus stylistics and cognitive poetics* by M. Mahlberg, P. Stockwell, J. de Joode, C. Smith and M.B. O'Donnell, Corpora, 11 (3), 2016, pp.433–463, http://clic.bham.ac.uk; An extract on pp.155–156 from ''Apple HomePod review'' by Gareth Beavis, *techradar*, February 2018, www.techradar.com/reviews/apple-homepod-review, copyright of or licensed by Future Publishing Limited, a Future plc group company, UK 2018. All rights reserved; An extract on p.186 from 'The Learning Challenge' by Mushtak Parker, in *New Straits Times*, 10/10/2017, https://www.nst.com.my/opinion/columnists/2017/10/289421/learning-challenge. Reproduced with permission; An extract on pp.192–193 from 'BBC is right to launch Pidgin language service as part of global expansion' by Ian Burrell, iNews, 29/08/2017, https://inews.co.uk/. Reproduced with permission; Extracts on pp.197, 200 from 'We must take back our stories and reverse the gaze' by Aminatta Forna, *The Guardian*, 17/02/2017; and 'That's the Way It Crumbles: The American Conquest of English by Matthew Engel – review' by Tim Adams, *The Guardian*, 03/07/2017, copyright © Guardian News & Media Ltd, 2018; An extract on p.209 from 'The Language of Apes' by Brian Duignan, copyright © 2007 by Encyclopædia Britannica, Inc, 2007. Reprinted with permission from Advocacy for Animals; The article on p.213 "How Does Our Language Shape the Way We Think?" by Lera Boroditsky, first published by Vintage Books in *What's Next? Dispatches on the Future of Science*, edited by Max Brockman, copyright © Max Brockman, 2009. Reproduced with permission of Quercus Editions Limited; and Vintage Books, an imprint of the Knopf Doubleday Publishing Group, a division of Penguin Random House LLC. All rights reserved; The article on p.224, 'It ain't what you say…' by Debuk (Deborah Cameron), 22/02/2018, https://debuk.wordpress.com/2018/02/22/it-aint-what-you-say/. Reproduced with permission of the author; An extract on p.224 from ''BBC debate sketch: Ed Miliband and Nicola Sturgeon... a romance for our times" by Michael Deacon, *The Telegraph*, 16/04/2015, copyright © Michael Deacon / Telegraph Media Group Limited 2018; An extract on p.228 from 'Men much more likely to ask questions in seminars' than women' by Rachael Pells, *Times Higher Education*, 12 December 2017, https://www.timeshighereducation.com. Reproduced with permission; An extract on p.229 from 'Language Pragmatics: Why We Can't Talk to Computers' by Cody Adams, *Big Think*, 17/02/2012, http://bigthink.com/floating-university/language-pragmatics-why-we-cant-talk-to-computers. Reproduced with permission of The Big think Inc.; An extract on pp.235–236 from "Derek Redmond: The Day That Changed My Life" by Derek Redmond, *The Daily Mail*, 27/07/2012. Reproduced by permission from Champions UK plc; An extract on pp.268–269 adapted from 'Thirteen Ways of Looking at English: This Language Gets Work Done in India' by Sreetilak Sambhanda, *Daily O*, 21/03/2018, https://www.dailyo.in/arts/english-language-day-india-obsession-works/story/1/22990.html. Reproduced with permission of the author; An extract on pp.271 adapted from "The Grand Divisiveness Of Political Correctness" by Aiya Madarang, *The Odyssey*, 16/08/2016. Reproduced by permission of the author; An extract on p.271 from *Nineteen Eighty-Four* by George Orwell, Martin Secker & Warburg 1949, Penguin Books 1954, 1989, 2000. Copyright © Eric Blair, 1949. Copyright © 1949 by Houghton Mifflin Harcourt Publishing Company 1949 and renewed by Sonia Brownell Orwell, 1977. This edition copyright © the Estate of the late Sonia Brownell Orwell, 1987. Introduction © copyright Ben Pimlott, 1989. Notes on the Text © copyright Peter Davison, 1989. Reprinted by permission of Penguin Books Ltd and Houghton Mifflin Harcourt Publishing Company. All rights reserved; An extract on pp.276 from ''Review: Memoirs: Tales From The Torrid Zone'' by Alexander Frater, *The Sunday Times*, 30/05/2004, copyright © Alexander Frater, News Licensing, 2004; An extract on p.277 from *The Snow Child* by Eowyn Ivey, pp.3–5, Headline Publishing Group, copyright © Eowyn Ivey, 2010. Reproduced by permission of Headline Publishing Group; Extracts on p.279 from *The Grasmere and Alfoxden Journals* by Dorothy Wordsworth, 2002, pp.109–110. Reproduced with permission of Oxford University Press; Extracts on pp.283–284, 285 from "From Seaspeak to Singlish: celebrating other kinds of English" by Rosie Driffill, *The Guardian*, 11/03/2017, and "There's nowt wrong with dialects, nothing broke ass about slang" by Stan Carey, *The Guardian*, 03/05/2016 copyright © Guardian News & Media Ltd, 2018.

Every effort has been made to trace the copyright holders and obtain permission to reproduce material in this book. Please do get in touch with any enquiries or any information.

Image acknowledgements

The publishers gratefully acknowledge the permission granted to reproduce the copyright material in this book. Every effort has been made to trace copyright holders and to obtain their permission for the use of copyright material. The publishers will gladly receive any information enabling them to rectify any error or omission at the first opportunity:

(t = top, b = bottom, r = right, l = left)

p: 7 SpeakingPix/ Shutterstock; p: 8 Wavebreakmedia/ Shutterstock; p: 10 HarperCollins*Publishers* Ltd; p: 10 HarperCollins*Publishers* Ltd; p: 13 Magic mine/ Shutterstock; p: 14 LightField Studios / Shutterstock; p: 16 SJ Allen/ Shutterstock; p: 17 The Granger Collection/ Alamy Stock Photo; p: 18 Andreja Donko/ Shutterstock; p: 19 Sumate Phakphian/ Shutterstock; p: 21 Stephen Coburn/ Shutterstock; p: 22 Green & Black's advertisement 'Acquire Taste'. Image Courtesy of the Advertising Archives.; p: 23 Paket /Shutterstock; p: 24 Antoniodiaz/ Shutterstock; p: 25 Andrey_Popov/ Shutterstock; p: 26 Matej Kastelic/ Shutterstock; p: 29 XiXinXing/ Shutterstock; p: 30 Mila Supinskaya Glashchenko/ Shutterstock; p: 31 George Philip/ Shutterstock; p: 34 Larina Marina/ Shutterstock; p: 35 Minerva Studio/ Shutterstock; p: 38 Monkey Business Images/ Shutterstock; p: 39 HarperCollins*Publishers* Ltd; p: 40 India Picture/ Shutterstock; p: 42 Michaeljung/ Shutterstock; p: 44l and 232l Art Babych/ Shutterstock; p: 44r and 232r David Boutin/ Shutterstock; p: 48 Davide Catoni/ Shutterstock; p: 50 WAYHOME studio/ Shutterstock; p: 51l Yossapong tulachom/Shutterstock; p: 51r Zephyr_p/Shutterstock; p: 53 The Print Collector/ Alamy Stock Photo; p: 54 Monkey Business Images/ Shutterstock; p: 56 MARKA/ Alamy Stock Photo; p: 60 Lookingforcats/ Shutterstock; p: 61t Stefan Pircher/ Shutterstock; p: 61b Leonard Zhukovsky/ Shutterstock; p: 62 Trabantos/ Shutterstock; p: 65 Marcos Mesa Sam Wordley/ Shutterstock; p: 67 Golden Pixels LLC/ Shutterstock; p: 68 Emily Kant/Shutterstock; p: 71 Chart on p.71 'The International Phonetic Alphabet (revised 2005)', IPA, http://www.internationalphoneticassociation.org/content/ipa-chart, copyright © 2015 International Phonetic Association. Available under the Creative Commons Attribution-Sharealike 3.0 Unported License; p: 74 Sarah Ansell/ Shutterstock; p: 77 Iurii Osadchi/ Shutterstock; p: 79 Xshot/ Shutterstock; p: 80 Kikovic/ Shutterstock; p: 81 Robert Kneschke/ Shutterstock; p: 88t Fizkes/ Shutterstock; p: 88b ITAR-TASS News Agency/ Alamy Stock Photo; p: 89 Justin Sullivan/ Getty Images; p: 91 Kristi Blokhin/ Shutterstock; p: 93 Racheal Grazias/ Shutterstock; p: 98 Efired/ Shutterstock; p: 100 David Hughes/ Shutterstock; p: 101 Bbernard/ Shutterstock; p: 102 One photo/ Shutterstock; p: 103 Collection Christophel/ Alamy Stock Photo; p: 104 Elnur/ Shutterstock; p: 105 Debby Wong/ Shutterstock; p: 109 paulista/ Shutterstock; p: 110 Monkey Business Images/ Shutterstock; p: 112 JeffG/ Shutterstock; p: 115 Everett Collection Inc/ Shutterstock; p: 117 CHAjAMP/ Shutterstock; p: 119t Dugdax/ Shutterstock; p: 120 Kozlik/ Shutterstock; p: 121 Lebrecht Music & Arts/ Alamy Stock Photo; p: 122t William Perugini/ Shutterstock; p: 122b Photographee.eu/ Shutterstock; p: 130t Granger Historical Picture Archive/ Alamy Stock Photo; p: 130bl The Picture Art Collection/ Alamy Stock Photo; p: 130br 2nd collection/ Alamy Stock Photo; p: 131 Iurii/ Shutterstock; p: 133t Heritage Image Partnership Ltd/ Alamy Stock Photo; p: 133b Chronicle/ Alamy Stock Photo; p: 134 and 149 World History Archive/ Alamy Stock Photo; p: 135 FL Historical 1D/ Alamy Stock Photo; p: 136 Granger Historical Picture Archive/ Alamy Stock Photo; p: 141 A proposal for correcting, improving and ascertaining the English tongue, by Jonathan Swift, 1712 (engraving), English School, (18th century)/ British Library, London, UK/ © British Library Board. All Rights Reserved/ Bridgeman Images; p: 142 Monkey Business Images/ Shutterstock; p: 145t Lilly Trott/ Shutterstock; p: 145b Monkey Business Images/Shutterstock; p: 147 Kevin Hellon/ Shutterstock; p: 148 Rawdon Wyatt/ Shutterstock ; p: 150 Hera Vintage Ads/ Alamy Stock Photo; p: 151 F8 archive/ Alamy Stock Photo; p: 157 Pixelheadphoto digitalskillet/ Shutterstock; p: 158 Marlon Lopez MMG1 Design/ Shutterstock; p: 162 Adamov_d/ Shutterstock; p: 167 Phovoir/ Shutterstock; p: 169 AlohaHawaii/ Shutterstock; p: 171 Dpa Picture Alliance Archive/ Alamy Stock Photo; p: 174 Antonio Guillem/ Shutterstock; p: 176 Dragon Images/ Shutterstock; p: 178t Figure 1. 'The plural allomorph in –z' from The Child's Learning of English Morphology by Jean Berko, WORD, 14:2-3, p.154, copyright © 2006. Reprinted by Permission of Jean Berko Gleason; p: 179t Wong sze yuen/ Shutterstock; p: 179b Phovoir/ Shutterstock; p: 182 Ultramansk/ Shutterstock; p: 184 IndoEuropeanTree, first version by Mandrak, 2008, https://commons.wikimedia.org/wiki/File%3AIndoEuropeanTree.svg. Licensed under the Creative Commons Attribution-Share Alike 3.0 Unported license; p:186 Faiz Zaki/ Shutterstock; p: 191 Rawpixel.com/Shutterstock; p: 192 AFP Contributor/ Getty Images; p: 197 London Red carpet/ Alamy Stock Photo; p: 198 Wong sze yuen/ Shutterstock; p: 200 GLYPHstock/ Shutterstock; p: 202 RosalreneBetancourt 12/ Alamy Stock Photo; p: 205 Koval Production/ Shutterstock; p: 207 Frans Lanting Studio/ Alamy Stock Photo; p: 208 Nolte Lourens/ Shutterstock; p: 210 Designua/ Shutterstock; p: 213 Fon Hodes/ Shutterstock; p: 214 Robert Crum/ Shutterstock; p: 216 alphaspirit/ Shutterstock; p: 218 Sally and Richard Greenhill/ Alamy Stock Photo; p: 220 Roman Samborskyi/ Shutterstock; p: 221 DFP Photographic/ Shutterstock; p: 222 Rawpixel.com/ Shutterstock; p: 224 WENN Ltd/ Alamy Stock Photo; p: 228 Sirtravelalot/ Shutterstock; p: 229 Piotr Swat/ Shutterstock; p: 231 ESB Professional/ Shutterstock; p: 235 Professional Sport/ Getty Images; p: 240 Vladislav S/ Shutterstock; p: 245 Ewilding/ Shutterstock; p: 248 Monkey Business Images/ Shutterstock; p: 253 Ray Evans/ Alamy Stock Photo; p: 259 Artokoloro Quint Lox Limited/ Alamy Stock Photo; p: 263 Classic Collection 3/ Alamy Stock Photo; p: 265 Frolphy/ Shutterstock; p: 268 CRS PHOTO/ Shutterstock; p: 274 Fizkes/ Shutterstock; p: 275 Panitanphoto/Shutterstock.